Praise for *Putting Wealth to Work*

"Joel L. Fleishman adroitly marshals his remarkable expertise and experience to provide actionable insights about the most important, contentious issues in twenty-first-century philanthropy. As philanthropy grows in size and significance, this book is a tremendous resource for donors, for those who are considering philanthropy, and for philanthropy professionals." —**Melissa A. Berman, president and CEO of Rockefeller Philanthropy Advisors**

"The vast amount of wealth directed toward social purposes by private individuals through their foundations has quietly altered the landscape of the post-1990 world. Joel L. Fleishman is our best historian of this development and our wisest assessor of its impact. Writing with an incomparable array of examples and his distinctive mix of generosity and shrewd discernment, Fleishman tells the story of this shift from its origins to the present day. Along the way, he gives a deeply thoughtful answer to the question facing any would-be philanthropist: Which does more good? A short-term attack on a problem in a single burst of energy? Or an effort with a far longer horizon?" —**Richard H. Brodhead, president of Duke University**

"A very valuable resource for those pondering whether to engage in limited life versus perpetual philanthropy. Joel L. Fleishman analyzes the various factors that need to be considered in making those decisions and adduces myriad examples to illustrate his analysis. Although Fleishman argues in favor of perpetuity, even those choosing otherwise will benefit from his efforts to tease out and test the strength of the relevant arguments on both sides of the question." —**Harvey P. Dale, founding president of the Atlantic Philanthropies and university professor of philanthropy and the law at New York University**

"Joel L. Fleishman's meticulously researched book, full of many supporting case examples, outlines why the type of foundation you use to put your wealth to work, and its duration, should be defined by and aligned with your underlying philanthropic objectives; there is no absolute right answer." —**Steven A. Denning, chairman of General Atlantic**

"At no point in the hundred or so year history of organized philanthropy has there been such unprecedented growth in both dollars, participants, options, and opportunities. And no book captures this dynamic moment in time so compellingly and completely as *Putting Wealth to Work: Philanthropy for Today or Investing for Tomorrow?* It is all here: from the rationale for the tax exemption to values-based missions, the variety of nonprofit and for-profit giving vehicles to impact investing, to a new era of collaborations and a reframed focus on communications and what it means to be effective. Joel L. Fleishman saves his most significant inquiry for what may be the trend likely to have the most enduring impact: whether a foundation should exist in perpetuity or for a more defined and limited period of time. Rigorous research is complemented by historical detail, anecdotes, and personal insights. Bold (often courageous) commentary—offered in a spirit of inquiry and humility—encourages readers to a more fulsome and thoughtful consideration of lifespan. Happily, Fleishman has no patience for a choice born of complacency or control, timidity or trend. He offers commendable examples of both the perpetual and the limited life foundation. But, in making our own choice, he urges us to give serious attention to our goals for philanthropic impact and governance participation for the near and long-term. *Putting Wealth to Work* is a must-read for anyone who gives, advises, and cares about the future of philanthropy. It is more than evident that Mr. Fleishman cares deeply about that future and, for that, I am both grateful and inspired." —**Virginia Esposito, president of the National Center for Family Philanthropy**

"Joel L. Fleishman is a leading scholar of philanthropy. He is also a practitioner who has lead a major limited life foundation and been an advisor to major perpetual foundations. Drawing on that deep experience, he articulates a vision of American philanthropy that has room for both but cautions against the current trend of new wealth to 'give while living.' He makes a solid case for the continued relevance of perpetual foundations based on deep evidence they continue to matter in confronting the world's most pressing problems." —**Jonathan F. Fanton, president of the American Academy of Arts & Sciences**

"*Putting Wealth to Work* illuminates a vigorous debate among twenty-first-century philanthropists: fund solutions to today's problems or leave a legacy for the future? With this question in mind, Joel L. Fleishman takes his readers on a highly informative guided tour of the American philanthropic sector. His deep mastery of the subject shines throughout as he introduces his readers to the organizations that are changing the landscape of American philanthropy and giving donors more options than ever to invest in social change. *Putting Wealth to Work* is a must-read for anyone who wants to understand America's philanthropic sector and the many ways it's shaping our world. If further confirmation were needed that Fleishman is the sage of American philanthropy, this is it." —**Paul Grogan, president of the Boston Foundation**

"Joel L. Fleishman's latest book will be useful to individuals and families seeking to design and execute on their philanthropic goals and strategies, including the determination of whether to give their wealth while living, versus over time after their death." —**Hubert Joly, chairman and CEO of Best Buy**

"Deftly, and with ample evidence, Joel L. Fleishman shows that either giving while living or establishing a perpetual foundation can have significant impacts for good. Even for those of us who can't create our own foundations, his book provides multiple insights into the comparative benefits of diverse ways of giving, and the possible targets of our philanthropy." —**Nannerl O. Keohane, former president of Wellesley College and Duke University**

"Based on a lifetime of working in philanthropy and researching philanthropy, Professor Fleishman has written a tour de force that resolves historical and analytic misconceptions and provides a new starting point for anyone who wants to understand philanthropy in the United States." —**Professor Michael Klausner, Stanford University**

"This book provides not just insightful analysis of the innovations and new players transforming the foundation and philanthropic sectors, but also offers strong opinions and clear advice from an expert who is able to place these developments in historical perspective." —**Robert D. Reischauer, distinguished institute fellow and president emeritus of the Urban Institute**

"*Putting Wealth to Work* is the latest in a wonderful series of books by Joel L. Fleishman that burrow beneath the shimmering surface of American philanthropy. This latest contribution to the field is a timely challenge to the recent trend of billionaire donors who trust their own judgment—sometimes to the exclusion of others—and who are skeptical that a donor's intent will be respected after they die. The book is enriched with history, with examples of today's extensive philanthropic ecology, and with some provocative views on what has contributed to this nation's rich loam of thoughtful giving, not to be lightly washed away." —**David Rockefeller Jr.**

"This latest book by Professor Fleishman is clear, well-documented, and important for shaping American philanthropy for the future. *Putting Wealth to Work* addresses the question: Is it better to give now or later? The end message is that both are important and honorable. There is also lucid, straightforward, and specific advice for both strategies. All sides of the issues are presented fairly, and evidence and data give true understanding of the alternatives." —**Robert K. Steel, CEO of Perella Weinberg Partners and chairman of the Aspen Institute Board of Trustees**

"The most fundamental question confronting philanthropists is when to commit their philanthropic resources. This complex and emotional issues is easily ignored or approached without the careful consideration it merits. In this provocative book, Joel L. Fleishman combines his extraordinary wisdom, deep experience, and personal beliefs in a manner that will greatly benefit both philanthropists and society." —**Thomas J. Tierney, chairman and cofounder of the Bridgespan Group**

PUTTING WEALTH TO WORK

PUTTING WEALTH TO WORK

Philanthropy for Today or Investing for Tomorrow?

JOEL L. FLEISHMAN

PUBLICAFFAIRS

New York

PublicAffairs
Hachette Book Group
1290 Avenue of the Americas, New York, NY 10104
www.publicaffairsbooks.com
@Public_Affairs

Printed in the United States of America

First Edition: September 2017

Published by PublicAffairs, an imprint of Perseus Books, LLC, a subsidiary of Hachette Book
Group, Inc.

The publisher is not responsible for websites (or their content) that are not owned by the
publisher.

Library of Congress Cataloging-in-Publication Data has been applied for.

ISBNs: 978-1-61039-532-8 (HC), 978-1-61039-533-5 (EB)

LSC-C

10 9 8 7 6 5 4 3 2 1

Contents

To the memory of Samuel J. Heyman, 1939–2009, Exemplary Philanthropist, Visionary Founding Donor, and Chairman of The Partnership for Public Service, the mission of which is to assist the US government in its efforts to recruit and retain the most talented individuals possible.

Acknowledgments

The debts I owe to the following friends and institutions are huge and many. Without the patient, generous, and never-failing kindnesses of each and every one of them, this book would not have been possible. Despite the inadequacy of the following words of thanks, however heartfelt they are, in conveying the profound gratitude that I feel on the completion of this book, I do salute all of you:

Tom Tierney for his wise counsel and enthusiastic colleagueship of over two decades, as well as the inspiration and great satisfaction of his co-authorship with me of *Give Smart*

Harvey Dale for his cherished friendship over 60 years and his wise and dependable mentorship in philanthropy, as well as computer tutoring over 30 of those years

The William and Flora Hewlett Foundation, The David and Lucile Packard Foundation, and the Ford Foundation for their support of the founding of the Center for Strategic Philanthropy and Civil Society, within the Sanford School of Public Policy, at Duke University, almost 15 years ago

The Kresge Foundation, the W.K. Kellogg Foundation, The Rockefeller Foundation, and the Knight Foundation for additional program support of the Center for Strategic Philanthropy and Civil Society

John and Mary Rayis for their generous support of the Center for Strategic Philanthropy and Civil Society, which helped make the time available for me to write this book

Alan and Jette Parker, as well as the other trustees of the Oak Foundation, whose support helps make possible all of the activities of the Center for Strategic Philanthropy and Civil Society

John and Ginger Sall for their unstinting support of Duke University, including the Center for Strategic Philanthropy and Civil Society

Adam Abram, long-time friend and trusted advisor, for his support of the Center for Strategic Philanthropy and Civil Society, as well as his former leadership role as Chairman of the Board of Visitors of the Sanford School of Public Policy

My assistants Pam Ladd and Cassie Lewis, without whose constant, always can-do generosity of time, energy, ideas, and, yes, infinite patience with me, nothing I undertake would be possible

Lisa Buckley, Program Coordinator for the Center for Strategic Philanthropy and Civil Society, who helped greatly to bring the copyedited version of this book to the level of perfection required by the copyeditors

President Richard Brodhead for his generous support of my efforts at Duke from the very beginning of his presidency through, alas, this, his final year of leading Duke in 2017

Kelly Brownell, Dean of the Sanford School of Public Policy, for his friendship and strong support of my initiatives from the beginning of his appointment as Dean

Professor Bruce Kuniholm, the inaugural Dean of the Sanford School of Public Policy, for his colleagueship over 45 years and his visionary intellectual as well as diplomatic leadership of the school throughout, with special thanks for his always strong support of all of my undertakings

Tony Proscio, my colleague, coteacher, coresearcher on foundation spend-down, and editor par excellence, Associate Director of the Center for Strategic Philanthropy and Civil Society, whose editorial assistance on this book has been indispensable because of his deep knowledge of philanthropy and his incomparable writing and editing talents

Arthur Fried, Trustee and former Chair of the AVI CHAI Foundation, who first drew my attention to the need for scholarly research on the subject of foundations spending down and whose talents for presiding over a foundation have made him a veritable model of visionary foundation leadership

Gara LaMarche, formerly President and CEO of The Atlantic Philanthropies, whose willingness to allow Tony Proscio and me to document the spend-down of Atlantic Philanthropies contributed substantially to the knowledge presented in this book

Peter Osnos, whose vision and willingness to make a bet on me led him to accept my first book on philanthropy for publication almost sight unseen and whose support for my work has continued throughout the discussions of this book's publication

Susan Weinberg, who succeeded Peter Osnos and now heads PublicAffairs' parent Perseus Group, as well as Clive Priddle, now publisher of PublicAffairs, with whom it has been a special joy to work from first discussion to the final publication of all three of the books published by PublicAffairs on which my name appears as author or coauthor

Mindy Werner, a gifted editor whose clear mind and deep reservoir of patience helped tremendously in tightening and focusing this book

Prologue

As the following chapters of this book make clear, philanthropy in America and the wider civic sector that it generously supports and significantly empowers are thriving as never before in American history. In Part One, I have documented the many aspects in which philanthropy and the civic sector have significantly changed for the better since 1990, and my intention in doing so is to provide a solid context of credible specific examples that both chart the present course and suggest desirable continuing efforts to increase their present effectiveness.

I have deliberately chosen to provide that heartening context in order to help the reader view and assess my concerns—indeed my fears—about the possible consequences for America's civic sector of the one major trend about whose wisdom I have serious doubts: the dramatic shift of donor preference away from accumulating wealth in presumably perpetual institutions—foundations that provide for America's charitable and philanthropic needs both in the present and for the future—and instead toward spending such wealth primarily in the present. Part Three of this book focuses on those concerns in great detail.

To enable the reader to gain an understanding about how philosophers of philanthropy, government regulators of philanthropy, philanthropic practitioners, and knowledgeable observers have viewed the pros and cons of perpetual endowments, in Part Two I review the evolution of such thinking starting with 18th- and 19th-century Europe and England. I then move on to describe how this early thought manifested itself in philanthropic decision-making during 20th-century America.

This, too, provides a background for the decisions, starting in 1970s' and 1980s' America, that gave a strong and still growing impetus to the trend I just described: the rejection by philanthropists and foundations of employing presumably perpetual entities for deploying philanthropic wealth and the corresponding adoption of time-limited entities. This preference for time-limited philanthropy is most often referred to, in this book and elsewhere, as "giving while living" and "spending down."

In the later sections of Part Two, I underscore how that change came to pass, what I think the dominant ideological and practical motivations were that brought it about, and why they very much concern me.

In summary, as described at much greater length later in the book, I think that a number of persons in philanthropy, animated by conservative leanings, seized on Henry Ford II's resignation in 1976 from the Board of Trustees of the Ford Foundation and succeeded in making it an emblematic example of a major foundation's departure from donor intent. Their focus on this story and, I would argue, their distortion of it have captured the attention of many prospective donors largely because of the prominence of the Ford Foundation. But the problem with this attempt to spin a morality tale out of a tangled bit of boardroom history is that the moral does not fit the tale, when accurately told. Put simply, it is logically impossible to have a departure from donor intent when, as in the case of the Ford Foundation, there was no concrete expression of donor intent in the first place.

Nonetheless, despite the shakiness of that example, those conservative-leaning individuals and groups proceeded to use Ford as an example of what is bound to happen to any perpetual foundation whenever a donor/founder passes from the scene. In my discussion of this sequence of events, I point out that, alongside several efforts to pin the "departure from donor intent" badge of shame on several perpetual foundations—attempts that, in my view, substantially failed in every case—those individuals and groups have also continued vigorously recommending to potential donors that they always include a clause in their foundation governing documents that permits their foundation to end its existence if the trustees decide to do so.

Why, one will ask, do these conservative-leaning individuals and groups have so strong an antipathy to perpetual foundations? Because their ideological inclinations have persuaded them that, irrespective of a founder-donor's meticulous efforts to ensure the foundation's fidelity to donor intent, any perpetual foundation is vulnerable to departure from that intent and, moreover, that any drift away from donor intent will be politically leftward.

The fact that many of America's largest, most successful, most-admired foundations are not characterized by any such departures from donor intent has not seemed to deter such opponents of perpetual foundations from continuing to believe as they do nor deterred them from opposing the creation of perpetual foundations. Nor does the continuing record of important achievements by such American foundations over more than 100 years dissuade them from waging their war against philanthropic perpetuity.

To be sure, the creation of doubt about presumably perpetual vehicles for philanthropic giving, based on the claim that they are vulnerable to drift away from donor intent, is only part of the explanation for the growth in the number of donors who today are choosing to give all their wealth while they are alive or soon after their death. Many donors who choose "philanthropy today" rather than "investing in philanthropy for tomorrow" are undoubtedly doing so out of an overwhelming conviction that the urgent problems of today merit as many of the philanthropic dollars available today as possible. I believe, however, that the successful effort to discredit the presumably perpetual vehicles has operated to cause many donors to dismiss perpetuity entirely and opt instead for a default position of "philanthropy today."

If the arguments by those who hold anti-perpetuity positions continue to dissuade prospective foundation-founders from endowing new perpetual institutions, as they appear increasingly to be doing, America will be at risk of losing its capacity to continue facilitating the birth and nurturing of the kinds of high-quality civic-sector organizations that have helped make this country the dynamic society that it has long been. It will have lost the source of financing for America's "passing gear," as the Ford Foundation's pioneering urban grantmaker Paul Ylvisaker called it. That would be a terrible loss indeed—for America and for the world!

Preface

Further, there are things of which the mind understands one part, but remains ignorant of the other; and when man is able to comprehend certain things, it does not follow that he must be able to comprehend everything.
—Maimonides[1]

More than at any time in nearly a century, America is awash in philanthropic dollars. Today's high-profile gifts are often given in spectacular amounts by famous, occasionally controversial donors. Now, as with the big gifts of the early 20th century, when such philanthropic notoriety occurs, criticism soon follows. Some of history's largest charitable gifts, or publicly expressed intentions to make such gifts, such as the announcement by Mark Zuckerberg and his wife, Dr. Priscilla Chan, mentioned in the next paragraph, have recently been announced as this book goes to press. As night always follows day, the many critics of American philanthropists, both cynical and sincere, have once again emerged in great profusion, as well as often in great confusion.

Ever since 2006, when Warren Buffett surprised the world with his extraordinary $31 billion gift to the Gates Foundation, philanthropy has regularly been in the headlines. In 2010, for example, Buffett and Bill Gates announced the creation of the Giving Pledge whereby all signers commit to giving away half of their wealth. From 2012 to 2016, David Rubenstein, cofounder of The Carlyle Group and one of the signers of the Giving Pledge, donated $7.5 million to help restore the Washington Monument after an earthquake, $5.37 million to restore the US Marine Corps Iwo Jima War Memorial, $10 million to restore President James Madison's home at Montpelier, $18.5 million to restore the Lincoln Memorial, and $50 million to the

Kennedy Center for the Performing Arts. In 2016, Philip Knight, founder of Nike, donated $400 million toward a $1 billion endowment to finance 100 three-year graduate and professional fellowships at Stanford University, to be named for himself and for former Stanford president John Hennessy. And, raising the bar to its highest point ever, in December 2015, Mark Zuckerberg, the 32-year-old founder and CEO of Facebook, and his wife, Dr. Priscilla Chan, announced that they would, over their lifetimes, put the $45 billion present worth of their Facebook stock to various kinds of philanthropic use.

All of these charitable acts drew exceptional media attention, both to the respective givers and to the idea of philanthropy writ large. With public and media attention thus heightened, this is an especially opportune moment to seek to clarify the significance of American philanthropy to American society, to American culture, and especially to America's flourishing civic sector. While American foundations, by and large, remain "The Great American Secret"—the subtitle of my first book on philanthropy[2]—public awareness of the existence of the wider philanthropic sector is now greater than at any time since Andrew Carnegie and John D. Rockefeller Sr. captured the attention of the public with their launch of the first great institutions of American philanthropy more than a century ago.

American entrepreneurs, as well as those who have invested early in their ventures, have accumulated ever-greater wealth, and a steadily expanding number of them are donating increasingly larger portions of their riches to charitable causes at unprecedentedly youthful ages. Moreover, less-wealthy Americans routinely make charitable donations to the best of their ability. Together, the rich and the far more numerous less-rich continue to sustain a remarkable multipurpose civic sector that runs schools and universities, owns hospitals, provides social services to the impoverished, supports the visual and performing arts, fosters think tanks and scientific innovation, and much more. Many people, myself included, have long believed that this sector is among the key sources of America's continuing robust dynamism.

The current philanthropic energy is reminiscent of—and more widespread than at any time since—the end of the 19th century and the early 20th, when the newly rich then began their huge giving and great foundations and universities began to be established. America's civic sector is once again being widely recognized as one of the authentic marvels of the world, which it assuredly is. Yet since about 1990, that civic sector has been steadily changing, not only because of outsized gifts and pervasive digital communication devices but also because of the invention of new vehicles to facilitate philanthropic giving, such as donor-advised funds. These tax-advantaged structures, which allow donors to control when they get tax advantages and when they or their heirs can direct philanthropy to different causes, have become a very significant presence; at the end of 2014, they contained about $70 billion in assets destined to pass through them to nonprofit organizations over the coming several years. The average annual payout rate from these funds to recipient organizations is about 22 percent of fund assets. If that continues, their aggregate contribution will be equal to almost one quarter of the amount paid out in 2014 by all private foundations in the United States. That same year, the approximately $19 billion contributed to donor-advised funds represented 7.6 percent of all giving by individuals.

Moreover, foundations and individual philanthropists are now combining philanthropy and advocacy in ways that even a decade ago were untried and considered likely to be illegal or close to it. Crusading attorneys on both the left and the right have spent more than two decades advising foundations that the US Tax Code's prohibition against lobbying—once thought to be a barrier against funding most direct appeals to voters and legislative bodies—actually permits a great many forms of aggressive political action. While some philanthropic structures (such as the LLCs of the Omidyar Network or the Chan Zuckerberg Initiative) will face no such constraints, traditional foundations have grown bolder in following that advice. Furthermore, foundations, corporations, individual philanthropists, and governmental agencies are working together to tackle thorny social and economic problems, and corporations are increasingly engaging in ambitious strategic nonprofit and even for-profit initiatives (such as B Corporations) to seek social transformation.

However, the single most important change that has taken place since 1990 has to do with the intentions of individuals who have great wealth and who want to deploy it philanthropically. One hundred years ago, the overwhelming majority of such people instinctively opted to create foundations that they expected would go on perhaps forever. At that time, not one of the largest foundations had a limited lifespan. Ever since 1990, however, prospective donors appear to be favoring either the creation of a time-limited foundation with a lifespan roughly concurrent with their own or the direct disposition of substantial gifts during their lifetimes without the involvement of a foundation at all. That is a seismic shift in philanthropic practice and one worth trying hard both to track and to understand.

In other words, over the past 25 years, it has become ever clearer that a fast-growing number of wealthy individuals have concluded that their preferred philanthropic option will be "giving while living," a phrase coined by early 20th-century philanthropist Julius Rosenwald[3] and popularized in the 21st century by Charles Feeney—successful businessman, entrepreneur, founder of Duty Free Shoppers, and donor/founder of The Atlantic Philanthropies.[4] Like Feeney, such donors usually express a passion for deploying all or a large part of their wealth during their lifetimes to help solve or mitigate urgent social problems. This impulse is understandable. Around the globe, human beings face enormous suffering from hunger, disease, displacement, discrimination, and countless other woes. While I wholeheartedly praise the determination to act now, as will become clear in the pages that follow, I have serious concerns about whether it is wise to spend all of one's philanthropic wealth in the short run.

My purpose in writing this book is to examine, assess, and explain the major changes in American philanthropy—beneficial, harmful, and still doubtful—over the past 25 years and to consider the significance of each of those changes for the future health and vibrancy of America's civic sector. For this book, I have drawn on my interviews with some 50 attentive observers of the American philanthropic and nonprofit sectors, along with my own experiences as a researcher, teacher, and writer on philanthropy and the nonprofit sector for more than 40 years and as a foundation officer for 10 of those years.

Introduction: America's Indispensable Civic Sector Dynamo

America's civic sector is substantially unencumbered by government regulation—much *freer* to act without the advance approval of government officials than America's famously vigorous and innovative for-profit sector. Moreover, America continues to be a notable exception, as many other countries have witnessed episodes of dramatic governmental intrusion on the very existence of nonprofit organizations.[1]

On November 30, 2015, Russia's General Prosecutor's Office issued a statement regarding two of the foundations created by financier George Soros, which are devoted to the promotion of free and tolerant societies with open, accountable governance: "It was found that the activity of the Open Society Foundations and the Open Society Institute Assistance Foundation represents a threat to the foundations of the constitutional system of the Russian Federation and the security of the state."[2] Between 1993 and 2012, 39 nations, including India, China, and Russia, enacted repressive legislation against some forms of non-governmental organizations (NGOs).[3] In India, the recent targets of such state "regulation" have included the global environmental organization Greenpeace and the Ford Foundation. In China, it has included many Christian churches and their leaders. In April 2016, China enacted a broad new law significantly burdening the functioning of foreign nonprofits operating there.[4]

In Russia, according to another study in the same publication, Russian "legislation passed in 2012 requires locally operating NGOs to register with a special government body before they can receive foreign aid. Although the legislation applies only to groups that engage in 'political activities,' the Russian government defines that term so broadly that it encompasses virtually any effort aimed at influencing Russian state policies. NGOs that receive funding from non-Russian sources, moreover, must identify themselves as 'foreign agents' in their communication material—a requirement that only heightens their sense of vulnerability."[5]

Protected by the US Constitution's First Amendment guarantees of free speech, assembly, petition, and association, along with the long-celebrated freedom of the press, America's nonprofit organizations are almost certainly the freest in the world to challenge government officials and agencies, to criticize as well as organize against powerful corporations, to call both majority and minority opinions to account, to propose innovative initiatives in every realm of public policy, to pilot new ways of solving public problems, and to propose and lobby for changes in the federal, state, or local governments.

John Gardner, the widely admired secretary of Health, Education, and Welfare under President Lyndon Johnson and president of The Carnegie Corporation of New York from 1955 to 1965, described better than anyone else I know the essential greatness and scope of America's nonprofit sector. One of the most creative and admired foundation CEOs, Gardner was not only a funder of nonprofits but also the founder of two well-known national nonprofit organizations: Common Cause and The Independent Sector. Here is how Gardner defined America's nonprofit sector:

> Every American knows some piece of the independent sector. . . . But very few people have glimpsed its extraordinary sweep and its possibilities. . . . At its best, it is a sector in which we are allowed to pursue truth, even if we are going in the wrong direction; allowed to experiment, even if we are bound to fail; to map unknown territory, even if we get lost. It is a sector in which we are committed to alleviate misery and redress grievances, to give reign to the mind's curiosity and the soul's longing . . . to honor the worthy and smite the rascals with everyone free to define worthiness and rascality, to find cures and to console the incurable, to deal with the ancient impulse to hate and fear the tribe in the next valley, to prepare for tomorrow's crisis and preserve yesterday's wisdom, and to pursue the questions others won't pursue because they are too busy or too lazy or fearful or jaded. It is a sector for seed planting and pathfinding, for lost causes and causes that yet may win.[6]

But Gardner also acknowledged the nonprofit sector's shortcomings:

> The nonprofit world does have its share of oafs and rascals. . . . If you can't find a nonprofit institution that you genuinely dislike, then something has gone wrong with our pluralism.[7]

How did America's civic sector come to be as independent as it is?

The short answer is that, unlike in European and many other countries older than the United States, America's nonprofit sector preexisted the establishment of the country's governmental institutions. Remember that the first settlers in Jamestown, Virginia, and Plymouth, Massachusetts, in 1607 and 1620, respectively, came to these shores in order to escape religious persecution in England and France, and on arrival they planted their churches wherever they settled in the New World. Those religious congregations provided not only spiritual sustenance but also a wide array of social services, including secular schooling, financial support for the indigent, medical services, and housing. Note too that, unlike the governance of religious congregations under the established Anglican Church in England and the Roman Catholic Church in France, each of these congregations was an independent, self-governing body. These churches were the first nonprofit organizations established in what later became the United States, and they, along with the schools, hospitals, and indigent care institutions they founded, continued to provide social services long after governments were gradually established in their areas. Essentially, they beat the government to the punch and they, as well as the governance models that they embodied, became the foundation of and precedents for the expansive civic sector that America now has.

THE SIZE OF AMERICA'S CIVIC SECTOR

America's civic sector is not only the freest but also the largest such sector in the world. As of mid-2015, there were approximately two million nonprofit organizations in the United States—1,059,150 public charities, 101,892 private foundations, 368,720 noncharitable nonprofits, and 315,629 nonprofit religious congregations.[8] As of 2013, the total revenues reported by US public charities were $1.74 trillion and the total expenses were $1.63 trillion. In addition, public charities reported owning assets worth over $3 trillion.[9]

To understand how significant America's nonprofit sector is, consider these figures: in the 2014 fiscal year, the United States had a gross domestic product (GDP) of about $17.4 trillion. In that same year, the annual expenditures of the federal government totaled $4 trillion, of which 66 percent ($2.6 trillion) was "mandatory" spending, 16 percent ($640 billion) was for national defense, 6 percent ($252 billion) was to cover interest on the national debt, and only 12 percent ($520 billion) was for "discretionary" spending. Within "mandatory spending" were $1 trillion for Medicare/health,

$900 billion for social security, about $106 billion for food assistance, about $47 billion for unemployment benefits, and $500 billion for "other." Within "discretionary" spending, $72 billion went to education, $61 billion went to housing and community development, $38 billion went to international-serving organizations, $38 billion went to energy and the environment, $26 billion went to transportation, and $284 billion was for "other."

So, if the total of "discretionary" expenditures by the federal government was $520 billion, the amount of money spent by the nonprofit sector ($1.7 trillion) was *three times* the amount spent by the federal government for roughly analogous purposes. I say "roughly" because medical services are not included in the federal "discretionary" purposes, and therefore, federal "discretionary" spending does not include entitlement expenditures for health and human services. The amount received from the federal government and spent by nonprofit organizations for health services, omitting entitlement support for Medicare and Medicaid, is estimated at $82 billion in 2015 dollars.[10] But even when we add $82 billion to the federal "discretionary" category to make it parallel with the full range of nonprofit domestic activities, we come to around $600 billion. Nonprofit expenditures, at $1.7 trillion, are still nearly three times larger than that adjusted federal "discretionary" figure.

The point is not substantially altered if we subtract from total nonprofit expenditures the portion that is funded by the federal government. Total federal contribution to nonprofit spending amounted to $597 billion (including Medicare and Medicaid entitlement spending), which would bring the nonprofit/nonfederal total down to about $1.1 billion. Even after that subtraction, the ratio of nonprofit expenditures to federal "discretionary" spending stands at almost two-to-one.

What are the sources of the revenues received by nonprofit organizations?

Approximately 40 percent are from income for services rendered, such as tuition paid by students to educational institutions and hospital fees paid by patients or their insurance companies. Approximately 40 percent are from federal, state, and local government contracts and grants, and about 20 percent are from charitable contributions and gifts from all sources.[11]

AMERICAN LARGESSE

American monetary generosity takes many forms, but what is most impressive is its consistency over the years. Charitable giving in the aggregate has been tracked by the Internal Revenue Service since 1956. Between then and 1972, donations from all sources were at or above 2 percent of the US GDP. From 1973 to 1998, charitable contributions' percentage of the GDP was between 1.6 percent and 1.7 percent. Between 1999 and 2014 it returned once again to at or above 2 percent of the GDP, with the exception of the four years in the aftermath of the Great Recession between 2008 and 2011, when it dropped to 1.9 percent of the GDP, and slowly rebounded to 2 percent in 2013 and 2.1 percent in 2015.[12] To put those figures in proper context, note that nearly the closest country for which comparable statistics are available is the United Kingdom, in which tax filers made contributions at the level of 0.84 percent of the United Kingdom's GDP.[13] In other words, over most of the past 40 years, American taxpayers gave almost two and a half times the share of GDP of the next most generous country.

Americans give huge amounts of money every year to the nation's non-profits. In 2015, total charitable giving from all sources was $373.25 billion. The breakdown is in Table I.1 below.

Compared with the size and growth of America's GDP, the growth of today's nonprofit sector and level of charitable giving, while large, is not out-sized. Between 1990 and 2015, the US GDP grew, in 2014 inflation-adjusted dollars, from $10.8 trillion to $17.4 trillion. During that same period, total US charitable giving from all sources, in current dollars, more than tripled, from $98.3 billion in 1989 to $373.25 billion in 2014.[14] In inflation-adjusted 2014 dollars, however, US charitable contributions grew from $178.6 billion in 1990 to $373.25 billion in 2015, slightly more than doubling.[15] More-over, if measured by personal disposable income in 2015 inflation-adjusted dollars, charitable contributions also grew only commensurately. The personal disposable income in the United States in inflation-adjusted dollars tripled from $4.254 trillion in 1990 to $13,403.2 trillion in 2015[16] while charitable contributions by individuals grew from $79 billion to $264.58

I.1 Total charitable giving from all sources[17]

Type of Giver	Amount Given	Percent of Total Given
Individuals during lifetime	$264.58 billion	71% of total
Individuals by bequest	$31.76 billion	9% of total
Foundations	$58.46 billion	16% of total
Corporations	18.45 billion	5% of total

billion, just a bit more than tripling.[18] In short, the share of Americans' real after-tax income devoted to charitable contributions has risen only modestly since the 1990s, on average, but that growth has come atop a consistently high base. In 2015, Americans gave 2.0 percent of their personal disposable income to charity.[19]

The fact that 80 percent of the dollar value of all contributions comes from individuals is a testament to Americans' devotion to nonprofit organizations as an important vehicle for community building. People give to express the values about which they care deeply. Thanks to their actions, many vital organizations, on the national level as well as in local communities, can regularly depend on the money (and time) of countless individuals of all income levels. This is powerful evidence of the commitment and altruism of Americans.

It is also significant that about two-thirds of those who file US tax returns—those who do not have income sufficient to make it worthwhile to itemize their deductions—contribute to charity without benefiting from any specific tax deduction for their donations. Instead, they benefit from the "standard deduction," which for many years was calculated at 10 percent of gross income but which now floats a bit depending on tax status and is intended to reflect all categories of otherwise deductible expenditures. They thus benefit from this provision whether they make contributions or not—meaning that their gifts earn them no financial reward.

After individual giving, the next largest percentage of civic-sector organization revenues—$58.4 billion in 2015—comes from American foundations.[20] As the late Paul Ylvisaker, the much-admired, long-standing senior program officer at the Ford Foundation, put it, "foundations are America's passing gear." They not only provide year-after-year support for existing nonprofit organizations, which are primarily the domain of midsized and smaller foundations' giving as well as community foundations, but they are also the "go-to" source for enterprising individuals who need start-up money for new nonprofit organizations.

For example, inspired by Rachel Carson's *Silent Spring*, which was published in 1962, four young men fresh out of Yale Law School decided in 1967 to try to create a national organization that would focus on strengthening America's capacity to conserve its natural resources and protect its environment from degradation by using their legal training. They turned to Mitchell Sviridoff, the Ford Foundation's visionary but highly practical vice president for national affairs; they were successful in persuading him to have Ford provide significant start-up and sustaining support for what became, in 1970, the Natural Resources Defense Council. In 1968, other like-minded individuals who had in 1967 gone ahead and founded the Environmental Defense Fund, a science-based environmental organization, approached the Ford Foundation and it, too, started to receive significant Ford support that year. Today, having been primed and sustained for several years by foundations, both of these organizations have attracted broad membership support across the nation, with the Environmental Defense Fund having more than 2 million paid members and the Natural Resources Defense Council having 1.5 million. Both are widely admired for their numerous, vitally important accomplishments in the creation and enforcement of a body of national and state legislation, informed by rigorous scientific research and evidence-based economics and public policy findings. These two organizations are continuing to confer extraordinary benefits on America, a very significant return on the investment capital provided by the Ford Foundation.

Foundations are in fact the only readily available source for financing innovation in America's civic sector. They have catalyzed, mediated, and facilitated many of the major social changes over the past century and have seeded new fields of research in universities and think tanks, such as that which led to the understanding of the human genome. They were "angel" as well as "mezzanine" investors in social change before the venture capital community as we know it today was born and invented those terms.[21] The list of large and small nonprofit organizations now playing vital roles in America that were founded and/or significantly funded by foundations is mind blowing, from Human Rights Watch, Human Rights First, and the NAACP Legal Defense Fund to the Center for Science in the Public Interest, the mission of which is to protect the safety of our food and medicine, often against decisions of both government agencies and corporations.

Where, other than foundations, could the creators of these and other organizations have gone to seek the funds to realize their visions for America's benefit? Of course, wealthy philanthropists can serve the same start-up purpose, but, unlike foundations, they are not as visible or as easily reachable. Moreover, with only a few exceptions, individuals tend not to be a fruitful source of early capital for new ventures. No matter how wealthy and philanthropically inclined, they do not readily opt to support untested ideas championed by people with whom they are not already acquainted.

Because the role of piloting new ways of tackling social problems and of fill-ing perceived niches in America's civic sector is among foundations' unique strengths, they often are the first and last resort of would-be social entre-preneurs.

One reason foundations have been relatively welcoming sources of sup-port for new methods of solving social problems is that they can be patient investors, testing the waters and observing and learning over time which approaches hold promise, which ones call for more nurturing and experi-mentation, and which are likely to be dead ends. They can underwrite orga-nizations whose mission must press on over long periods of time and adapt to new information and circumstances. The ability to make such judgments and to stick with them over many years is among the forms of wisdom—or, at least, of strategic judgment—that can accumulate in a secure and long-lasting institution. To be sure, not all old or perpetual foundations have shown such canny judgment or consistently managed their risks so wisely. But experience, discernment, and a willingness to persevere and learn all de-pend on a time frame unrushed by some fast-approaching day of reckoning. Are funders with a much shorter time horizon able to apply these long-term approaches? If the goal is to expend all of one's charitable wealth in a few years or decades and then depart the field, is there time enough to master philanthropy's subtler and slower arts?

It is too early in the evolution of time-limited philanthropy—whether "giving while living" donors or spend-down foundations—to know whether they, too, will be willing and able to play the same role of discerning and pa-tient backer of new and long-range projects. In principle, both "giving while living" donors and foundations that are deliberately spending themselves down must spend larger amounts in a foreshortened period of time than would be appropriate if they instead were to create permanently endowed philanthropies. Thus the large amounts and shortened time frames put a premium on dramatic gestures over the slower, more methodical approaches that can lead, by and by, to big discoveries. But the evidence that now exists suggests that they are more interested in making novel "big bets" on complex problems than on supporting and enlarging the infrastructure of existing nonprofits and birthing new ones. It is this question that I will investigate in the pages ahead: since we are so reliant on the health and impact of our diverse weave of independent sector activities, does the recent shift to "giving while living" support or threaten the well-being of, and innovation within, our pluralistic civic sector?

TAX INCENTIVES, BENEFITS, AND EXEMPTIONS

Charitable nonprofits are exempt from many forms of federal and state taxation, including taxes on their income and, in most states and localities, on their real property; individual and corporate contributions to these organizations are also deductible, with certain limitations, against income taxes. This means that when citizens give in large amounts, as Americans do, government treasuries lose significant revenues that, but for such tax exemption and the deductibility of contributions, they would otherwise receive.[22]

Many persuasive reasons exist for government to provide tax incentives to individuals and corporations to encourage them to donate to civic-sector organizations. To begin with, while the loss to the US Treasury from the deductibility of contributions to nonprofit organizations is less than $50 billion annually,[23] the amount donated at present to nonprofit organizations by living individuals and by bequest at death is almost $300 billion. Add in the amounts donated by corporations and foundations, and the total annual giving is above $373 billion. In other words, for every dollar the Treasury loses because of the tax deductibility of contributions only by individuals to charitable organizations, Americans give about *seven* dollars to charity, for a net gain to society of about $250 billion with only a very modest loss to the Treasury's capacity to serve the public good.

Moreover, I strongly believe that, in most countries but especially in America, there is much greater comparative social benefit in incentivizing individuals, corporations, and foundations to allocate discretionary dollars to public purposes than for government to reserve to itself the privilege of spending a comparable amount of money. Considering the trillions of dollars that government will spend for various purposes and the half-trillion it already spends for purposes analogous to what the civic sector itself spends, encouraging the contributions of nongovernmental actors seems like a healthy balancing of the sources of civic-sector revenues. Incentivizing citizens by means of tax benefits to make gifts to tax-exempt organizations in appropriate circumstances, therefore, seems much more conducive to the public good than is direct government spending for the same purposes authorized by elected officials and doled out by the executive branch.[24] Doing so permits the diverse values of millions of individual American citizens to balance and temper the collective judgment of majorities, as well as elites, about how best to advance the public good.

As noted by countless scholars and observers, the dynamism of America's for-profit sector is powered by the ability of individuals and groups to test out and shepherd their ideas into organizations that prosper or perish on their own motion. Aside from ministerial government approvals, entrepreneurs of business ventures are unencumbered by significant substantive restraints upon what they choose to launch. That same freedom is what has enabled America's not-for-profit sector to thrive steadily. Innovative ideas for social problem-solving almost always originate with individuals, think tanks, civic organizations that specialize in particular problems, university researchers, activists, or others rather than from committees within government. Even when government appoints and convenes problem-oriented task forces or commissions, most of the members recruited for such groups are from outside government. They are selected because of their expertise, usually as members of an organization or as researchers in an educational institution substantially supported by the charitable contributions of individuals, corporations, or foundations.

Ideas that are critical of government policy or that aim at changing such policy almost inevitably require a test run before being found worthy of and ready for scaling with government funds. Because their goal is to alter public policy or practice, they are very unlikely candidates for being piloted initially by the federal government itself. The very same factors that have created gridlock in Congress make it extremely unlikely that that legislative body would appropriate funds for such pilots. Consider, for example, the Patient Protection and Affordable Care Act, also known as Obamacare. It was designed by a nonprofit think tank—The Urban Institute—and piloted by the State of Massachusetts before it gained enough traction to be advanced as a national program by the Obama administration. Another example is the Personal Responsibility and Work Opportunity Reconciliation Act of 1996, recommended by President Bill Clinton and enacted by a Republican Congress, which transformed public assistance from "welfare" grants to work incentives. That transformative program's provisions had been piloted and evaluated for 20 years under the direction of the Manpower Demonstration Research Corporation, a civic-sector nonprofit organization created by the Ford Foundation and supported by other philanthropies as well as the US Department of Labor. Still another example is the Obama administration's Race to the Top initiative in education reform. In that program, states wishing to compete for US Department of Education dollars to implement reform of their K–12 education systems received substantial planning grants from the Bill and Melinda Gates Foundation to prepare their proposals for submission to the US Department of Education.

Some of the most important public policy initiatives of the federal and state governments over the past 50 years have been developed, honed, and advocated by civil society organizations. For example, the equal housing and fair lending laws of the 1970s were substantially designed by nonprofit organizations before they were enacted, as were the Low-Income Housing Tax Credit and the New Markets Tax Credits of the 1990s. Organizations supported by the Robert Wood Johnson Foundation and other health funders played a decisive role in the development of state and federal antismoking policies in the 1990s. The environmental groups mentioned earlier created the scientific, policy, and legal staff infrastructures of the environmental conservation and protection movement. Those and other like-minded organizations have initiated, advocated, and litigated such important national legislative provisions as the Environmental Protection Act, the Clean Air Act, and the Clean Water Act, along with their updates and improvements since the 1970s and 1980s. Another example is the growing number of states that have enacted legislation to prohibit or severely constrain payday lending, for which the Center for Responsible Lending, a nonprofit organization supported by foundations and individual philanthropists and based in Durham, North Carolina, has supplied the energy and strategic direction. On the political right, the American Legislative Exchange Council, funded by conservative donors, has provided many state legislatures with draft bills on social and economic issues ready-made for them to enact into law—which they have done repeatedly.

Given the critical role that public-interest organizations play in the development of public policy, it is peculiar that the US Tax Code constrains those very organizations from many forms of communication with lawmakers and voters who would benefit from hearing their views. No such barriers bar corporate interests, of course—which leads to a strange and unhelpful imbalance in the range of messages legislators may hear and citizens may express. Corporations, both individually and collectively, have long recognized the critical role that government at all levels plays in regulating their business interests, practices, and decisions, and they have accordingly built often huge advocacy and lobbying staffs to protect their interests in Washington and in many state capitals across the United States. Corporate officials have often banded together in political action committees to make campaign contributions to candidates for public office, and they continue to do so today. Therefore, while corporations are free to lobby for their interests, with after-tax dollars, foundations, ostensibly because of their tax exemption, cannot. Foundations, however, which often find themselves on the opposite side of corporate interests with respect to many issues, have been prohibited by the Internal Revenue Code from engaging in lobbying, with four minor exceptions—one of which is where the foundation's own existence is at stake—and of course foundations themselves cannot use their funds to support or oppose candidates for political office, which recent Supreme Court decisions permit corporations to do.

Moreover, operating charities continue to be limited in the amount of money they can spend on advocacy regarding legislation and remain prohibited from spending any organizational money on behalf of or opposed to candidates for political office. Because much of what corporations seek to do in their public policy advocacy is regarded by many as less in the public interest than in their own private interest—such as their efforts to protect themselves from tighter environmental regulation or stricter consumer protection legislation—it is all the more important that the ability of civil society organizations and foundations to engage in advocacy and lobbying be widened. No persuasive logic exists to support permitting corporations to lobby without limit while stringently prohibiting foundations and substantially limiting operating charities from doing so. The ostensible rationale for such a distinction is that charities are tax exempt and therefore should not be able to lobby at will, while corporations, even if they receive tax subsidies, are permitted to do so with after-tax dollars. Like many other scholars and tax lawyers, I am persuaded that this is another distinction without a difference.

Another arena in which tax exemption is the only way of publicly supporting an essential function in American public life is religion. The nearly half-million nonprofit organizations that are religious institutions cannot receive general operating funds from the federal government because of the constitutional separation of church and state derived from the First Amendment's two clauses dealing with religion: the Establishment Clause and the Free Exercise Clause: "Congress shall make no law respecting an establishment of religion, or prohibiting the free exercise thereof." If private contributions to religion were not incentivized by federal tax policy through the deductibility of such contributions against individual income taxes, a major source of funding for religion would be diminished. Religious organizations now receive about one-third of all the money contributed to charity each year by Americans; providing tax deductibility for such contributions is the only way government can constitutionally facilitate the flow of unrestricted financial resources to this wide diversity of organizations that support both spiritual and civil society. While government has been permitted by the courts to provide funds to religion-supported nonexplicitly religious secular activities, such as housing for the homeless, soup kitchens, and job training, such nonexplicitly religious service activities by religious organizations are estimated as consuming 30 percent or less of religious organization budgets.

Along similar lines, consider the many other kinds of objectives on which it is technically permissible for government to spend public revenues but for which there is often little or no public or political agreement to do so. The visual and performing arts are a good example of this reluctance, and the bitter controversies over some of the grants made by the National Endowment for the Arts are reminders of how diverse Americans' definition of art can be and how passionate Americans can be about the differences reflected in certain kinds of art. If there were no charitable deduction for fostering the artistic pursuits, and if the representatives of the public remained reluctant to appropriate funds for them, America would be impoverished culturally.

All of which is to say that providing tax exemptions for organizations and permitting tax deductibility for charitable donations to them are powerful—and, I would add, indispensable—ways of providing significant benefit to the American public as a whole, when government either cannot or will not make funds available for those purposes.

Whether the benefits conferred by America's civic sector outweigh the revenue loss to government is clearly subject to disagreement. Many on the left of the political spectrum quarrel with the provision of generous tax benefits to organizations such as art museums, symphony orchestras and opera companies, private K–12 schools, elite private and public universities, and hospitals, some of which are patronized primarily by Americans who are well-off. Many on the right and in the center of that spectrum see such organizations as benefiting society as a whole, and therefore view their tax-exempt public support as appropriate, but may still want to use the levers of the tax code to enforce certain directions among the beneficiaries (such as arguing that university endowments should be used to lower today's tuition rates).

Proposals have been made by countless policy wonks and various interest groups whereby more generous tax benefits could be provided to organizations and their contributors serving only America's least well-off, with lesser benefits to organizations that do not specifically benefit that demographic. So far, however, no one has been able to figure out how to distinguish persuasively between the two kinds of organizations. The many opponents of establishing preferential tax benefits for organizations that focus on serving

America's least well-off argue that such distinctions are difficult, if not impossible, to calculate persuasively and that the very act of differentiating between them is inherently invidious when, for almost four centuries of English and American law, *all* nonprofit organizations have been regarded as of equal worth to society as a whole.

Making persuasive distinctions between "poor-serving" and "all-serving" nonprofits is in fact challenging analytically. For example, in most of the elite universities, as many as half of the enrolled students receive financial aid; penalizing such universities by reducing or eliminating the tax benefits extended to them or their donors would inevitably harm the least well-off students who benefit from those institutions' financial aid programs, as well as all the other students enrolled there. The very same problem plagues calculations with respect to religious institutions and their contributors. Most of these kinds of institutions devote about one-third of their incomes to soup kitchens, charity given to the poor, mentoring programs, housing for the homeless, retraining for former criminal offenders, rehabilitation for those addicted to illegal drugs, and the like. Curtailing tax benefits to them would therefore harm those now receiving help from these places, as well as all members of their congregations, irrespective of their financial situation. A third kind of analogous problem is raised by how tax officials might characterize organizations that benefit people regardless of need—such as medical research, environmental protection, and efforts to improve governance—for purposes of being regarded as "poor-serving" versus "all-serving."

Because of the difficulty of making persuasive distinctions of social merit between one kind of historically charitable undertaking and all others, most observers, scholars, tax policy specialists, and politicians have been opposed to giving more generous tax deductions to organizations that benefit the least well-off than to other groups.

The consequent standoff led only to proposals by President Obama—and by some Democratic representatives and senators—to cap the benefit to donors at the level prevailing for those in the 28 percent marginal tax bracket, which would diminish the value of the deduction benefit available to any taxpayers whose income is federally taxed at higher levels (now subject to rates as high as 39.6%). When such proposals have come up for review in Congress, they have been roundly defeated. They simply decrease the loss to the US Treasury but do nothing to incentivize charitable contributions to flow to a greater degree toward America's poor rather than to institutions that benefit the American population without regard to socioeconomic status.

Many good reasons exist for Americans' long-term commitment to empowering, as well as to supporting by generous tax breaks, the nation's civic sector in benefiting *all* Americans. While America's first nonprofit organizations—the freestanding Protestant churches in New England that delivered comprehensive services to their local community—operated independently because they preceded the establishment of government, today the role of most nonprofits is a collaborative one that includes countless partnerships with both government—federal, state, and local—as well as often with for-profit corporations along with other nonprofit organizations in implementation and in funding. It is no exaggeration to describe today's civic sector—operating charities and the philanthropic individuals and foundations that support them—as playing a key role alongside the public and the for-profit sectors in striving to solve the many problems facing individual citizens and groups, as well as in sustaining all manner of citizens' voluntary activities and organizations that contribute to the public good in innumerable ways. As I have proposed, it is tricky to try to impose a "control panel" on how this wide range of important causes is supported. The splendidly diverse tapestry of public-serving institutions and organizations makes big differences in all of the "in-between" spaces of our national fabric.

WHAT ABOUT ENDOWED FOUNDATIONS?

Criticisms similar to those advanced above regarding the monolithic treatment of all kinds of nonprofit organizations have been revived, around the turn of the new century, regarding the institution of endowed foundations. The reasons have been much the same, although with a different twist. The core of the criticism is an attack on the idea of endowing foundations and requiring them to pay out to operating charities only an annual specified minimum (5%) of their endowment. The critics argue that it is inherently discriminatory against the present, and perhaps especially the poor of the present, to allow warehousing of such capital assets, presumably perpetually, while enabling donors to benefit from the full value of their charitable gifts at the time the gifts are made. Thereafter, present and future society are permitted to benefit only from modest annual payments from the income on those assets.[25]

By describing all perpetual foundations as "restricted-spending philanthropy," Professor Brian Galle of Georgetown Law School has attempted to load the dice at the outset. In essence, he disagrees strongly with the idea of creating perpetual foundations that preserve their "purchasing power" over the years in order to serve society's needs at any time over the long run. He argues that public policy, by exempting foundation earnings from taxation, actually encourages foundations to spend as little as possible and that board members tend to regard the preservation of purchasing power in their endowments as an obligation of prudent management. The result, in his view, is a systematic bias in philanthropy in favor of the future at the expense of the present.

In fact, virtually all perpetual foundations are unrestricted in how much they can spend annually. During the Great Recession of 2008–2011, many foundations often paid out as much as 7 percent or 8 percent of their assets to ensure that grantees could continue their work despite the decline in the economy. Furthermore, in my interviews for this book, I often asked whether a particular foundation's trustees would be able to spend its assets completely down if they chose to do so, and virtually all of my subjects answered yes—if the board found an initiative that would convincingly serve the mission of the foundation.

In truth, what such critics are attacking is the fact that founders of, or contributors to, foundations are able to receive a tax deduction for the value of their gifts in the year that the gifts are made, while the public will benefit only from the income earned on such gifts that is spent year by year in the future. The same criticism is now also being made against the donor-advised funds that have come to flourish since 1990, discussed at greater length in Chapter 3. Here, again, donors receive a tax deduction in the year the gifts are made to the organizations hosting the funds, whether national for-profit firms or regional community foundations, but their donations are not paid out until future years. Of greatest importance, however, is that the argument made by such critics could be applied equally to a gift that is immediately donated to an operating charity, if the recipient organization does not itself put the money to instant use. If the organization receives the money in Year 1 but spends it only in increments in Years 2, 3, and 4—or perhaps uses the money for its own endowment, spending only the income and not the principal—it would surely run into the same objection.

The argument for favoring the needs of the present over those of the future is arbitrary and almost certainly difficult to define and utilize practically. Moreover, if acted upon and extended to its full logical consequences, such a regulatory preference as forcing perpetual foundations to pay out more than the federally required annual amount or requiring universities to spend stipulated percentages of their endowment for particular purposes such as scholarships, would have devastating effects not only on foundations but on all nonprofit organizations whose existence depends in part on endowments. Indeed, recent years have also seen calls for taxing large university endowments or mandating that some portion of such endowments be spent to lower tuition. Such a change in America's tax policies would in effect kill the goose that laid the golden eggs and threaten the very existence of these institutions that are indispensable to America's continuing dynamism.

No one has made the point more forcefully or cogently than the late Nobel Prize–winner Professor James Tobin of Yale University. In mandating that endowment asset managers must not spend more annually than the endowment's "after-inflation rate of compound return, so that investment gains are spent equally on current and future constituents of the endowed assets,"[26] he wrote, "The trustees of endowed institutions are the guardians of the future against the claims of the present. Their task in managing the endowment is to preserve equity among generations."[27]

The American civic sector, whatever its eccentricities and imperfections, plays a critical, if not always well understood, role in the quality of our common life. It has proven to be a durable asset but it's not indestructible. The current ferment in early 21st-century philanthropy—much like that in the early 20th century—suggests profound changes ahead, both for the organizations that do the hard labor of serving the public interest and for the donors and foundations that furnish them with the means to do their work. Those changes may be thoughtful or reckless; they may take due note of the richness and complexity of the American public-interest landscape or proceed only to disrupt and dismantle. In the following pages, I will propose some means of recognizing and choosing among these different courses and suggest ways that American philanthropy can innovate and adapt, serving both the present and the future, without sacrificing the principles that have made it the envy of the world.

PART ONE

THE CHANGING LANDSCAPE OF AMERICAN PHILANTHROPY

The amount of change that has already taken place in America's philanthropic sector just since 1990 is mind-boggling. Taken together, these changes have transformed philanthropy in fundamental ways, most of them for the better. In Part One, I describe the components of that transformation and hope that I've made clear why each of them is making a significant contribution for the better.

In the first chapter of this section, I highlight the sharpening of discipline and focus among foundations—making them, on average, more strategic and ambitious, more intent on achieving clear impact, and more attuned to measurement, including benchmarks and indicators of progress. The second chapter deals with the new ways in which individual philanthropists, foundations, and corporations are operating, including their greater willingness to collaborate and the innovative uses of their wealth beyond pure grantmaking. Chapter 3 examines the newly developed infrastructure organizations that underlie and assist charitable giving, including such giving vehicles as donor-advised funds, the creation of numerous consulting firms to advise foundations and donors, and the impact of the Internet and social media in particular on philanthropy.

chapter one

A More Disciplined Focus

A new spirit is enlivening perpetual foundations. This change is best epitomized by what the Kresge Foundation writes in its 2014 Annual Report:

> Those of us invested in community—the public, private, nonprofit and philanthropic sectors—are stepping up, electing to participate beyond our traditional boundaries and areas of interest. What is emerging is a style of philanthropy that is visionary and strategic. It is unafraid to ask hard questions and fearless in the face of great challenge. Unlike our practices of the past, almost nothing is off limits today. We are willing to take risks and propose solutions commensurate with the size of the challenge at hand. This new way of working has become central to the ethos at The Kresge Foundation. We believe this approach represents the next generation of philanthropy for us and for the entire sector. . . . Bold is not a goal; it is a byproduct of collective effort. Bold is the urban future that awaits us.[1]

An example of this energy is the role that Kresge played, together with other large and small foundations, in helping the city of Detroit emerge from bankruptcy, as recounted in the same annual report:

> In 2013, with $18 billion in debt, the city of Detroit entered the largest municipal bankruptcy in U.S. history. Rip Rapson, president and CEO of The Kresge Foundation, was on the front lines of efforts to bring about a speedy resolution, one that protected the pensions of city retirees and safeguarded the world-class art collection at the Detroit Institute of Arts, the city's most valuable asset.
>
> Rapson and 10 other philanthropic leaders, together with the state of Michigan and the Detroit Institute of Arts, created an $816 million

fund, the Foundation for Detroit's Future—what has become known as the Grand Bargain. The fund enabled the art to be sold to a nonprofit trust, with the proceeds nearly fully funding retiree pensions. Equally as important, it prevented litigation that would have delayed indefinitely the essential and imperative work of city building.[2]

The kind of dynamism represented by Detroit's Grand Bargain—a willingness among foundations to depart from established practice and familiar roles and to seize opportunities to make a dramatic difference—reflects what the Kresge Foundation calls "Six Core Beliefs [that] have the power to reshape the philanthropic sector for the challenges of the 21st Century":

- Belief #1: Philanthropy has to be prepared to cut from its safe and secure moorings to embrace a level of risk commensurate with the magnitude of the challenge at hand.

- Belief #2: Philanthropy, by shedding its territoriality, can multiply its efficacy by recognizing the potency of its undeniable interdependence.

- Belief #3: Philanthropic leaders must be willing to act; they must create space to hear and internalize the wisdom of our community's collective voice.

- Belief #4: Philanthropy must increasingly become comfortable in engaging the vicissitudes and ambiguities of public-sector policies and practices.

- Belief #5: Philanthropy can find key acupuncture points that trigger the power of places to reflect community identity and create the map for vibrant, equitable civic life.

- Belief #6: There is a moral imperative for privately endowed philanthropies like Kresge to stitch together the other beliefs in ways that will improve outcomes for low-income people living in America's cities.[3]

Other large foundations have begun to express the same aspirations. Julia Stasch, who in 2015 was elected president of the John D. and Catherine T. MacArthur Foundation, wrote an essay in her first annual report, covering the previous year, entitled "Time for Change." The essay was posted on the foundation's website in 2015 and includes the following:

> [W]e need to change. . . . Be bolder and aim higher. Embrace indepen-
> dent, even unconventional, thinking. Act with greater urgency, even as
> we remain patient for the fruits of real, lasting change. Be more open,
> curious, and experimental, and take more risk. Set ambitious goals that
> are clear and practical, and seek significant, measurable progress.
>
> In the future, we will work primarily through programs and projects
> that are larger in scale, time-limited in nature, or designed to reach spe-
> cific objectives. We will place less emphasis on program areas with an
> indefinite lifespan.
>
> While this solution-driven approach is a topic of debate in philanthro-
> py, we believe it is right for MacArthur and the depth of impact we strive
> to achieve. Its application means focusing our not-unlimited resources,
> our leadership, and other assets in fewer areas where we believe real and
> lasting progress may be possible. More focus will require hard choices
> about some fields where we have long been active.
>
> Higher ambitions also will require a greater tolerance for risk and fail-
> ure. We will need to be even more flexible and innovative in our strat-
> egies and tactics in response to new circumstances, and ready to enter
> into alliances with unexpected partners. We will observe closely and listen
> carefully as we adopt an even more rigorous practice of reflection and
> learning.[4]

Other private foundations have expressed similar intentions, albeit without the trial by fire that Kresge and its Grand Bargain partners encountered
in the furnace of Detroit's financial collapse. But at this point, most of those
intentions are just that—intentions—and it remains to be seen whether and
how they will be translated into achievements. I quote Kresge at length because it has already demonstrated its determination to transform itself. The
animating principles that emerged from and guided—indeed were shaped
by—the achievements it reported in its 2014 Annual Report give its stated
intentions greater credibility. The same might fairly be said about some of
Kresge's partners in the Grand Bargain, including the Ford, Knight, Mott,
and Skillman Foundations and the Community Foundation of Southeast
Michigan. Moreover, in Darren Walker's first two years of leading the Ford
Foundation, he has created a comparable degree of excitement and optimism

about the changes taking place there, some of which are discussed in the following pages.

A NOVEL GRANTMAKING PARADIGM

For all of the 100-year-long history of American foundations, the prevailing pattern of decision-making was to choose among grant proposals that "came in over the transom," as newspaper and magazine editors used to say about unsolicited manuscripts. Leaving aside the fact that foundation offices no longer have any doors with transoms above them through which incoming proposals could come, the analogy as well as the practice continues to dominate foundation behavior. Clearly there are exceptions, as a growing number of foundations' websites prominently advertise "unsolicited proposals not accepted." Whether the proposals arrive randomly or are requested by the foundation, however, the criteria by which they are considered, granted, or rejected is based on the nature and quality of the particular substantive request and how well it fits with the priorities of the foundation considering it.

However, the Edna McConnell Clark Foundation has changed that grantmaking pattern, and its initiative seems slowly to be catching on. After becoming president of that foundation in 1996 and spending four years administering programs in five different areas, Michael Bailin came to the conclusion that, if social impact was to be the measure by which a foundation should assess its success, that foundation could achieve much more by honing its decision-making model. In 2000, he persuaded the foundation's trustees to spin off or close down four of its historic programs and concentrate on only one: Youth Development, broadly defined.[5]

Then, instead of doing what foundations had done for years—letting others make the initial move to send in proposals—he decided to reverse course by having the foundation itself take the initiative. By soliciting a wide range of knowledgeable informants around the country, Bailin set out to identify those organizations within the Clark Foundation's program catchment area that were demonstrably performing well already and then to help strengthen those organizations by providing general operating support and relevant consulting advice on strategy, management, business and financial planning, evaluation, board-building, and marketing, with the goal of enabling them to serve even more people at the same if not a higher level of quality. Obviously, rigorous evaluation criteria were essential for determining whether an organization was performing well in the first place and is achieving even more once support by the Clark Foundation kicks in.[6]

That change—shifting the focus of foundation grantmaking from the merits of a particular substantive program to the success of a whole *organization*, based on its established track record of success in delivering those substantive programs—was revolutionary. It has already begun to achieve traction, not only with other foundations but also with newly emerging institutions such as the Robin Hood Foundation in New York, the Tipping Point Community in San Francisco, and A Better Chicago—antipoverty funds supported mainly by the financial sector and concentrating on particular metropolitan areas. Robin Hood was founded by hedge fund manager Paul Tudor Jones in New York in 1988, Tipping Point by philanthropist Daniel Lurie in 2005, and A Better Chicago by Liam Krehbiel, a former Bain & Company consultant, in 2010.[7]

Solid evidence persuades like nothing else, including eloquent rhetoric. And, as in the Goldman Sachs example below, it was the Bridgespan Group that designed the evidence-generation system for the Edna McConnell Clark initiatives.[8]

Another example of how evidence-based data are influencing decisions to scale initiatives is Goldman Sachs' *10,000 Women*, an innovation discussed at greater length in a later section. Under the leadership of Chairman and CEO Lloyd C. Blankfein and Managing Director of Corporate Engagement Dina Habib Powell, the company established this initiative to identify, train, and facilitate the financing of women's businesses in developing countries. Before it was launched, Ms. Powell engaged The Bridgespan Group, America's preeminent nonprofit management consultancy,[9] to plan and execute the program's outcomes research and evaluation. By 2015, the data generated by Bridgespan documented achievements of the participants in *10,000 Women* that were so impressive that the World Bank decided to join the cause. In fact, the World Bank upped the ante by creating a $600 million Women Entrepreneurs Opportunity Facility, which is expected to raise the number of target beneficiaries from 10,000 to 100,000 women worldwide. What made such a scale increase possible was the existence of carefully designed research that produced persuasive evidence of the success of the original initiative.

A PREOCCUPATION WITH MAXIMUM IMPACT: THE DOWNSIDE

These days, it seems that "impact achievement" has become *the* goal of many philanthropists, especially the wealthiest ones. They seem to have become obsessed with achieving the greatest social impact, sometimes without much concern about which field or area of need benefits. Rather than striving specifically to feed the hungriest or to assuage the poor's most pressing needs, they seek, in a variation on Jeremy Bentham and John Stuart Mill, to produce the greatest good for the greatest number. On December 23, 2015, for example, the Bloomberg.com website featured an article by Sangwon Yoon entitled "From Ackman to Musk, Charity Giving Takes on Stock-Picking Feel."[10] The article's two subheadlines are "'Effective altruism' seeks to maximize returns from charity," and "Gates and Gross fans of a data-driven approach to giving." The author goes on to write the following:

> Econometrics is the new buzzword in charity circles with a growing number of nonprofit organizations applying a more scientific methodology to lure the rich and powerful to give more. GiveWell, for example, studies academic research and data to test a given approach and applies metrics such as "cost per life saved" or "financial benefits to recipients per dollar spent by donors."
>
> "When the end of the year comes, people prefer not donating than donating badly," said Alexandre Mars, a tech entrepreneur and venture capitalist-turned-philanthropist.
>
> Which is why Mars set up Epic Foundation, where he manages a portfolio of 20 youth-focused social enterprises for donors. The idea is that high net-worth individuals may not have the time to do the homework themselves but want guarantees they are getting value for money. Mars vets the charities by analyzing their data, ranking them through an algorithm and producing reports for each based on on-site visits and interviews.
>
> "We want to track what we've donated," he said. "In the non-profit world, this doesn't exist: You would have to wait six months or a year for a brochure or get invited to a gala you have to pay" to attend.
>
> GiveWell, which was founded by two former analysts at Bridgewater Associates, have their top picks each year.[11]

In another article earlier in 2015, Bill Gross, former CEO of PIMCO, the huge fixed-income investment firm, was quoted as saying that he intends to devote his entire net worth to giving to those organizations, which appear to promise the greatest amount of social impact as measured by data, irrespective of the kind of social good the organizations are doing. Similarly, Elie Hassenfeld, a hedge fund manager and cofounder of GiveWell, sums up this attitude toward doing good by asking, "What charity will give me the biggest bang for my buck?"[12]

This all seems benign enough. Who can possibly object to donors striving to achieve maximum impact with their charitable dollars? But is impact the only criterion? Is the nature of the problem on which impact is achieved irrelevant? In *Give Smart: Getting Results from Your Philanthropy*, my coauthor Tom Tierney and I list "What do you really care about?" as the very first question donors should ask themselves before supporting an organization or cause. Unless a person believes that no hierarchy of human needs, as ranked by one's own priority of values, is possible, how can one adopt a decision criterion based on quantifiable impact alone, without respect to the values one cares about?

A skeptic might reply that, while it is appealing to rank human needs according to a donor's own judgment of priorities, it would be wrong to do so. Placing so much importance on one's own particular values and beliefs, such a person might say, can tend toward narcissism. Someone who takes this view might go on to argue that tax-privileged philanthropic dollars are so scarce that any warm feelings the donor might derive from their use in one preferred field or another must pale in importance compared with the volume of benefit to humanity that could be derived from a dispassionate calculation of each dollar's most productive use.

To me, however, a decision-making goal that elevates the quantity of impact above the substantive good of the impact seems to be the truer form of narcissism, motivated only by a competitive drive to be the "impact king" of the universe. It also seems inhuman, indeed downright robotic. Personally, I would prefer to be known as someone who cares deeply about feeding the hungry or about perpetuating the glorious legacy of Mozart, for example, than someone who simply wants to wring the most impact out of my charitable dollars. If all that counts in trying to do good is the achievement of maximum impact, without regard to what one achieves impact in doing, philanthropy will have emptied itself of its humanity.

If the utility maximizers were somehow to win the day and philanthropy became entirely bound up with calculations of social return, imagine what a depressing effect it would have on the propensity to give. What moves most human beings to give wealth for the benefit of others that they could otherwise have spent on themselves is rarely the quantity of impact their gift might achieve but rather their caring for other human beings; their sense of gratitude to institutions that gave them a break, educated or healed them; or in general for endeavors that uplift or benefit large numbers of other human beings in countless—and sometimes uncountable—ways.

The fact is that the institutional and individual philanthropists who are most effective in achieving beneficial impacts are those who possess a great deal of knowledge about the problem area they wish to tackle. They may have come into philanthropy with such knowledge, but, more often, they must acquire it by extensive consultation, research, travel, and learning. Is it likely that donors will invest the time and energy—both physical and intellectual—that acquiring this knowledge requires if the focus of their giving is not something of great personal, emotional, or philosophical importance to them? Those who lack such knowledge and experience tend to be easily swayed to part with their dollars by smooth-talking, charismatic leaders who promise greatly but are able to deliver little.

Finally, an exclusive focus on getting the biggest bang for one's philanthropic dollars without regard to subject matter is bound to lead some prospective donors away from the most challenging problems and toward the easily solvable ones. That would undo one of the principal strengths of the civic sector and one of the principal rationales for exempting donations from taxation: the unleashing of myriad forms of human ingenuity and creativity in pursuit of elusive and neglected goals. My overall point is that not all philanthropy should be thought of as "effective" even if it aspires to a particular measure of effectiveness. We need collectively to consider what really matters about philanthropy and the causes that it supports rather than giving in to a reductive approach.

ORGANIZING, MANAGING, AND INVESTING FOR IMPACT: THE UPSIDE

Like so many of the other changes in philanthropy over the past 25 years, the growing organizational focus on mission, goal, strategy, performance benchmarks, and measurable results can be traced back more than 100 years to Andrew Carnegie and John D. Rockefeller. Both men's philanthropic credos were based on "scientific philanthropy," designed to cure problems at their roots, rather than on traditional charity, which both of them regarded as merely palliative. Neither Carnegie nor Rockefeller gave their institutions "express organizational missions" to tackle any specific problems, but they did (at least implicitly) give their foundations a mission of tackling problems at the root. Today, however, thinking has evolved to the point that, if a foundation or nonprofit organization is to tackle a problem at its root, it must adopt an express organizational mission dedicated to doing so, as well as an articulation of one or more goals, the choice of one or more strategies whereby the mission-serving goal is thought to be capable of being implemented, along with mechanisms for generating benchmarks that reveal whether or not one is in fact achieving the intention presupposed by the organizational mission.

Like the idea of maximizing impact, foundations' preoccupation with mission, strategies, and so on has both advantages and disadvantages. As a means of focusing an organization's energies and building its knowledge of a field, the discipline of setting a few well-defined goals, charting paths to achieving them, and measuring progress along the way is an excellent management device. It can easily become an end in itself, however, with the mechanics of benchmarking and performance-tracking occupying more and more time, at the expense of firsthand observation, learning, and interaction with people on the front lines.

The idea of a mission-goal-strategy-benchmarks-measurable-results-logic model for nonprofit organizations and foundations was first spelled out in public and professional discourse in Peter Drucker's 1990 book, *Managing the Nonprofit Organization: Practices and Principles*.[13] Part One of that book is "The Mission Comes First: and Your Role as a Leader," and Part Two is "From Mission to Performance: Effective strategies for marketing, innovation and fund development."

Three years later, the idea of a mission-driven nonprofit enterprise was given a significant boost by a 1993 gift to Harvard Business School (HBS) from John Whitehead's Fund for Nonprofit Management, which helped the school found its Social Enterprise Initiative (described more fully in Chapter 3). The dominant themes of the initiative, and of the HBS faculty's teaching about nonprofit management more generally, were clarity and focus on mission and strategy. The creation of this initiative soon inspired similarly oriented programs at other elite schools.

In 1994, Jim Collins and Jerry Porras published *Built to Last: Successful Habits of Visionary Companies*, some of whose lingo—such as "Big Hairy

Audacious Goals," familiarly known as "BHAGs"—quickly jumped over from business to nonprofits and foundations. When The Atlantic Philanthropies went through its strategic planning process at the turn of the 21st century, the main mission the institution's leaders assigned to the head of the working group was to come up with BHAGs—literally!

The next major step in the evolution of these concepts was the establishment of The Bridgespan Group in 2000 by Thomas Tierney, then Worldwide Managing Partner of Bain & Company, and Jeff Bradach, a professor at HBS, for the purpose of providing high-quality strategic consulting advice to foundations, individual philanthropists, and nonprofit organizations. Then in 2005 came Jim Collins's book *Good to Great and the Social Sectors*, which has had a great deal to do with importing the usage of both "mission-driven" and "strategies aligned with mission" into the nonprofit mantras that they have become today. So have Bridgespan, FSG, Arabella Advisors, and the several business strategy consulting firms, which have pro bono nonprofit consulting practices.

This same period has also been a fertile time for philanthropic advising, starting with The Philanthropic Initiative, a nonprofit in Boston (now the TPI division of The Boston Foundation), founded in 1989 by the now legendary, as well as, alas, late Peter Karoff, and two years later in 1991 with the creation of Rockefeller Philanthropy Advisors, also a nonprofit, headed by Melissa Berman. The knowledge and training reach of all these organizations, as well as many others, has been greatly extended by the proliferation of webinars that focus on an infinite variety of skills useful in governing and managing philanthropy and nonprofits. I will have more to say about the nonprofit and philanthropic advisory industry in Chapter 3.

The steadily increasing focus on mission inevitably has led to an explicit quest by donors and foundations to ascertain nonprofits' measurable results in fulfilling whatever mission they have been supported to pursue. The chain of steps starts with meticulous articulation of a goal, then to the development of one or more strategies for achieving the mission-serving goals, then to designing logic models that trace the nonprofit's or foundation's course in moving from the present state of a problem to the imagined state in which the problem has been solved, along with the generation of performance benchmarks along the way to reveal the extent of progress in achieving the goals, so that fine-tuning of the strategy can be done at any point if warranted by the benchmarks. For foundations, grantmaking initiatives can be chosen based, partly or wholly, on the expected measurable value of their results.

The quest to ascertain measurable outcomes has received a strong boost from the very recent creation of "social impact bonds" and other "pay-for-success" experiments. Those experiments promise financial returns to, or impose financial losses on, the for-profit and/or philanthropic investors who financed them, based on a venture's ability to meet certain carefully measured and consensually agreed-upon metrics. In a typical case of social-impact bonds, for instance, a nonprofit organization receives an infusion of cash from investors in exchange for delivering a service that will, if successful, create some form of public benefit—even, perhaps, a reduction in some government cost. An organization might receive such an investment, for example, to run a program helping homeless adults find housing or jobs. If the program is successful—if, say, a rising number of formerly homeless people achieve a more stable life and cease to need city-funded shelter—the government would repay the investors and share a portion of the savings with them. If not, the investors would lose some or all of the money and presumably stop funding the service.

It is not yet clear whether these arrangements could really transform the normal pattern of funding for public services, and the skeptics are plentiful. But one result is becoming clear: all parties to the "pay-for-success" experiments acquire an entirely new respect for the determining power of hard data to justify the undertaking of social policy experiments.[14]

On the other hand, the skepticism about and resistance to the increasing focus on metrics of results have been growing for some time. Most large foundations are committed to measuring results, quantitatively if possible and qualitatively if not. However, virtually all foundations have declared an implied, even if not expressed, allegiance to Albert Einstein's famous observation, "Not everything that can be counted counts, and not everything that counts can be counted." The quest for metrics should not be allowed to deter foundations from grantmaking in fields for which metrics are not easily obtainable. James Canales, president and CEO of The Barr Foundation in Boston, summed up this concern admirably in a 2016 comment to *The Chronicle of Philanthropy*:

We have made a decision as a foundation to stay invested in a significant way in arts and creativity. Arts and creativity are not the first areas you'd think of when you think of hard metrics. Ultimately, we are making a judgment as a foundation that inspiring the kind of creativity that creates a thriving, dynamic region is important. Part of that is about nourishing the soul and part of that is about elevating our aspirations. Those are things that are hard to measure. If we were driven by metrics and needing to point to certain numbers to say we've made progress, that might not be the first place we'd gravitate.[15]

Even so, the tug of business-school doctrine on philanthropic thinking continues to draw foundations ever more deeply into the quest for performance and outcome measurements. Within the past 25 years, social entrepreneurship and venture philanthropy have become subfields of their own and appear to be gaining traction steadily. The former is the application of entrepreneurship skills to social problem-solving, and the latter is the application of venture capital skills to philanthropic decision-making. The faculty members teaching and researching in the HBS Social Enterprise Initiative are among the pioneers of both of these subfields, especially the late Professor Greg Dees, who later founded The Center for the Advancement of Social Entrepreneurship at Duke's Fuqua School of Business. His pioneering paper, "The Meaning of 'Social Entrepreneurship,'" is among the most frequently cited papers on that subject.[16] Another influential paper on the subject is that of Christine W. Letts, William P. Ryan, and Allen S. Grossman, "Virtuous Capital: What Foundations Can Learn from Venture Capitalists."[17]

As this book goes to press, foundations and corporations are slowly adopting another high-finance approach to philanthropy: practices that have been variously described as "mission investing" and "impact investing." Both of those terms refer to investing a foundation's or donor's assets in ventures that pursue a public benefit rather than making grants to these institutions solely from the income on those assets. The antecedents of such practices reach back to the 1970s, when, under the leadership of President McGeorge Bundy, the Ford Foundation launched its program-related investments (PRIs) as a complementary category of Ford Foundation grantmaking support available to nonprofit organizations. Such PRIs were not grants but investments, which obligated the recipient organizations to repay the principal of the investment at some specified point as well as meanwhile to pay income to Ford, although at usually below-market rates. The resources used for PRIs could either be endowment assets or grantmaking budgets. Irrespective of the source of the resources used to make PRIs, they count toward a foundation's minimum annual payout.

"Mission investing" and "impact investing" constitute PRIs writ large. At the time of this writing, only about a dozen foundations—notably The

F.B. Heron Foundation and the KL Felicitas Foundation—have made significant commitments to the practice. Such investments may be made in the equity of individual corporations that meet certain criteria for contributing positively to society; in mutual funds holding such society-benefiting stocks and/or bonds; or in direct investments in eligible nonprofits or businesses that are substantively focused on programs of priority to the investing foundations. In short, the goal is to put into society-benefiting investments not only the mandatory 5 percent a foundation is required to pay out annually to eligible tax-exempt nonprofits, but some portion—in Heron's case, eventually all—of the foundation's capital assets as well.[18]

It is no understatement to describe the mission/impact investing trajectory growth of foundations as having been glacial until recently, but unquestionably it now seems to be steadily increasing. The Kresge Foundation announced in 2015 that it would invest $350 million of its approximately $3 billion endowment in what it calls its "Social Investment Practice," which will use "tools including debt, equity, guarantees and deposits to make investments that further the foundation's mission and programmatic priorities."[19] On April 5, 2017, the Ford Foundation announced "it is committing up to $1 billion from its $12 billion endowment over the next 10 years . . . to mission-related investing."[20]

However, for-profit banks and investment management firms, with JPMorgan Chase in the lead, appear to be doing just the opposite of the hitherto slow-moving foundations. JPMorgan Chase is rushing to get into the mission/impact investing field with products designed to attract socially motivated investors. Other financial institutions that are now offering such products include Morgan Stanley, AXA, UBS, and BlackRock. So far as foundations are concerned, the pace of adoption is indicated by a *Chronicle of Philanthropy* article by Ben Gose: "Foundations Wary of Impact Investing."[21] It is amusing to note that, on December 1, 2015, when this article was first posted on the *Chronicle of Philanthropy* website, the headline descriptor was "cautious." By the time the publication appeared in hard copy, the headline descriptor had changed to "wary."

Undoubtedly, philanthropy has much to learn from Wall Street and the business schools—both the portion of philanthropy that manages endowments and the portion that distributes the proceeds to worthy causes. The management and financial innovations described here have all arisen from an earnest search for greater effectiveness, stricter fidelity to mission, clearer strategic thinking, and greater certainty about results and their value. But, it is essential to remember that many of these techniques and doctrines were designed for the very different environment of for-profit enterprise, with its mostly unambiguous reckoning of profits and losses, the disciplining force of competition and market share, and long-established means of calculating risk and return. In the nonprofit world, where such ideas have other, less consistently defined meanings and where many goals and values are difficult or impossible to value quantitatively, ways of managing and investing that have served businesses admirably may have unforeseeable and unintended consequences. In this context, some caution—if not outright wariness—is surely called for. If some of these strands of innovation are proceeding slowly, with only a few pioneers in the lead and many skeptics still on the sidelines, that may well be just as it should be.

OPERATIONAL SUPPORT AND INCREASED ALLOWANCE FOR OVERHEAD

For as long as I can remember, leaders and observers of the philanthropic and nonprofit sectors have criticized foundations for confining their grants to meticulously itemized budgets that support specific program activities but not the strength and durability of the organizations operating the programs. Critics castigated foundations for being unwilling to provide nonprofits with the budget flexibility that comes with general operating support and for refusing to reimburse indirect costs like executive and financial management, information technology, rent, fundraising, and other expenses that contribute to the success of whatever program is supported. Indeed, for much too long, foundations have been unreasonably rigid, even unthinking, in their micromanagement of how, upon what, and in what amounts their grantees spend foundation dollars, and they have been downright parsimonious in significantly underreimbursing the real costs to the grantee of carrying out the programs for which funds are being provided. At long last, those practices are beginning to change, again albeit slowly. According to a 2015 article in the *Chronicle of Philanthropy*, "Foundations are gradually awarding more general operating core support to nonprofits to strengthen their organizations: e.g. The Weingart Foundation in Los Angeles awarded $100 million in general operating support to some 90 nonprofits since 2008, and its unrestricted grants rose from $1.8 million in 2008 to $19.2 million in 2014."[22]

The evidence is mounting. Darren Walker, the Ford Foundation's president, wrote this in his Second Annual Letter in November 2015:

> According to Nonprofit Finance Fund's most recent State of the Nonprofit Sector Survey, the single greatest challenge facing organizations today is "achieving long-term financial sustainability." So much of the feedback we've received echoes that sentiment.
>
> In light of this, we have decided to invest in organizations as partners—and to give them the kind of trust, flexibility, and additional support they need to do their best work. As incubators for both individuals and ideas, organizations are essential to developing a robust ecosystem of actors addressing inequality around the world.
>
> For this reason, we are aiming to double our commitment to supporting key anchor organizations in our six program areas. Over the next five years—from 2016 to 2020—our trustees have authorized us to allocate up to $1 billion for a concerted effort [called "BUILD"] to support stronger, more sustainable, and more durable organizations.
>
> In some cases this may mean larger, longer-term grants that can be used more flexibly. In other cases it may mean support for wraparound services that help an organization develop, adapt to change, or even merge with others. Whatever form it takes—depending on context and the needs of each organization—our aim is to ask not, "How do we make this grant successful?" but rather, "How do we help make this organization successful?"[23]

Then, in a widely distributed letter to the public that same month, Walker revealed that the Ford Foundation would henceforth double the rate it had historically allotted to cover its grantees' overhead costs. The foundation will, he wrote, now allow up to 20 percent of its grant award value to be used for such purposes, rather than the former ceiling of 10 percent. Most foundations have long imposed a very low cap on the amount of overhead they allow grantees to recover on program grants. Some foundations allow no overhead at all. Others arbitrarily impose a 15 percent to 20 percent ceiling on overhead. In announcing the change in Ford's policy, Walker wrote:

> All of us in the nonprofit ecosystem are party to a charade with terrible consequences—what we might call the "overhead fiction." Simply put, because of this fiction, foundations, governments, and donors force

nonprofits to submit proposals that do not include the actual costs of the projects we're funding.

I recently learned of one local government request for proposals that gave extra points to applicants that submitted proposals with lower overhead, resulting in the winning groups receiving overhead payments of 5 percent—an absurd and self-defeating outcome.

The overhead fiction also results from well-intended metrics developed by nonprofit watchdog groups that have equated lower overhead with organizational effectiveness when, in fact, the opposite may be true.

At Ford, we have been willing participants in this charade. Our policy of 10 percent overhead on project grants in no way allows for covering the actual costs to administer a project. And, to be honest, we've known it.

This number does not reflect what it takes actually to manage a project; nor does it help those we support effectively to run robust organizations capable of executing projects. Thus, beginning January 1, [2015,] we will double our overhead rate on project grants to 20 percent. We hope to encourage more honest dialogue about the actual operating costs of nonprofit organizations working in the US and internationally.[24]

Foundations' growing awareness of the "actual costs" of running successful programs may even mean they are paying more attention to—and in some cases, at least, providing more support to—voices in the field that have been clamoring for a more realistic approach to covering basic organizational costs. In October 2015, a group of major foundations made the surprising announcement that they had collaborated in awarding separate $1 million general operating support grants to two of the key infrastructure-strengthening organizations in the nonprofit sector: the Center for Effective Philanthropy and Grantmakers for Effective Organizations.[25] Both organizations have been influential in drawing foundations' attention to what Walker called the "overhead fiction" and inspiring more and more funders to confront reality.

On the surface, this trend may seem to be merely an adjustment—admittedly belated—to an almost self-evident reality: organizations that have too little to spend on management are likely to be poorly managed. If foundations want to fund excellence, then they need to fund excellent organizations, which does not come free. But I think there is more to the changing attitudes on this issue than just a belated reckoning with elementary organizational arithmetic. Many of the trends I have described thus far—the preoccupation with measurable performance, outcomes, and impact; the appetite for more sophisticated consulting services; the willingness to employ new and more complicated forms of financial support—all have at least one prerequisite in common: they demand better-run, more-data-savvy organizations that can make effective use of all the technical advice and the fancy financing and that can track and analyze and report on all the metrics demanded of them.

In short, it's not just that foundations have suddenly awoken to their long-standing stinginess about operating expenses—although that would be a positive development all by itself. More to the point, they have come to the realization that well-run, well-equipped, technically up-to-date nonprofit organizations are the only way that *foundations themselves* can achieve the kind of philanthropic results they say they want and need. When funders see a value *to themselves* in providing adequately for organizational management, then perhaps the days of the "overhead fiction" may finally be numbered. This partnering approach can thrive when both recipients and grantmakers understand what being effective means. It is not the case when one side of the partnership—the grantmakers who asymmetrically hold the power due to their resources—are the only ones in the equation who deem what is effective.

chapter two

New Players in Philanthropy and More Avenues by Which to Achieve Concerted Social Change

THE NEW WORLD OF THE YOUNG PHILANTHROPIC BILLIONAIRES

The number of immensely wealthy individuals and couples with publicly declared philanthropic intentions has grown steadily since 1990, and new vehicles for charitable giving by persons of even less wealth have come into being and are now being regularly utilized by larger numbers of people. Moreover, what individuals, foundations, nonprofits, and corporations do with their charitable dollars has taken significant leaps forward with more frequent engagement in public policy advocacy as well as with more collaboration among funders, with the goal of achieving greater, longer-lasting impact. Those are the topics explored in this chapter.

Staggering amounts of personal wealth are being created and accumulated today, especially by individuals in the high-tech, biotech, and financial investing fields. The new golden age of philanthropists is upon us. Bill Gates, Warren Buffett, Mike Bloomberg, Charles and David Koch, George Soros, Jeff Bezos, Eli Broad, David Rubenstein, Mike Milken, Mark Zuckerberg, Dustin Moskovitz, Jeff Skoll, Pierre Omidyar, Tom Steyer, Marc Benioff, Laurene Powell Jobs, Elon Musk, Sean Parker, Bernard Marcus, and Stephen A. Schwarzman: these people are now virtually household names. All the evidence suggests that there are far more philanthropic billionaires today, often deploying more philanthropic dollars individually, than there were in the age of Rockefeller and Carnegie.

While John D. Rockefeller Sr. started tithing at age 16 and Andrew Carnegie decided at age 36 to spend the rest of his life giving away the money he had already accumulated, the current generation of young philanthropists has raised the ante considerably. As of this point, certainly the most memorable example is the 2015 publicly released letter, written by Mark Zuckerberg and his wife, Dr. Priscilla Chan, to their newborn daughter announcing their determination to give away 99 percent of their Facebook shares, then valued at $45 billion. More recently, Dr. Chan and Mr. Zuckerberg announced the first allocation of their promised gift—$3 billion over the next three years "to cure, prevent, or manage all diseases in our children's lifetime."[1] Their startling generosity highlights two powerful and poignant points. The couple is celebrating their good fortune at the same moment that they have been blessed with a newborn daughter, which underscores their youth. In addition, unlike wealthy parents in most other countries who are dynastically driven, they are deliberately *not* passing along to their progeny the great wealth they have created. Instead, they are dedicating it to the alleviation of some of the critical social problems facing humankind. As dramatic as was the Zuckerberg-Chan decision, it is hardly unprecedented, either in history or in contemporary times. About 125 years ago, Andrew Carnegie made public, in *The Gospel of Wealth*, his determination to give away all of his wealth to philanthropic causes during his lifetime. In contemporary times, Zuckerberg's Facebook associate Dustin Moskovitz, whose net worth is estimated by *Forbes* to be about $8 billion, and his wife, Cari Tuna, pledged in 2010 to give away most of their wealth for philanthropic purposes during their lifetimes.[2]

The public declarations of many of these individuals, especially those in their 20s, 30s, and 40s, to give away most or all of their wealth while living is striking indeed.[3] Controlling such phenomenal wealth at such a tender age, they must find it difficult to imagine how that wealth would best be used, or the causes on which it ought to be spent, 30 or 40 years into the future—a time when they would have just crossed into retirement age—much less 100 or more years from now. Having made so much money in such a short time, and as a direct consequence of rapid economic and technological change, such young philanthropists might well conclude that their giving should be concentrated on the present and the near future, under circumstances that are known, and for needs that are clearly visible, rather than held in reserve for a future they can scarcely imagine.

Whether that is true or not, it seems likely that the existence of vast philanthropic fortunes in the hands of very young entrepreneurs—creatures of the tech age and reared in a climate of sudden, unpredictable developments—will lead to a future of charitable giving that is markedly different in pace and tenor from those of past generations. That cultural shift, if it happens, could be as consequential for philanthropy as anything that has happened since today's great foundations were created more than a century ago.

The Impact of the Buffett–Gates Pledge

But even the older among today's wealthy have done something that has never been done before in America: to create a "club," membership in which is acquired by vowing to give away at least half of one's wealth. Founded by Warren Buffett and Bill Gates in 2010, the Giving Pledge remained an American-only club until it started attracting givers from other countries in 2013. As of June 30, 2016, it still predominantly comprises Americans, but there are now pledgers from Australia, Brazil, Canada, England, Germany, India, Indonesia, Malaysia, Russia, South Africa, Scotland, Taiwan, Turkey, Ukraine, United Arab Emirates, and the United Kingdom—157 people in total, as of the writing of this book. (See Appendix B for the complete list.) While the pledge may have started in America, its greatest impact is likely to be outside the United States, because philanthropy on any scale comparable to what is found here simply does not exist elsewhere. Why do the non-US pledgers sign up? Brad Smith, president of The Foundation Center, a nonprofit clearinghouse of information, data, and analysis on philanthropy, explains:

> Billionaires are a culture unto themselves—As much as they may be African, Asian, European, or Latin American, [these people] are also part of a growing, global culture of the ultra-rich. They are densely networked through business and investment ties and "hang" together in places like Davos, Aspen, and at the Clinton Global Initiative. In deciding to join something like the Giving Pledge they are more likely to look to the example of their fellow billionaires, wherever on the globe they may be from, than to pay credence to the skeptics in their own backyard.
>
> Philanthropy is an aspiration—Whether the Giving Pledge billionaires started out poor or were born into wealth, they see their fortune as a form of immense privilege. And, as their public pledges reflect, they recognize that they are in a position to do something about things in the world they feel could be better. As the ranks of the world's billionaires grow, we have the Giving Pledge to thank for elevating philanthropy to the level of a higher calling to which they can aspire.

The Giving Pledge is a social movement—When the Giving Pledge was first announced, I blogged about it being akin to a billionaire social movement. Several years later, it has become one. Its ranks have swollen to over a hundred, it has its own website, an independent resource in the Foundation Center's "Eye on the Giving Pledge," and periodic gatherings where pledgers share their experiences in philanthropy. As a movement, the Giving Pledge provides identity, recognition, and—above all—a network through which philanthropists can learn from one another. When you think about it, as wealthy as they are, the only place Giving Pledge members can turn for advice without being sold a service or pitched a project is probably to each other.

The most surprising thing about the globalization of the Giving Pledge is that anyone should be surprised that it is happening. Information is global, technology is global, many of the world's most pressing challenges are global, and ultra-wealth is global.[4]

While I continue to believe that the greatest impact of the Giving Pledge will be outside the United States, the Zuckerberg and Chan's decision to give away the bulk of their assets, which was likely influenced to some degree by their experience from having signed the Pledge, has forced me to reconsider. They, along with Dustin Moskovitz and Cari Tuna, Sean Parker, and Bill Gross, are the only pledge members I know of who have committed to give away virtually all of their wealth. If their example raises the bar for other pledgers (or for wealthy non-pledgers) or, perhaps even more likely, for other young billionaires, their actions could have very significant consequences within the United States.

The Informal Philanthropic Conglomerate

Increasingly, wealthy philanthropists are choosing not to limit their philanthropic efforts to tax-exempt foundations but are engineering new kinds of vehicles for giving and investing for social purposes. The first signal that a new form of philanthropic enterprise was emerging came from Pierre Omidyar, the cofounder of eBay. In the early days of his philanthropic efforts, he established a tax-exempt foundation, but, within a few years, realized that such a structure unnecessarily constrained his opportunities to support a variety of undertakings, especially investments in for-profit ventures created for the purpose of solving social problems or achieving certain kinds of public benefit, such as changes in public policy. In 2004, he created what he calls a "philanthropic investment firm," the Omidyar Network, consisting of a grantmaking foundation and a social-purpose investing arm.

In the early 21st century, significant experimentation with hybrid for-profit/not-for-profit/governmental initiatives was already under way, including social-impact bonds and "pay-for-success" undertakings. Quickly, Omidyar seized on these ideas and incorporated both for-profit and not-for-profit ventures in the Omidyar Network. The Network's website describes itself as being "structured to support the notion that philanthropy is more than a type of funding. In its truest sense, philanthropy is about improving the lives of others, independent of the mechanism. Consequently, we work across the social and business sectors, operating both a Limited Liability Company (LLC) and a 501(c)(3) foundation." That website also explains that "We invest in entrepreneurs and their visionary ideas that create opportunities for people to improve their lives, their communities, and the world around them."[5] Significantly, the website is a ".com," not a ".org," which is the designation for a tax-exempt organization.

Laurene Powell Jobs, the widow of Apple founder Steve Jobs, has done something similar by establishing The Emerson Collective, an organization that supports education and social-justice initiatives, as an LLC rather than a foundation. Such an LLC can advise Ms. Jobs in making charitable gifts for which she can receive a charitable deduction, while also investing in for-profit ventures with a social purpose that would not offer such a deduction. An intention to make both kinds of expenditures is clearly the reason that the Zuckerberg–Chan initiative has been established the same way. The criticisms that were leveled by some when it was announced were clearly unfounded, based on a lack of knowledge about the new possibilities now available for philanthropists to achieve their social change objectives whether by for-profit or nonprofit vehicles of change.

Another example of the "network" framework for philanthropy, while not specifically so described, are the philanthropic initiatives of Jeff Skoll, the other cofounder of eBay. The center of his network of organizations is the Skoll Foundation, which is the leading worldwide foundation focusing on the advancement and support of social entrepreneurship. In addition to that foundation, Jeff Skoll's other initiatives include the Centre on Social Entrepreneurship at Oxford University's Said School of Business and the Institute for Social Entrepreneurship at Zhejiang University in China, which together organize an annual World Forum on Social Entrepreneurship. In addition to the not-for-profit components of his network, Skoll created a for-profit corporation, Participant Media, for the purpose of producing "entertainment that inspires and compels social change."[6] This company has produced over 70 films since its founding in 2004, including *An Inconvenient Truth*, about Al Gore's efforts to combat climate change, and *Spotlight*, about *The Boston Globe*'s investigative reporting on clerical sex abuse. Many of Participant Media's films have been nominated for major honors in the film world. The company uses traditional and social media to inform and activate citizens interested in many areas of social change.

The growth of these complex hybrids of for-profit/nonprofit social investment vehicles is a major advance that builds on the simpler, straightforward 20th-century models of philanthropy. Moreover, such a hybrid "network" form has an additional value for living donors in giving them the freedom to engage in advocacy and lobbying initiatives, which, if their philanthropic efforts were confined to a charitable foundation, would be either prohibited by law or much more difficult to achieve. Such unlimited lobbying and advocacy initiatives cannot be done through foundations, but foundations can play an important role in social-change efforts in which the lobbying and other restricted activities are funded separately by a donor or a non-tax-exempt institution using after-tax dollars. Foundations can, for example, support extensive research and public information on social issues, provided they do not fund appeals for specific legislation or campaigns for or against candidates for office. The more directly political activity can be funded separately with after-tax dollars. The two efforts, if harnessed to the same cause, can be far more effective than either would be on its own.

The structure can be very effective in enabling living donors to coordinate the strategies of their tax-exempt foundations with non-tax-benefited political entities that can engage freely in lobbying and that support candidates in elections. It is no longer unusual for wealthy individuals to coordinate their personal, individual giving with that of the foundations they have created, in order to achieve greater impact for their social policy aims. Julian Robertson, the pioneering hedge fund manager, has done so by personally paying the salary, with non-tax-benefited dollars, of his foundation president. That person can thus engage in lobbying, primarily on environmental issues, which he would not have been permitted to do if he were on the foundation's payroll. Pete Peterson, founder of the Blackstone Group, has used the same structure but with a focus on reducing the US national deficits and cumulative national debt.

Business entrepreneur and former mayor of New York City Michael Bloomberg has created Bloomberg Philanthropies, which encompasses his foundation giving, the charitable work of his company, Bloomberg LP, and his personal giving (including to political advocacy). This umbrella arrangement lets Bloomberg tackle complicated problems (such as climate change, tobacco control, gun safety, and obesity prevention) through multiple approaches, which allow him to capitalize on his unique status as a global figure, both in business and politics, to build both domestic and international coalitions around issues of concern.

George Soros has likewise combined his personal giving and that of his tax-exempt Open Society Foundations on a variety of subjects, as has hedge fund manager Tom Steyer with the TomKat Foundation on environmental regulatory matters. These mixed models offer a different version of ambitious innovation in philanthropy than the sole focus on a charitable, tax-exempt foundation as one's philanthropic vehicle. The flexibility is giving givers a new and wider reach.

INCREASING COLLABORATION AMONG FOUNDATIONS

The history of foundation collaboration in the United States is brief. Prior to 1990, in fact, it is difficult to identify any significant true collaborative partnerships among foundations. When I wrote *The Foundation* in 2006, I could name fewer than five of any consequence. I noted then that every foundation "is happy to have its favorite initiatives supported by others, but few are eager to volunteer support to programs launched by others. Blame it on ego, politics, turf, or desire for control, basic factors of human motivation that make partnership-creation unusually difficult."[7]

As of this writing, however, the number of such partnerships is clearly growing, which suggests that the urgency of the socioeconomic and environmental problems facing America have finally caused at least a temporary—one hopes rather a permanent—breach in the preexisting psychological and practical barriers to such collaborative decision-making.

Detroit: A Case Study in Large-Scale Cooperation

Consider, once again, the Grand Bargain that eased Detroit out of bankruptcy. It was catalyzed by CEOs Darren Walker of the Ford Foundation, Rip Rapson of the Kresge Foundation, and Alberto Ibargüen of the Knight

Foundation, at the urging of the bankruptcy court's chief mediator. It is certainly the most dramatic of such recently established collaborations.[8]

As often happens when foundations decide to pool their resources, the three institutions came to the Grand Bargain for different (though not conflicting) reasons. The largest single contribution to that collaboration—$125 million—was given by the Ford Foundation. The size of that figure may be partially explained by the fact that Ford was incorporated in Michigan and still remains a Michigan corporation under the supervision of that state's attorney general. In fact, Ford has a long history of fraught relationships with Michigan attorneys general and other officials who have felt, rightly or wrongly, that the foundation has not been generous enough to the state where it was founded in 1936 and where it still maintains its legal domicile. In any case, Ford has a legal and historic connection with Michigan, which made it possible to justify a grant of such magnitude for a single city in distress while also discouraging other troubled American cities from hoping for comparable Ford largesse.

But the main reason that Ford decided to join this collaborative effort when it did was because of the passionately held values of its then new president, Darren Walker. Walker had taken office in June 2013, just months before the Detroit bankruptcy began to emerge as the nationally urgent crisis it ultimately became. He believed that Detroit's festering socioeconomic and racial problems were an opportunity for Ford to reaffirm its historic commitment to struggling cities and their residents, as well as for him to signal his own priorities for the foundation. I think it is also likely the case that, once the Kresge Foundation's president Rip Rapson and its board of trustees expressed a willingness to commit $100 million to the Grand Bargain, Ford, with a fortune founded and based in Michigan, could not be seen as doing less and indeed *had* to do more. As a matter of size, Kresge's commitment is much heftier in relation to its $3.5 billion endowment than Ford's $125 million is to its endowment of $11 billion.

The Knight Foundation, too, had a long history in Detroit by virtue of Knight Newspapers' purchase of the *Detroit Free Press* in 1940 (Knight later merged with Ridder Publications to form the Knight Ridder chain, which was in turn sold to the McClatchy Company in 2006). Since its founding, that foundation has had a policy of focusing the bulk of its giving on the metropolitan areas in which Knight Ridder–owned newspapers, so its leadership in the Grand Bargain was fully consonant with its history and mission, even though a significant departure from its usual grantmaking procedures and priorities.

A word here about Rip Rapson's philanthropic leadership is also appropriate. In my view, he has not received the credit fairly due for leading the way in envisioning, implementing, and nurturing the antecedents of the Grand Bargain. Rapson is widely admired for his many prior initiatives to improve the financial, transportation, and socioeconomic circumstances of Detroit from the moment he first arrived in Michigan as president of Kresge on July 1, 2006. The Grand Bargain is hardly the first of Kresge's efforts under Rapson to rebuild Detroit, much less the only one. Kresge's commitments to Detroit's schools, arts scene, small businesses, transportation, neighborhood redevelopment, and civic leadership ballooned dramatically when Rapson took the reins of the foundation. Nor is the effort in Detroit the first comparable initiative for Rapson, who led similar initiatives as leader of Minneapolis's McKnight Foundation before coming to Kresge.

The Grand Bargain was a major event in the slender history of foundation collaborations, mainly because of its size and its powerful effect in hastening the end of the Detroit bankruptcy while protecting most of the pensions of Detroit's municipal retirees. Still, it was essentially a one-time arrangement, brought about under extraordinary circumstances and designed so as to rule out any expectation that it would be repeated elsewhere. Although less spectacular in their origins or (thus far) their outcomes, other multifoundation collaborations are becoming both more numerous and more durable. If it lasts, the trend is as welcome as it is overdue.

A Lengthening Roster of Philanthropic Alliances

Partnerships among foundations are now sprouting with regularity. They include the Energy Foundation, launched in 1991, which focuses on building "a strong, clean energy environment"[9] globally. It grew out of a project of The Trust for Public Land. The original foundation partners were The Pew Charitable Trusts, The Rockefeller Foundation, and the John D. and Catherine T. MacArthur Foundation, which together provided a $20 million endowment. Joining the founding foundation partners later were the Mertz-Gilmore Foundation in 1996, the McKnight Foundation in 1998, the David and Lucille Packard Foundation in 1999, and the William and Flora Hewlett Foundation in 2002. Subsequently, about a dozen other foundations have joined in supporting the Energy Foundation and one or more of its five initiatives, one of the earliest of which was an effort targeted at enabling China to reduce its energy use. As of 2016, the Energy Foundation has assisted China in announcing a plan "to reduce its energy use per unit of GDP by at least 40 percent from 2005 levels, and increase the share of renewable energy to 15 percent."[10]

There's also Living Cities, which was conceived in 1991 by Peter Gold-mark, then president of The Rockefeller Foundation, as a partnership of foundations and financial institutions to help provide capital for community economic development in cities. The initial funds of $62.5 million contributed by the partner institutions were originally distributed by the nation's two leading sponsors of community redevelopment: the Ford Foundation-founded Local Initiatives Support Corporation and Enterprise Community Partners, which was cofounded by James Rouse, the much-admired real estate developer, city planner, and urban activist. Originally called the National Community Development Initiative, it changed its name to Living Cities and broadened its mission to focus on the transformation of urban governance, planning, and development. As of 2015, its members included roughly a dozen private foundations along with nine large corporations and corporate foundations, mostly from the financial industry.[11]

Another example is ClimateWorks, a global partnership to combat climate change, which was founded in 2008, initially by the Hewlett and Packard Foundations, each of which committed around half a billion dollars over five years. The combined $1 billion commitments made ClimateWorks by far the largest foundation collaboration ever, but, as other foundations joined, it grew even larger. Thereafter, the MacArthur, Oak, and KR Foundations joined as core funders. As of 2017, both Hewlett and Packard have renewed their support for another seven years, and, with other donors' contributions, ClimateWorks' annual expenditures are about $400 million.[12]

In August 2013, The Kavli Foundation spearheaded the creation of The Science Philanthropy Alliance, the purpose of which is to increase the flow of financial resources from individuals, foundations, corporations, and government to basic scientific research conducted by those in universities and elsewhere in the United States. The Alliance includes nine member institutions as of 2016, with three more as associate members.[13]

In March 2014, the Hewlett Foundation launched the Madison Initiative, a three-year exploration to identify possible ways to overcome the polarization that is plaguing American politics and governing institutions, especially at the federal and state levels. Hewlett committed $50 million toward grants focusing especially on Congress but also sought to recruit other foundation partners from across the political spectrum to work with it on specific components of the problem. Sixteen others have joined as of the time this is written.[14]

The five-member Improving Foundation Effectiveness Collaborative was launched in 2015 with the two $1 million general-operating support grants, mentioned earlier, to the Center for Effective Philanthropy and Grantmakers for Effective Organizations.[15]

The Freedom Fund to End Slavery in the World, established in 2013, describes itself as "the world's first private donor fund dedicated to identifying and investing in the most effective front-line efforts to end slavery." It was conceived by Humanity United, The Legatum Foundation of Dubai, and the Walk Free Foundation, three private funders dedicated to antislavery initiatives. As of this writing, seven foundations are participating.[16]

In response to the recent conflicts over police shootings of African Americans spread across the country, and as the drumbeat of alarms over racial, ethnic, and socioeconomic inequality grew louder and more frequent, foundations and nonprofits have begun to collaborate, sometimes formally and sometimes informally, to identify and pilot possible ways of mitigating the problems. In April 2013, led by Robert Ross, president of the California Endowment, a group of foundations established the Executive Alliance to Expand Opportunities for Boys and Men of Color. About a year later, President Obama established a national public-private initiative called My Brother's Keeper to bring together foundations, corporations, and government at all levels to improve education and opportunity for young African American males.[17] The California Endowment pledged $50 million to that effort over seven years, and 42 other foundations have made pledges to bring the present total to more than $300 million. Other foundations have made gifts to organizations that are affiliated with My Brother's Keeper, and many foundations have revisited their program priorities to focus, to one degree or another, on such inequalities.

Global Ocean Legacy Collaborative, which was catalyzed by The Pew Charitable Trusts in partnership with the Sandler Foundation and the Tubney Charitable Trust, has established "the world's first generation of great marine parks by securing the designation of large, fully protected reserves." Its website reports that "To date, our efforts have helped to safeguard 5.2 million square kilometers of ocean—an area 10 times the size of Central America."[18] Six foundations were participating in the collaborative as of 2015.[19]

Since 2007, the Edna McConnell Clark Foundation has been attracting individual philanthropists and other foundations as investors in Growth

Capital Aggregation Funds, which, according to its website, have "leveraged $155 million of the Clark Foundation's funds to add nearly $487 million in additional private and public funding for 14 youth-serving organizations."[20] Some 18 foundations have been partners in these funds. But then, on January 29, 2016, the Clark Foundation took the idea to unprecedented scale. It announced a new $1 billion partnership, called Blue Meridian Partners, the members of which have already committed $750 million to "invest in high-performance nonprofits that are poised to have truly national impact for economically disadvantaged children and youth." In her letter announcing Blue Meridian, Clark President Nancy Roob wrote that the partnership would make "big bets. They will be flexible, unrestricted, long-term (5–10 years), tied to performance, and total up to $200 million for each grantee. They will help grantees to expand their impact directly, by allowing them to strengthen their work, grow and serve greater numbers of youth, as well as indirectly, by helping them increase their influence on the child welfare, educational, judicial, and other systems that affect children's lives."[21]

Each of the six general partners in Blue Meridian has committed $50 million. Four limited partners have pledged a minimum of $10 million each. To have assembled a mix of so many individual philanthropists and private foundations, at such a high minimum level of financial commitment, to tackle so huge and complex a social problem, is nothing short of pioneering.

Then, on December 13, 2016, the chair and CEO of the Edna McConnell Clark Foundation announced that they had "decided to 'sunset' the Foundation itself and spend all of its resources (approximately $1 billion) over the next decade," including topping off Blue Meridian Partners, the goal of which was to raise $1 billion in all.

The Fund for Shared Insight, initiated in 2014 by the William and Flora Hewlett Foundation's Effective Philanthropy Group, is a collaborative effort aimed at improving the functioning of philanthropy itself. It is the first effort I know of to seek ways of eliciting reliable and meaningful feedback from philanthropy's ultimate beneficiaries: those who are served by the nonprofits that foundations support.[22] The fund's eight founding partners note, in their mission statement, that "Private foundations with two or more paid staff control nearly $40 billion of giving. We believe we can make an even bigger difference in the world with that $40 billion dollars if foundations encourage and incorporate feedback from the people we seek to help; understand the connection between feedback and better results; foster more openness between and among foundations, grantees, and those we seek to help; and share what we learn with one another and the field."[23]

The lure of collaboration has now extended even to film and sports celebrities. For example, in September 2015, two celebrities—the actor Kevin Spacey and the Baltimore Orioles Baseball Hall of Fame shortstop Cal Ripken Jr.—announced that their respective foundations would organize a joint fundraising event and divide the proceeds between the two organizations. In doing so, they pointed out that both of their foundations aim to benefit at-risk children, Kevin Spacey's through theater and film and Cal Ripken's through sports.[24]

While many of the collaborations discussed here were formed in the early 2000s and thus are of fairly recent vintage at the time this is written, the State Priorities Partnership (SPP) is much older. It was founded in the early 1990s by the Ford Foundation, one of whose program officers, Michael Lipsky, was the primary catalyst, along with the Annie E. Casey Foundation and the Charles Stewart Mott Foundation. Its mission is to support research and advocacy to make state governments more responsive to the needs of their less-advantaged citizens, in areas such as education, health care, criminal justice, and the environment. In recent years, it has achieved a steady annual budget of $20 million, contributed by 8 national and about 400 state and local foundations from across the country. In 2009, the Council on Foundations honored SPP with its award for Distinguished Grantmaking Through Collaboration.[25]

Overcoming Centrifugal Forces

The evolution from virtually no partnerships in 1990 to today's cooperative environment involving many foundations, individual philanthropists, public charities, financial institutions, and government is an important change in the way foundations conceive of their role and increasingly do their work. Moreover, the list of formal partnerships described here does not include the many arrangements in which a single foundation works with multiple individual donors who wish to piggyback on its expertise by donating funds to be spent on specified initiatives. This is, in effect, what Warren Buffett did with the Gates Foundation and what several other funders have done in joining initiatives of The Pew Charitable Trusts, which has attracted more than half a billion dollars in this kind of arrangement. Nor does the list include the pioneering Social Innovation Fund established by the Corporation for National and Community Service with funds appropriated by Congress. The Innovation Fund has used $241 million in federal funds to leverage $516 million from private philanthropy and other civic-sector organizations working on innovative solutions to major social problems, including a major component of pay for success experiments. Around a dozen foundations and philanthropic funds have received grants from the fund.[26] Also omitted are the partnerships between individual for-profit corporations and foundations for particular purposes, such as the partnership between the Kaiser Family Fund and National Public Radio to support NPR's coverage of various health policy issues affecting Americans.

The need for collaboration among foundations ought to have been glaringly obvious all along—and to many scholars and outside observers it has been. Among many simple, irrefutable arguments for working together is that few foundations are large, and none is as large as the problems it seeks to solve. The American foundation sector in its entirety, applying every penny of every endowment, could not fund the federal government's health care budget for even nine months before running out of money and vanishing. To tackle gargantuan problems of poverty, inequality, disease, inadequate education, an imperiled environment, or pick any other serious challenge, any one foundation's resources—even those of the mighty Gates Foundation, the largest in history—would meet only a tiny fraction of the need. For foundations, the failure to pool effort and money is a dangerous step toward insignificance.

Yet as Hodding Carter III, a former president of the Knight Foundation, acknowledged in a 2010 interview, for most foundation leaders, collaboration has long been "just an unnatural act, frankly." "At all times and in all ways," he explained, "the various pressures of just doing your own business, focusing just on your own mission, your own staff's capabilities, your own opportunities—all that is hard enough" for leaders of most foundations. The extra effort required to get to know other funders, understand their interests, blend one's own priorities with theirs, and create mechanisms to share control of one another's resources has, for most foundations of the 20th century, consistently been seen as prohibitive.[27]

If that has now begun to change—and the evidence presented here strongly suggests that it has—then something genuinely remarkable is afoot in philanthropy. All the centrifugal "pressures of doing your own business" that Carter described remain in full force, and yet an emerging generation of donors and foundations is finding ways to overcome them or at least to counterbalance them with incentives to join forces and share leadership. (It should be noted that Carter managed to overcome these pressures himself, having been an early participant in Living Cities as well as other collaborative efforts while at the helm of the Knight Foundation.) If that trend continues, foundations will not only be operating differently in the coming decades, but they will also be achieving much more and inspiring new donors to follow suit.

FINDING A PHILANTHROPIC VOICE IN PUBLIC POLICY

In the early 1990s, when the Robert Wood Johnson Foundation spent millions of dollars on prime-time television advertising to counter the insurance industry's campaign attacking the Clinton health care plan, everyone in the foundation world was surprised. Foundations simply did not do that. Now, 20 or so years later, independent philanthropists, foundations, and quasi-foundations (institutions that raise and regrant money rather than spending the proceeds of an endowment) do this all the time. As many foundations focus their substantive programs on public policy change, especially in education or environmental protection, they are devoting large proportions of their program expenditures to public policy advocacy.

As with collaboration, the impetus behind this trend has to do with money and with the relative size of the foundation sector compared to government. A typical foundation can invent and test a new way of educating children or treating disease, but only federal and state governments can afford to deliver that innovation to large numbers of actual students or patients. For a good part of the 20th century, governments tended to pay close attention to foundation programs and to adopt the most successful ones, often in close cooperation with the foundation. Since the 1980s that has become much less common, and the appetite for philanthropic influence among government agencies has waned. As a result, foundations have discovered that it is no longer good enough to produce compelling ideas and promising innovations; they must promote their ideas to an often-unheeding public sector. Hence, a growing embrace of public policy advocacy. According to a recent study informed by anonymous interviews with program officers of four leading foundations heavily involved in education, from 2010 to 2015 the Gates Foundation spent 20 percent of its education budget on advocacy efforts, and the Broad Foundation, founded by Eli and Edythe Broad, is now allocating 40 percent to 50 percent of its budget to policy-related expenditures.[28]

Other examples abound. The Atlantic Philanthropies, which since 2001 has been on a path to spend itself out of existence during the lifetime of Charles Feeney, its donor, devoted $25 million in 2008 in support of advocacy efforts to achieve the enactment of the Affordable Care Act.[29] In addition, between 2008 and 2014 it devoted some $60 million to a multifoundation effort to end the death penalty in the United States. Although that goal has not been achieved, the effort contributed significantly toward a dramatic reduction in executions nationwide and abolition of the death penalty in 11 states. Moreover, the Gates Foundation established the Race-to-the-Top competition, eventually supported by the US Department of Education, to encourage state governments to adopt long-stymied desirable education reform initiatives.

For over 25 years, the Gill Foundation and the Evelyn and Walter Haas Jr. Fund have collaborated with a group of other foundations on efforts, ultimately successful, to legalize same-sex marriages.[30] Bloomberg Philanthropies' obesity prevention, road safety, tobacco control, and education reform programs are heavily concentrated on advocacy, and its $50 million self-described "Counterweight to the NRA" effort in 2014 was explicitly aimed at making more stringent the laws regulating background checks for gun ownership.[31]

In 2004, The Pew Charitable Trusts changed its legal form from that of a private foundation to a public charity, with the result that it is now permitted to lobby and otherwise advocate on matters of public policy within specified dollar limits.

Considering all of these advocacy initiatives, it should not be surprising that some living foundation founders are using their own money, without the benefit of tax exemption, to establish 501(c)(4) "social welfare" organizations, which have a much freer hand to engage in advocacy, lobbying, and electoral politics than do private foundations, which are 501(c)(3)s. In 2014, The Atlantic Philanthropies announced that among its final gifts would be the establishment of a Civic Participation Action Fund, a spinoff 501(c)(4) organization that would make grants for lobbying and for political campaigns on issues that had been central to the foundation's mission over the past 30 years.[32] The Eli and Edythe Broad Foundation, which is deeply engaged in K–12 education reform, has created such a 501(c)(4) and, just as some of the Robertson Foundation's employees who engage in lobbying are paid with the founder's non-tax-benefited dollars, so are some of the Broad Foundation's officers who engage in lobbying and other advocacy.[33] Because of the Broad Foundation's energetic national role in supporting charter schools, it has increasingly become a target for the many critics of such schools, as documented in considerable detail by Motoko Rich on the front page of the *New York Times* on March 5, 2016, under the headline "Oakland Is Flash Point in Billionaire's Push for Charter Schools."[34]

It must be acknowledged that, given the heated partisan and ideological battles that are commonplace today, the freedom that foundations and philanthropists now enjoy to engage in advocacy is hardly guaranteed for the future. Tony Proscio, a highly knowledgeable consultant to foundations and my colleague as Associate Director of the Duke Center for Strategic Philanthropy, offers the following caution:

> Twice in the 1990s, members of Congress threatened to provoke an IRS review of the Robert Wood Johnson Foundation's tax exemption because of its support for two controversial causes: health care reform and anti-smoking policies. The foundation's grants were entirely, scrupulously legal. They involved research and public information on issues central to the foundation's charitable mission: improving health and health care in the United States. They did not pay for lobbying, or for encouraging others to lobby, nor did they support or oppose any candidate for office. The political assaults on RWJF were unsuccessful and not even very vigorously pursued, but they cost the foundation a lot of time and money in defensive legal maneuvers. The lesson of this story is that staying within the law is no protection for foundations and nonprofits that insert themselves into hot public controversies. They still emerge with a target on their backs. That may explain why this kind of activity has been slow to develop, why it tends to be undertaken only by the most fearless and politically passionate donors and institutions, and why many utterly guiltless foundations will speak candidly about this only on deep background.[35]

In recent years, charitable operating nonprofits have also been engaging in much more direct advocacy initiatives than in the past, often using general operating funds provided by foundations—a practice permitted by the relevant tax law.[36] For example, the recent spread of state and local $15-an-hour minimum wage laws has been powered by the National Employment Law Project.[37] That organization is a nonprofit with support from many foundations, including The California Endowment, Annie E. Casey Foundation, the Ford Foundation, The Joyce Foundation, Charles Stuart Mott Foundation, Open Society Foundations, Public Welfare Foundation, and The Rockefeller Foundation.[38]

In addition, more foundations are supporting lawsuits on matters affecting public policy.[39] Given the partisan paralysis of the US Congress, more and more social issues in the 21st century have been making their way through the judiciary rather than through the legislative process. These cases come from both the right and the left, and foundations of both persuasions have become more sophisticated and aggressive in backing legal organizations that can identify potent cases, formulate winning arguments, and battle their way successfully through the courts.

Although not for the faint of heart, supporting advocacy to change public policy is a potent philanthropic tool. When employed on the national stage, it can produce effects that influence millions of lives, as Gates has done in education, Gill and Haas in gay rights, and Bloomberg and Robert Wood Johnson on smoking and other public-health issues. But taking a creative and influential role in public policy is not only a national strategy. In fact, foundations at the community and regional level have in some cases been the earliest and most successful practitioners, though their stories are less well known outside their communities. Let's now look more closely at some of them.

Community Foundations as Civic Leaders

Until 1914, when the Cleveland Foundation was established, there were no community foundations in either the United States or elsewhere in the world. From their founding, the primary purpose of such foundations has been to provide a group of citizens in a specific geographical area a vehicle for receiving contributions from donors who wish to improve the circumstances, public-benefiting institutions, and the environment in the locality in which they live. Their ability to aggregate the contributions and civic leadership of many local donors and to speak with an authoritative voice in the public interest has made them a powerful—and popular—presence in local civic life. Over the past 100 years, America's pioneering creation of community-focused foundations has spread to about 800 metropolitan areas nationwide and, more recently, to many other countries as well. The idea has proved so attractive to The Bertelsmann Foundation, one of Europe's largest philanthropies, that it has adopted an initiative to seed community foundations in several countries in Europe and elsewhere.

As of the end of 2015, American community foundations have endowments aggregating almost $80 billion and give out about $5.2 billion a year. While these foundations vary widely in their individual missions, what they share is an imperative to identify and give high priority to the civic problems that can be addressed with concerted community action, and then to tackle those problems by utilizing financial resources that they raise locally from individuals, private foundations, and corporations. In the metropolitan areas in which community foundations have been most effective, their staffs have come to be recognized as the central node of the communications and activist networks focusing on the social good of the region, providing objective advice and financial resources with which to tackle the area's most important problems. The original pattern of activity, charted by the Cleveland Foundation, was to identify the community's problems; commission evidence-based studies about their nature, extent, and possible solutions; and recommend courses of action which the community might pursue to solve or mitigate them. The Cleveland Foundation also supported community organizations regarded as important contributors to the Cleveland area, such as the world-renowned Cleveland Clinic, and often those with the potential to help ameliorate or solve the city's problems in following up the studies.

During the past 25 years, many community foundations have received major infusions of unrestricted endowment assets that have multiplied the worth of their endowments. Most of that growth has been in the form of donor-advised funds, such as the $1 billion gift by Mark Zuckerberg and Dr. Priscilla Chan to establish a donor-advised fund at the Silicon Valley Community Foundation. At some community foundations, such funds represent an overwhelming proportion of their assets. In the case of the Greater Kansas City Community Foundation, for example, that figure is greater than 90 percent. Other community foundations have been more fortunate in attracting large unrestricted endowment gifts from wealthy local citizens, such as the $200 million given to the California Community Foundation upon the 2006 death of Los Angeles resident Joan Palevsky.[40] More recently, in 2015, the San Antonio Area Foundation received a donation of $605 million, 90 percent of the income of which is unrestricted, by the estate of John L. Santikos, a wealthy San Antonio movie theater owner.[41]

Until recently, it was rare for a community foundation to undertake publicly a course of action to solve a particular problem in its community, especially one that called for political or legislative change. The reluctance to do so stemmed from the hesitancy of the community foundation leadership to appear less than impartial on what often were, or might become, controversial proposals for change. That reluctance is understandable. After all, since community foundations depend on raising endowments or current operating funds from their local communities, taking a controversial stand might well have a negative impact on those sources of funding. As a consequence, most community foundations played low-profile roles in their communities, content with doing as much social good as possible without unnecessarily stirring the waters. The few exceptions, such as the Cleveland Foundation's championing of neighborhood redevelopment in the 1980s, under successive CEOs Homer Wadsworth and Steve Minter, stood out starkly against an otherwise gray backdrop.

But things are changing. Consider The Boston Foundation, which was founded in 1915. Like the Cleveland Foundation, TBF has won admiration for its long service to the area it assists—in this case, metropolitan Boston. With an endowment of over $1 billion, The Boston Foundation (TBF) is now one of the wealthiest community foundations in the country. Over its 100-year history, it has made grants totaling about $1.6 billion. But its conventional pattern of operation, involving intentionally low visibility and a tendency to deflect attention and controversy, changed in 2000 when a new president, Paul Grogan, was named. Grogan had been president of the Local Initiatives Support Corporation, now America's largest nonprofit investor in urban development and community revitalization, for 13 years. Grogan emphasizes that the transformation he led occurred under the guidance of the directors of TBF, who strongly articulated the need to rethink their methods of operating before they chose him. He quotes one of TBF's directors as asking: "If we want to have impact and want to be influential, just exactly how does it help us that nobody knows who we are or what we are doing?"[42] Now, 16 years after Paul Grogan took the helm, many Bostonians definitely know what TBF is and what it does.

The foundation has become a public convener on some of the most controversial issues affecting the city. To the traditional low-key community foundation model it has added an in-house think tank, which does objective, evidence-based research on public problems. As Grogan points out, the objectiveness of the data "allows leaders to cross ideological boundaries and have one conversation about common problems."[43] TBF instituted a Boston

Indicators Project hosted at the foundation, which continuously tracks change and progress in 10 sectors across 150 specific measures. As Grogan described it in 2015:

> The Indicators Project not only provides large amounts of data in one place, but it also helps create a story line about the region's challenges and opportunities. Moreover, it provides important legitimacy to the Foundation, justifying our involvement in the public discourse and stances on sometimes controversial issues. Beyond the Indicators Project, we regularly commission research into specific areas that we are interested in. . . . TBF Media staff vigorously market to the media and [to] both the elite and wider public the results of the think tank studies. We seek to drive the conversation and keep key issues in public view. . . . [W]e also bring together key stakeholders and convene coalitions to create momentum for change on key issues. This is not just hosting meetings—it is serial mobilizations of civic, business, and community leaders. . . . We see it as our contribution not only to lead the group, but to handle back-office support to make the engagement possible for busy individuals. We can either complement work done by the public sector or challenge the practices and offer alternatives. In doing so, we can help create better choices for the public sector . . . and embolden our leaders to make difficult or controversial decisions. At TBF, we work closely with all three levels of government. We have three lobbyists on staff and work on a wide range of issues.[44]

Grogan's explanation makes clear how the civic leadership model radically differs from the traditional low-profile community foundation model of operating. In February 2016, TBF published a summary of the progress of its new initiatives from 2009 to 2015, highlighting its achievements as well as its shortcomings. The report underscores the extraordinary changes in foundation practice during those years, such as nearly doubling its median grant size from $40,000 to $75,000, raising the percentage of funding going to general operating support grants from 20 percent of all grants to between 70 percent and 80 percent, and the percentage of funding going to multiyear grants from 0 percent of the grants budget to between 50 percent and 80 percent. Those are remarkably impressive changes in crucial indicators of behavior by any kind of foundation with regard to the way in which a foundation deals with its grantees![45]

While The Boston Foundation has been a pioneer in such civic leadership, it is no longer alone. A number of other community foundations have reached out to Grogan and TBF to understand firsthand how this foundation has been operating and are beginning to follow suit, including the Baltimore Foundation, the Buffalo Foundation, the Boulder Foundation, the San Francisco Foundation, the Rhode Island Foundation, the Greensboro Foundation, the Foundation for the Carolinas (based in Charlotte, NC), the New Hampshire Foundation, and the Miami Foundation.

The changes sparked by Paul Grogan and The Boston Foundation have reached almost half way around the world to the Honolulu headquarters of the Hawaii Community Foundation and its president and CEO, Kelvin Taketa. In his own words, these are some of the foundation's exceptional initiatives in civic leadership, involving such controversial issues as the environment, education, and voter participation:

> We convened a panel of experts and stakeholders, many of whom had been adversaries in the courts for years, to work for 16 months [on] a blueprint to create a stable and increasing source of fresh water, the precursor to any hopes we have of building a more sustainable food and energy economy in the face of climate change. The blueprint has been completed, and most of the panel has committed to working on a number of policy and investment strategies in Phase II.
>
> We partnered with 14 funders on an $8 million, three-year effort to work with a cohort of public schools and the department of education to develop successful strategies to increase the number of at risk middle school kids who complete 9th grade on track (as an early indicator for high school graduation). Still underway. . . .
>
> We also organized a funder collaborative during the great recession to help stave off foreclosures and increase access to government benefits. . . . Working with a number of nonprofit partners, we increased their capacity to help those families and the $3 million deployed resulted in over $20 million in benefits alone. We have several other civic initiatives in the design phase right now: civic engagement focused on turning around an abysmal voter participation rate, launching a statewide effort for prenatal screening and referrals (Hawaii has one of the highest rates of substance use by pregnant women) and a system of screening, referral and treatment for early childhood developmental and behavioral health and an initiative to advance nonprofit excellence.

All of these efforts share a couple of key design elements (learned the hard way): 12–24 months of strategy development with key stakeholders and outside expertise, a group of funders who pool resources and are willing to think long term, a network of actors (funders, public policy and government leaders, nonprofits) who have a shared goal that lends itself to measurement to assess progress, accountability and performance improvement. [What is challenging is] extracting useful and timely data from government.[46]

In 2005, with support from the Charles Stewart Mott Foundation and the Ford Foundation, Lucy Bernholz, Katherine Fulton, and Gabriel Kasper, three highly regarded researchers/writers on nonprofit and philanthropy matters, published a major report, entitled "On the Brink of New Promise: The Future of US Community Foundations," which documents some of the changes that are under way among the US community foundations and which encourages emulation by others. Among other trends that echo the examples cited here, the authors foresee among community foundations "a shift in focus from the institution to the community, . . . from managing financial assets to long-term leadership, [and] from competitive independence to coordinated impact."[47]

Because of the growth in the number of community foundations already committed to civic leadership, a new freestanding nonprofit called "CF Leads" was established in 2006 and now advocates the adoption of varying forms of that model by other community foundations.[48]

City-Based Antipoverty Foundations Supported by the Financial Community

An entirely new form of community-focused philanthropy was created in New York City in 1988 by Paul Tudor Jones, a wealthy hedge fund visionary, who first saw the possibility of raising large sums of money from a local area's financial community to deploy and using that money to support metropolitan nonprofits that seek to solve or ameliorate some of the problems of poverty-stricken citizens. The fund would adopt state-of-the-art venture philanthropic giving principles as described above in Chapter 1, including the exacting use of performance benchmarks and outcome metrics. Jones's creation, the Robin Hood Foundation, has proved its success dramatically over the past 28 years by amassing huge sums of money primarily from large benefit dinners attended by wealthy financial sector stars and entertained by celebrities. In 2015, the Robin Hood fundraising dinner yielded $101 million in a single night. Four thousand wealthy donors packed the Javits Center, Manhattan's convention center, while 2,000 wealthy but younger people from the world of finance attended two parallel events, both of them sold out. The foundation's fundraising might is matched by its skill in deploying its philanthropic assets to support metropolitan New York nonprofit organizations serving disadvantaged members of the community in such fields as education, health, housing, and employment.[49]

This model—drawing large contributions from the local financial community, depending at least in part on one or more big fundraising dinners, and using the proceeds for general operating support to nonprofits with outstanding track records based on performance metrics—is slowly spreading to other cities. Daniel Lurie, a San Francisco native who worked for two years at Robin Hood, returned home and launched The Tipping Point Community in 2004. Its first gala raised about $400,000; 10 years later, after steadily increasing the take at its dinners year after year, it raised $12 million at its May 2014 gala, for an annual 2014 total raised of $20.9 million. In 2015, the Tipping Point annual dinner raised $14 million, and the total raised in the 2015 fiscal year was $21.6 million.[50] Because of his impressive entrepreneurial track record with Tipping Point, Lurie was tapped by the mayor of San Francisco to chair San Francisco's committee to attract the 2016 Super Bowl. When the site selection committee chose San Francisco over South Florida, Lurie guided his committee to put a philanthropic overlay on Super Bowl 50, called "50Fund.org." It promised to return 50 percent of all funds raised by Super Bowl 50 back to San Francisco nonprofits and fulfilled that promise with grants totaling more than $13 million.[51]

As noted above, other cities that have launched initiatives similar to Robin Hood and Tipping Point, although not yet as well-established as either of them, are Chicago (A Better Chicago); Washington, D.C. (Lever Fund); and Detroit (The Detroit Children's Fund, an affiliated organization of The Skillman Foundation).

All of the above organizations are committed to identifying and nurturing "high-performing" nonprofits, with a track record that suggests their greater effectiveness in fighting poverty than other organizations with similar missions.

Collaborative Philanthropic Giving on
a Regional Basis

Similar to the Robin Hood Foundation but different from it in important ways is Venture Philanthropy Partners (VPP), a collaborative launched in 2000 by Mario Morino, a wealthy software pioneer. He succeeded in attracting 29 wealthy individuals, foundations, and corporate leaders in Northern Virginia and the Washington, D.C., area to invest more than $30 million in VPP's first fund to provide both financial support and consulting advice to strengthen and grow high-performing organizations that serve low-income youth and children. VPP launched fundraising for its second fund in 2007 and began investing in recipient organizations in 2009.

VPP is like the Robin Hood Foundation and Tipping Point Community in its state-of-the-art practice of giving strategically to organizations with a track record of achieving impact, but unlike them it attracts financial support from a wider and more diverse group of investors. It is also different in having recruited four major organizations to work with VPP as strategic partners: The Community Foundation for the National Capital Region, Community Wealth Ventures (a nonprofit-owned management consulting firm that provides services to nonprofits on ways of achieving financial sustainability), the McKinsey & Company Social Sector Office, and Mario Morino's own Morino Institute, which is dedicated to spurring entrepreneurship. VPP is also different in how it follows through on its initiatives. It actively uses publications and social media to spread word about the successes of the model organizations it supports in hopes that activists in other locations will be inspired to follow suit in their respective localities.

Morino has a thoroughly admirable zeal for intelligently evangelizing about what VPP is doing and how it is doing it through the energetic writing of well-crafted, reader-friendly publications and an imaginative use of social media. His book, *Leap of Reason: Managing to Outcomes in an Era of Scarcity*, has attracted many enthusiastic reviews, and his regular short essays, which appear on the VPP website, have a wide following among foundation professionals, nonprofit leaders, and philanthropists. Early on, Morino recruited a talented and knowledgeable writer, Lowell Weiss, the founder of Cascade Philanthropy Advisors, to be coeditor of the Leap of Reason initiative, which publicizes and updates the examples from the book. Weiss is also an advisor to Venture Philanthropy Partners.[52]

Corporate Social Responsibility

The transformations previously described regarding foundations are mirrored by comparable changes in the ways that corporations seek to tackle important social problems facing the nation. The two corporations that exemplify that change most markedly are IBM and Goldman Sachs. At IBM the corporation uses its most significant assets, the time and talent of its employees, to create innovative solutions to societal problems and then brings them to scale and makes them sustainable. The 25-year continuity of Stanley S. Litow's leadership of IBM's corporate engagement, which began in 1993 when Louis V. Gerstner became CEO and which has continued through the administrations of the two CEOs who succeeded him, has undoubtedly contributed to the sustained trajectory of IBM's high quality and innovativeness.

Starting with significant initiatives and IBM leadership in US education reform, IBM itself planned and managed three widely admired national education summits, which included the nation's governors, many corporate CEOs, and leaders in education as well as President Bill Clinton, all of them hosted at IBM. Those widely representative conferences led to a consensus on the need for higher standards and the creation of a new national organization, ACHIEVE, which was chaired by IBM Corporation, to put its weight behind specific education reform initiatives chosen by the conferees.

In 2008, IBM established its Corporate Service Corps, which has often been referred to as the corporate version of the Peace Corps. It sends teams of IBM employees to help developing-world communities and NGOs solve pressing social problems. As of 2016, approximately 3,000 IBM midcareer and younger employees had participated in over 1,000 team projects across 37 countries, tackling challenges such as reducing mother-to-child AIDS transmissions in Ghana and creating management systems to expand food bank programs in Latin America.

In 2010, IBM launched "The Smarter Cities Challenge," a $50 million competitive grant program to provide teams of IBM employees to 130 cities around the world to help them become more efficient in providing public services and more effective in solving their problems. An IBM "Smarter Cities" challenge team in Memphis used data analytics to help transform the city's 911 system. IBM also created a virtual supercomputer called "World Community Grid," which pulled power from millions of computers so as to provide hundreds of millions of dollars of free computing power to fuel important research studies on health challenges such as treating Ebola and the Zika virus.

Yet another example of IBM's creativity and commitment has been the establishment of a new kind of high school known as P-Tech (Pathways in Technology Early College High School), first in Brooklyn, New York, and now in six states. The P-Tech schools run from 9th grade through what the program calls "14th grade"—ending in a two-year associate's degree. They are established within the public school systems as collaborations among IBM, the school system, and individual corporate partners. The students, all from disadvantaged backgrounds, are given technology education that equips them to fill tech-intensive jobs in business. Successful graduates are then first in line for jobs at IBM and other companies. P-Tech results are exceeding the national average for college completion and have resulted in a push to alter the distribution of federal funding for career and technical education programs across the United States consistent with the P-Tech design.

Such schools have spread rapidly since they were first launched by IBM in September 2001, with 60 in operation at the start of the 2016 academic year.[53] In addition, IBM has launched a new effort to use its Watson supercomputer to help physicians diagnose difficult health problems by loading all the relevant clinical trial results into the computer and enabling physicians to have access to the data by apps for smartphones. The company is now using the Watson supercomputer to provide to school teachers, again via smartphone apps, materials on discrete subjects that they wish to use in their classroom instruction. Beginning with elementary school math, the Watson technology becomes a personalized coach to assist teachers with finding the best academic course materials, customizing them for use in their classrooms, and answering questions about the best teaching strategies. In each case, IBM frames a solution to a critical problem using Watson technology and cloud computing, as well as data analytics and mobile technologies, to develop innovative solutions and then bring them to scale and make them sustainable.[54]

Since 2008, Goldman Sachs has committed more than $1.6 billion in high-impact, strategic philanthropic initiatives. That was the year it launched the aforementioned *10,000 Women* initiative, the first of its two major strategic programs to drive economic growth and opportunity. The company started by identifying women-owned small- and medium-sized enterprises as a "white space" in need of investment. Based on Goldman Sachs's research demonstrating the significant economic and social benefits to investing in women's education—published in reports such as "Womenomics" (2005)[55] and "Women Hold Up Half the Sky" (2008)[56]—*10,000*

Women was established as a five-year, $100 million program to identify and train women entrepreneurs in developing countries. Goldman Sachs partnered with educational institutions in 56 countries to provide high-quality business and management education to the women entrepreneurs, as well as technical assistance and the opportunity to access working capital in accordance with their business plans.

By the end of 2013, the 10,000th woman had entered the program. Babson College released an independent evaluation in 2014 and determined that "training and education for women entrepreneurs positively affect emerging economies by increasing revenues and creating jobs, expanding women's contributions to their communities, and informing their leadership styles."[57] Within 18 months of graduating, nearly 70 percent of graduates increased revenues, 60 percent added new jobs, and 90 percent were "paying it forward" by mentoring other women in their communities.[58] Graduates' sustained growth was significant. However, many confronted challenges accessing capital to take their businesses to the next level, highlighting the massive credit gap that exists for women entrepreneurs in developing countries.

To address this market need, in 2014, Goldman Sachs, in partnership with the World Bank Group (through the International Finance Corporation), created the first-ever loan facility for women entrepreneurs to enable up to 100,000 women around the world to raise capital for their enterprises.[59] This partnership was also driven by research: IFC estimates a $285 billion global credit gap for women entrepreneurs, and Goldman Sachs's research publication "Giving Credit Where It Is Due" (2014)[60] found that closing this gap in many developing countries could increase per capita income by up to 12 percent by 2030 and as much as 25–28 percent in Brazil and Vietnam.

With an anchor investment of $50 million from the Goldman Sachs Foundation, the facility has attracted coinvestment from commercial and public institutions, including a $100 million commitment from the Overseas Private Investment Corporation, announced by President Obama in July 2015.[61] Two years later, this public-private partnership, spurred by for-profit-sector innovation, has continued to attract new funders and highlighted the increased interest in investing in this space to close the gap and make progress. As of 2016, the facility has committed $420 million to financial institutions in 15 countries, making capital available to more than 25,000 women entrepreneurs. Among the major new investments are those from commercial investor AP2, the Second Swedish National Pension Fund, demonstrating the evolution of the women's economic empowerment space from a philanthropic investment to an impact investment.

Incorporating the lessons learned from *10,000 Women*, Goldman Sachs launched *10,000 Small Businesses* in 2010, a $500 million initiative to support small business owners in the United States and the United Kingdom with access to education, capital, and business support services.[62] With an advisory council cochaired by Goldman Sachs CEO Lloyd Blankfein, former New York mayor Michael R. Bloomberg, Berkshire Hathaway chairman and CEO Warren Buffett, and the founder of Initiative for a Competitive Inner City, Michael Porter, *10,000 Small Businesses* has also seen remarkable results, as detailed in a 2016 progress report released by Babson College in May 2016, which found that "*10,000 Small Businesses* participants consistently increase revenues and create jobs over a longer period of time. Six months after completing the program, 47.9 percent of participants reported adding new jobs. This number increased to 55.7 percent at 18 months and to 60.9 percent at 30 months after the program," significantly exceeding the extent of new hiring among small businesses generally.[63]

Other corporations, including Coca-Cola, have followed suit with similarly ambitious plans that are related to the business activities of those companies. In the case of Coca-Cola, the focus is on creating clean water in the countries in which Coca-Cola is using water to produce its beverages.

In the past, corporate social responsibility mainly consisted of writing checks to nonprofit community groups in the vicinity of the company's manufacturing plants and offices. The difference between that and the robust, cutting-edge initiatives of some of today's corporations, as exemplified by IBM and Goldman Sachs, could not be more striking. Today's pioneering efforts are bold, strategic, and measured by impact data.

chapter three

New Vehicles for Giving and New Organizations That Enable Philanthropy to Be More Effective

In addition to the evolving and expanding roles and practices of individual philanthropists, foundations, and corporations described in the previous chapter, very significant additions to the philanthropic landscape have appeared since 1990 that increasingly play beneficial roles in improving philanthropy and enabling it to become more effective and efficient. This chapter explores the ones that I think are most important.

DONOR-ADVISED FUNDS

Tax-exempt donor-advised funds—long offered by community foundations but since 1991 a frequent offering of some for-profit financial service institutions—have become major vehicles for charitable giving. I have mentioned these funds in earlier contexts but they deserve a closer look. They are essentially intermediary mechanisms that hold funds or securities for some period of time for individuals who desire to devote financial resources to one or more tax-exempt operating charities but who have not yet selected the recipients. By transferring assets to a donor-advised fund, individuals part with the ability to use such funds for anything other than IRS-certified tax-exempt entities but reserve the right to advise the fund administrator as to the specific charities that are to receive the funds. By relinquishing legal ownership of the funds, the donor receives a tax deduction in the year in which the gift is given, notwithstanding the fact that it may be several years before the funds are designated to a specific operating charity. When Fidelity Investments persuaded the Internal Revenue Service in 1991 to recognize its Fidelity Investments Charitable Gift Fund as a 501(c)(3) public charity, a major new national vehicle to facilitate optimally tax-planned charitable giving by individuals was born.[1]

It was a community foundation, The New York Community Trust, that in 1931 pioneered the establishment of donor-advised funds, and by 1991 most other community foundations had begun offering them. Some had grown dramatically from contributions to these funds. Consequently, community foundations vigorously protested the extension of public charity status to the charitable gift funds of for-profit entities. For perhaps a decade after the IRS opened the door for for-profit financial institutions to create and be custodians of such national funds, the community foundations fought the battle but ultimately gave up, and some of them began forming joint ventures with commercial firms.

In 2014 and 2015, however, criticism from scholars and others began to mount. Some community foundations began urging Congress and the Internal Revenue Service to reconsider the current regulations that treat commercial firms hosting donor-advised funds the same as community foundation hosts.[2] The critics argued that, because community foundations are public charities by law, and because they provide donors with professional guidance regarding the making of grants to nonprofits from the donor-advised funds, they are entitled to more favorable payout regulations than are the national commercial firms. This was no small matter: by 2015, some of the largest for-profit financial investment-managing institutions had followed Fidelity's lead by creating their own donor-advised funds. Examples include the Schwab Charitable Fund, the Vanguard Charitable Endowment Program, and the Goldman Sachs Philanthropy Fund, although Fidelity has far more assets than any of the others. The debate over the merits of this competition between community foundations and investment firms continues, though the growth of these funds in the commercial marketplace seems unlikely to be reversed.

The fact that a large proportion of the gifts to donor-advised funds occurs each year during December underscores the degree to which such funds have come to be a critical component of many individuals' annual income tax planning and charitable gift-making. Individuals highly value the convenience of making tax-deductible annual gifts when they have surplus cash or publicly traded securities available for philanthropic purposes but have not identified, or don't have the time to identify, the ultimate recipients of such philanthropy. One consequence of such year-end calculations is to create a rush in December of deposits to donor-advised funds and of gifts from such funds to charities.[3]

As of the end of 2015, the total value of all donor-advised funds in community foundations, federations, and for-profit corporations in the United States was $78.64 billion. Of that amount, about one-sixth was in the Fidelity Charitable Gift Fund, whose assets were $13.2 billion, and it alone hosted 66,829 giving accounts. In calendar year 2015, Fidelity's fund made 733,000 grants to about 106,000 operating charities totaling more than $3.1 billion.[4] The cumulative value of charitable contributions given through Fidelity since the fund's inception in 1991 has ballooned to $18 billion. The amount given in 2014 alone was $2.2 billion.[5] For comparison purposes, as of the same date, the total assets in all US private foundations were about $700 billion. It is significant that the year-to-year growth of donor-advised funds from 2013 to 2014 was 23.9 percent, of course on a much smaller base figure than foundations, while the growth in assets in private foundations was a mere 3 percent.[6] It is also worth noting that, throughout the first eight years that systematic figures on donor-advised funds were collected, the annual payout rate has been consistently higher than 20 percent of assets in those accounts.[7]

Some observers of the philanthropic scene have criticized the fact that donor-advised funds are not subject to any minimum annual payout requirement like the one imposed on private foundations, which must pay out 5 percent of their asset value annually. Such critics argue that it is not wise public policy to allow a deduction for gifts that benefit donors instantly and that earn management profits for the funds' host institutions but that may take years to benefit the ultimate intended beneficiaries—nonprofit organizations and the individuals they serve.[8] The data cited in the preceding paragraph suggest that such a potential requirement may not be needed if donor-advised funds continue voluntarily to pay out 20 percent or more of their asset value every year. Nonetheless, critics say that those figures are aggregates, meaning that some funds pay out more than that, and others may pay out nothing.[9]

In my considered judgment, the criticism of Fidelity and other national hosts of donor-advised funds is the result of renewed effort by a combination of ideology-grounded, self-interested organizations motivated by envy-based resentment of the rapidly growing success of the commercial entrants into the field. Clearly those new players have identified among potential clients a widespread desire for national reach, a higher quality of service befitting a large financial institution, and greater flexibility for the tax planning of their philanthropic giving than they find available from their local community foundations.

Let me stress, however, that many community foundations are in fact providing a level of service for their donor-advised funds that is comparable to, or perhaps even superior to, that of national financial institutions. Furthermore, they are also offering experienced professional guidance about the charitable needs in their communities, which the national, commercial hosts are not. The recent success of the national hosts suggests, however, that a large portion of Americans wishing to make some or all of their charitable giving via donor-advised funds does not feel the need for such substantive guidance and find the convenience of national scope of giving an advantage that community foundations do not offer competitively. Most community foundations will accommodate fund-holders' desire to make grants from their funds outside the local or regional areas, but of course the community foundations do not usually have any substantive knowledge about the needs of the nonlocal geographies where such grant recipients are located.

One final point worth noting is that, for calendar year 2014, the average size of donor-advised funds at community foundations was double the average size of such funds housed at the national hosts—$420,155 versus $256,626—which suggests that donors use their local community foundations for their longer-term giving and for their support of local causes and needs, whereas donors using the national hosts may be more transaction focused. It is also likely that some donors prefer the national donor-advised fund hosts, sensing that they provide more anonymity to donors than the local community foundations, which typically have boards and distributions committees made up of a number of local residents. The national hosts, however, can ensure no exposure of donors to others.[10]

A STEADILY GROWING PHILANTHROPY-IMPROVING INFRASTRUCTURE

Along with the rise of donor-advised funds and the increased focus on metrics, over the past quarter-century there has been a marked growth in the number of institutions and organizations focused on improving the functioning of foundations and nonprofit organizations. Some of them develop and provide expertise to individual philanthropists, families, foundations, and nonprofits in hopes of increasing the effectiveness of charitable gifts to organizational recipients. Others seek to fill niches in the organizational infrastructure supporting nonprofits and philanthropy to facilitate the improved functioning of the kinds of organizations each seeks to serve. The expanding availability and quality of these services, combined with the fact that more and more donors, especially wealthier ones, are pursuing more reliable prospective as well as retrospective knowledge about the impact their philanthropy can possibly have suggests a deepening concern among donors for knowledge, strategy, and evidence of impact. If so, that is an important trend for the field, one that may well contribute to significantly greater achievements for philanthropy in the future. Following is a description of the major players as of the writing of this book. Some of them have been mentioned earlier, but each is worth considering in more detail.

Harvard Business School Social Enterprise Initiative

In 1993, John Whitehead, formerly co-CEO of Goldman Sachs, made a multimillion-dollar gift to Harvard Business School (HBS) to found an entirely new kind of entity in the world of business schools, the Social Enterprise Initiative. Its mission was to enable students and faculty members to bring to bear on the problems of society and their solutions the rigorous intellectual and analytical capital that business schools had developed in the 20th century. That Initiative quickly attracted the involvement of more than a dozen HBS faculty members and proved so enticing to Harvard MBA students that the Social Enterprise Club almost instantly became the largest of the dues-requiring student clubs at HBS. The Initiative gradually inspired other American business schools either to create similar programs, as Duke University, for example, has done, or to strengthen existing programs that focus on solutions to social problems, as Northwestern and Yale have done. Over the past 25 years, the intellectual capital generated by HBS through the Social Enterprise Initiative has steadily enriched public policy discourse on a wide range of subjects, including how to achieve greater social impact, with a particular focus on nonprofit organizations and philanthropy. The Initiative's existence has contributed substantially to a new body of research on the strengths and weaknesses of nonprofit practices, including many HBS cases on individual nonprofit organizations and on major corporate social responsibility initiatives, as well as influential books on venture philanthropy and social entrepreneurship.

Grantmakers for Effective Organizations

For several years after commencing grantmaking, the David and Lucile Packard Foundation was a pioneer, under the leadership of its program officer Barbara Kibbe, in providing support for the strengthening of the organizational effectiveness with which their grantees made their decisions, implemented their strategies, and sought to achieve their substantive program goals. By 1997, several foundations were coming to the recognition that organizational skills of high quality were indispensable to their grantees' impact. As a result, they, together with Packard, established Grantmakers for Effective Organizations (GEO), originally as an affinity group of the Council on Foundations and later as an independent nonprofit organization in its own right. The Packard Foundation quickly realized that the training it had been providing to its own grantees was needed by all nonprofits and therefore widened its focus by supporting the expansion of the new GEO. That organization now has a dues-paying membership of over 500 grantmakers and is the leading advocate for individual foundation financial support for the training of grantmakers in all aspects of organizational effectiveness. GEO runs a variety of research, training, and outreach programs that serve all foundations, whether GEO members or not; publishes some excellent how-to-do-it reports; and offers many webinars on those subjects. As the focus of many foundations has broadened to include emphases on clarifying strategy in their fields of interest, measuring outcomes, and other process goals now thought to contribute to a foundation's impact, GEO has become ever more influential in raising the standard of both foundation and grantee organizational effectiveness.

New Profit, Inc.

New Profit, Inc. is an ingenious social venture capital investment bank-cum-management consultancy that was founded by Vanessa Kirsch in Boston in 1999. She envisioned the raising of a large pool of financial resources supplied by individual philanthropists, foundations, and corporations that would be regranted to promising or already high-performing start-up nonprofits to enable them to achieve greater scale and sustainability. Kirsch invited the Monitor Group, a strategy consultancy, to partner with her organization to provide strategic consulting advice to its grantees.

Among New Profit's early grantees were such successful social enterprises as Kickstarter, Right to Play, Citizen Schools, and Jumpstart. In 2012, the Monitor Group was acquired by Deloitte, which committed its much greater resources and depth of expertise to New Profit (the consultancy is now called Monitor Deloitte). Two years later, New Profit became a founding investor in the Massachusetts Juvenile Justice Pay for Success Initiative, and New Profit's America Forward arm helped achieve the July 2014 passage by Congress of the Workforce Innovation and Opportunity Act, "which provides funding for social innovation through its landmark Pay for Success and other provisions." Since 2007, New Profit has provided $120 million and 35,000 senior staff hours to the organizations it supports, and it estimates that those organizations have touched some 10 million lives through their work.[11]

Foundation Center

The Foundation Center was created in 1956 as an intermediary between foundations and the public; it collected the foundations' annual reports and published periodic volumes with information on the purposes of grants made by those foundations. With the onset of the Internet and the corresponding capacity to create searchable digital databases, the center gradually expanded the range and detail of information collected and digitized the repository, enabling widespread access by the public. Starting in 2008, with the appointment of a new president, Brad Smith, the center began to establish partnerships with various organizations to undertake new initiatives in research, publishing of reports, and educational offerings in many aspects of philanthropy and fundraising, making it an active participant as well as a catalyst in countless forms of outreach to nonprofit organizations, foundations, and the public. The Foundation Center has become one of the major creators of information for and about philanthropic initiatives broadly conceived. It has devised a stronger analytic capacity to apply to the data it receives, resulting in a steady stream of well-designed, imaginatively visualized print and digital publications. In recent years, it has also created, merged with, or adopted a growing number of initiatives, such as Philanthropy News Digest, GrantCraft, IssueLab, and Glasspockets. In anticipation of the adoption by the United Nations of the 2030 Agenda for Sustainable Development Goals, the Foundation Center, in partnership with the United Nations Development Program and Rockefeller Philanthropy Advisors, created the SDG Philanthropy Platform in September 2015, the first activity of which was to organize a conference at the Ford Foundation entitled "Philanthropy Engaged: Implementing and Achieving the Post-2015 Agenda."[12] That kind of forward thinking characterizes today's Foundation Center.[13]

National Center for Family Philanthropy

The National Center for Family Philanthropy was founded in 1997 by Virginia Esposito, a long-time staff member of the Council on Foundations, with the goal of helping family foundations, which constitute by far the largest proportion of private foundations in the United States, to be ever more effective in achieving the impact to which their trustees and staff aspire. Since then, the NCFP has become the primary advocacy organization on behalf of the value of family philanthropy. It has published more than 50 books and issued briefs and articles on such matters as various forms of governance of family foundations and different ways of bringing new generations of children and grandchildren into their families' philanthropic endeavors. In addition, the NCFP periodically conducts research to determine best practices for family foundations and organizes conferences, seminars, and webinars to disseminate that information to family foundation trustees, family members, and staff. All told, as of 2016 the NCFP had organized more than 750 workshops, created a searchable database on family giving, and devised peer learning networks to help guide families in making their way through intrafamily decision-making challenges and leadership transitions. The fact that the NCFP is now supported entirely by families and family foundations is credible testimony to the value its primary beneficiaries place on the services it provides.

The Center for Effective Philanthropy

With the founding of The Center for Effective Philanthropy by Harvard professor Michael Porter and Mark Kramer of the Foundation Strategy Group (now FSG) in 2001, and their recruitment of Phil Buchanan as the Center's Chief Executive, America's foundations came to be blessed with the capacity, for the very first time, to learn how their grantees perceived their performance. During the past 15 years, the Center, under Buchanan's visionary and dynamic leadership, has become an energetic force for greater foundation accountability. The mechanism that enabled that change in accountability to occur was Buchanan's vision, with a significant contribution of ideas by his associate Kevin Bolduc and the Center's Board Chair Phil Guidice, which they named the "Grantee Perception Report."

The Grantee Perception Reports grow out of confidential surveys of an individual foundations grantees and measure how well the grantees believe to the foundations are doing in supporting and working with grantees. It is no exaggeration to describe these Grantee Perception Reports as having revolutionized the relationships between those who make grants and those who seek and receive them. For the first time, foundation trustees now have a way of obtaining independent views of how well their executives and program officers are doing, and many surprises have emerged from those surveys. Before the founding of The Center for Effective Philanthropy (CEP), the Robert Wood Johnson Foundation, for example, had conducted its own "customer" surveys for many years without obtaining any significantly critical comments about the performance of its program officers. Trustees and management were therefore shocked by the first Grantee Perception Report (GPR) it received from the CEP, which revealed that, in the opinion of the foundation's grantees, its communication with them left a great deal to be desired, euphemistically speaking. In fact, the president of the Robert Wood Johnson Foundation was so stunned that she wrote a letter to every grantee to apologize for the foundation's shortcomings in relating to them.

When the GPR on The Kresge Foundation revealed that about three-quarters of its grantees felt that the foundation did not have a very good idea of what the grantee organizations were all about, the foundation did not hesitate to post the findings on its website, which, of course, shook up the foundation's trustees. Many other foundations have now made a habit of having a GPR done on them every few years and then including the report on their website, whether positive or negative.

The consequence of this increasing transparency is that foundations, which have heretofore rarely admitted that their performance leaves anything to be desired, have at long last been emboldened by the GPR to be more forthcoming about how well or badly they are actually doing their jobs.

Moreover, because many foundations now choose to commission Grantee Perception Reports, the Center has accumulated a great deal of information on the standards of foundation–grantee relations across the field. This enables it to provide to individual grantmakers precise data comparing a specific foundation's performance with that of others. Therefore, the GPRs are not only useful in uncovering shortcomings by any fixed standard but are perhaps even more helpful in enabling individual foundations to assess their accomplishments against those of other foundations. The data obtained by the GPRs are sufficiently granular that a foundation can learn the quality of performance by individual members of its program staff. That, too, is a major lever for foundations to use in improving their performance. As the CEP has acquired more information on the strengths, weaknesses, and effectiveness of foundations, it has become a frequent source of carefully researched, well-written, hard-hitting, objective reports on how and what foundations are doing. Phil Buchanan writes op-ed pieces regularly, speaks often, and even does TED-like talks aimed at correcting public misunderstandings of nonprofits and philanthropies.

The Philanthropic Initiative

Like so many of the organizations discussed in this chapter, The Philanthropic Initiative (TPI) was founded in Boston, in this instance in 1989 by the remarkable Peter Karoff, a philanthropic advisor who moonlighted by publishing poetry. He launched TPI as a for-profit organization but quickly realized that philanthropic consulting alone, however valuable it might be, could not generate financial profits. Therefore, with the aid of The Rockefeller Foundation, he converted the organization into a nonprofit consulting firm and obtained 501(c)(3) status from the Internal Revenue Service. According to an article on the Fidelity Charitable Gift Fund website, TPI was the first such organization to be created.[14] Others listed as of this writing include the aforementioned Rockefeller Philanthropy Advisors, Arabella Advisors, Charities Aid Foundation of America (CAF America), Cascade Philanthropy Advisors, Entrepreneurs Foundation, Excellence in Giving, Growth Strategy Inc., Paragon Philanthropy, Philanthropy Advisors, Philanthropy Directions International, Strategic Philanthropy, and The Chambers Group.[15] At one time in TPI's history, it was advising individuals, foundations, and corporations on their annual charitable giving in the total amount of about $100 million a year. Some years later, Karoff went into semiretirement and in 2012 the organization became an independent operating unit of The Boston Foundation, discussed in Chapter 2. But the fact that so many other organizations followed TPI's example testifies not only to the foresight that Peter Karoff clearly had but also to his skill in running that firm so effectively for so many years. Karoff died, alas, March 9, 2017.

The Bridgespan Group

In Chapter 1, I briefly told the story of the founding of The Bridgespan Group in 2000 by Tom Tierney of Bain & Company and Harvard Business School professor Jeff Bradach and how it has since become the gold standard of philanthropic strategy consulting. It serves many of the largest foundations in the country, wealthy individuals contemplating philanthropic initiatives, and operating charities that are seeking to improve their functioning. Bridgespan was created as a nonprofit affiliate of Bain & Company, with a separate board of directors and with 501(c)(3) certification from the Internal Revenue Service. Headquartered in Boston, it then added offices in San Francisco and New York and, as of 2015, one in Mumbai, India, its only office outside the United States. In addition to providing consulting services, Bridgespan has developed a robust research-based program with the goal of providing to the civic sector field as a whole, as well as to the general public, empirical data amassed through its individual consulting engagements. That information is widely and continuously disseminated by means of articles in various journals, including especially the *Stanford Social Innovation Review,* a lively website (www.bridgespan.org), and vigorous outreach to both print and digital media. Bridgespan also hosts the Nonprofit Job Board, which posts employment opportunities in nonprofit organizations.

FSG

FSG, also founded in 2000, was created as the Foundation Strategy Group, a for-profit partnership between Harvard Business School professor Michael Porter and Mark Kramer, an experienced philanthropic advisor. Starting with a focus on advising foundations on how to develop and implement strategies to achieve greater impact in their grantmaking, FSG broadened its mission to include partnerships aimed at improving both philanthropy and nonprofit organizations. It has worked with the Council on Foundations, the Clinton Global Initiative, The Rockefeller Foundation, the Aspen Institute Forum for Community Solutions, Grantmakers for Effective Organization, and the United Way Worldwide, among others. In 2006, FSG converted to nonprofit status with 501(c)(3) certification by the Internal Revenue Service. Beginning with an office in Boston, it steadily added offices in Geneva, Switzerland, San Francisco, Seattle, and, in 2015, in Mumbai, India. Porter and Kramer have frequently published widely read and highly regarded articles in both *The Harvard Business Review* and the *Stanford Social Innovation Review*. According to its website, FSG now has more than 150 staff members.

McKinsey Social Initiative

In March of 2015, McKinsey & Company announced the creation of a new nonprofit affiliate, which focuses on solving difficult social problems worldwide. The firm allocated $70 million from its own funds for this initiative, which also received support of $15 million from the US Agency for International Development (USAID) and $3.2 million from Walmart. In addition, McKinsey assigned 25 of its consultants to work on projects with the Social Initiative and designated 10 of its partners to provide advice. To lead the initiative, it appointed Helene Gayle, formerly CEO of CARE, Inc. In January 2016, the Social Initiative announced its first major program, Generation, which was tasked with training and placing in jobs one million unemployed young people from five countries over five years.[16] That McKinsey decided to undertake this initiative, following the lead of Bain & Company in founding Bridgespan, is another major step forward in increasing the worldwide infrastructure of public problem-solving.[17]

Rockefeller Philanthropy Advisors

Rockefeller Philanthropy Advisors (RPA) was founded in 2002 by the investment management firm Rockefeller & Company as a nonprofit organization with 501(c)(3) certification by the Internal Revenue Service for the purpose of offering philanthropic advisory assistance to individuals, families, foundations, and corporations. Its primary service is to advise those seeking to achieve impact through their philanthropic giving on how to do so, but it also operates a charitable giving fund through which, according to its website, individuals and organizations "can make gifts outside the United States, participate in funding consortia and operate nonprofit initiatives."[18] It also offers "program, administrative, and management services for foundations and trusts."[19] It currently "manages or advises on more than $200 million in annual giving by its clients" and has "facilitated more than $3 billion in grantmaking to nearly 70 countries."[20] Among those who follow charitable giving advisory services, RPA is widely regarded as one of the very best organizations because of the depth of experience of its professional staff, led by CEO Melissa Berman.

A NEW "GOLDEN AGE" OF PHILANTHROPY?

Social media and the Internet have the potential to bring about radical changes in the world of philanthropy, from the nature of volunteering and the ease of making donations to the facilitation and scaling of new events to raise those funds. The fact that the technology exists and has been adopted widely by Americans does not alone, however, translate into a predictor of philanthropic benefit. Simply because there is a new way to give does not mean that there exists a new level of will, which is prerequisite to any kind of charitable act.

Facebook is a good example. It now has a Social Good Team, which is developing a variety of ways in which the one billion people worldwide who use the site daily can donate to the nonprofits of their choice. In 2013, when Facebook originally piloted the "Give Now" button, prospective donors could make their gifts directly on the nonprofits' Facebook pages. While easy enough for the givers, the recipient charities quickly realized that they were being deprived of important information—the donors' e-mail addresses—because in making the gifts through an organization's Facebook page, those e-mail addresses remained with Facebook.

Implementation is everything. In August 2015, the company announced that it would initiate a "Donate Now" button on some nonprofit organizations' Facebook pages, which, when clicked, would redirect the user to the particular nonprofit's web page, where a contribution could then be made. What seemed easy in fact required three transaction steps: from inclination through search to completion.[21]

The simple existence of so many Facebook members does not necessarily translate into many charitable contributions at all. In fact, at least at present, the specialists in online fundraising tell us that "only one percent of all online fundraising is attributed to social media."[22] It is clearly premature to conclude, on the basis of the information now available, therefore, that social media have much promise any time soon of adding much gold to American philanthropy.

Nonetheless, I choose not to believe that the present lack of interest among Facebook members or other Internet users dooms the possibility that social media-facilitated generosity will increase in the future. PayPal, for example, reported that the charitable donations it processed to nonprofit organizations in 2014, $212 million, were 50 percent higher than in 2013.[23] Network for Good, which facilitates charitable giving by individuals to any nonprofit registered with the Internal Revenue Service, publishes a periodic Digital Giving Index. Its 2014 figures show a 9 percent increase over 2013 in online giving through Network for Good's giving platform, for a 2014 total of $233 million distributed to 45,000 nonprofits, 55 percent of which came through the giving pages of the nonprofits themselves.[24] The *Nonprofit Quarterly* reported that the M+R Strategic Services Benchmark Study, which surveyed the online experience of 84 nonprofits, reported a 14 percent overall increase over 2013 in online giving to those organizations.[25] Finally, the fundraising-software company Blackbaud reported that online charitable giving in 2014 to the 3,724 nonprofits in its survey grew 8.9 percent over 2013, for a total of $2 billion in donations. For those nonprofit organizations surveyed, Blackbaud's data showed that only 6.7 percent of their income had come from online donations in 2014.[26]

In analyzing these growth figures, it is essential to keep in mind that giving to the US nonprofit sector in 2014 from living individuals—obviously the only donors who use online giving—was $258.5 billion and that the increase in their giving from 2013 to 2014 was 5.7 percent.[27] Measured in dollars, that is a year-to-year increase from 2013 of $18 billion in individual contributions alone, which puts into context how tiny today's amount of online individual giving is, even when using the highest figures for it as reported above.

Regardless of how much money is donated online, social media might turn out to have a beneficial effect on how much *time* users donate to charity. It is heartening to know that a substantial portion of Americans give generously of their time: 62.6 million adults, about a quarter of all Americans, "donated" 7.7 billion hours to nonprofit organizations in 2013, or 32.5 hours per individual during that year.[28] The research also tells us that volunteering has spillovers among charitable contributions. According to the Corporation for National and Community Service, "Nearly eight in 10 (79.2 percent) volunteers donated to charity, compared to four in 10 (40.4 percent) of non-volunteers."[29] To the extent that volunteers use social media to help attract other volunteers, then, that would likely increase both the number of those volunteering and the amount of funds given to charity.

Whatever the statistics indicate, something is clearly afoot that was not even imaginable in 1990. Indiegogo, which declares itself "the Largest Global Crowd-funding & Fundraising Source Online,"[30] announced on October 21, 2015, the launching of a site that nonprofits can use to solicit funds without cost. According to an article in *The Chronicle of Philanthropy*, "The new website, Generosity by Indiegogo, will also house individuals' personal crowdfunding campaigns for needs like medical and education expenses, replacing the company's earlier offshoot site for personal crowdfunding, Indiegogo Life."[31] Go-FundMe, a pioneer of online crowdfunding that launched in 2010, had raised $3 billion from more than 25 million donors by the end of 2016.[32] Many other organizations devoted to facilitating online giving and finding volunteering opportunities continue to be founded and are flourishing. Universal Giving, founded about 2006, invites individuals to "donate and volunteer with vetted opportunities all across the world." It promises that "100% goes to the cause."[33]

Other organizations are relying on the rapid utilization of social media on mobile phones and apps to connect potential donors and recipients from around the globe. An excellent example of this is Kiva, which authors Roger Martin and Sally Osberg described this way:

> [A] global microfinance organization, a spiritual descendant of [the pio-neer microcredit institution] Grameen Bank with a technology-enabled twist. Rather than acting as a bank that [makes] loans . . . Kiva channels funds to micro-entrepreneurs through crowdsourcing, matching lenders with as little as $25 to lend to small business-builders around the world. Using field partners to vet potential entrepreneurs and micro-finance or-ganizations to distribute and monitor the funds in their relevant geogra-phies, Kiva focuses on providing an online marketplace through which lenders and borrowers can match themselves up.[34]

Another organization working in this vein is GiveDirectly, which "sends money directly to the extreme poor" abroad.[35] On our shores, social media have been the principal reason that "Giving Tuesday" exists. That is a day similar to the American Thanksgiving Day but intended to encourage Amer-icans not only to give thanks but "to give back." Its website explains that "We have a day for giving thanks. We have two for getting deals. Now, we have #GivingTuesday, a global day dedicated to giving back."[36] On that day in 2015, 699,000 donors made 1.08 million online gifts averaging $108. Twitter had 1.3 million tweets mentioning #GivingTuesday during that day, which was an increase of 86 percent over the number of 2014 tweets.[37] Without social media, a "Giving Tuesday" would be, if not unimaginable, much less effective in attracting ever-increasing amounts of support, especially but not only from small givers. In total, online giving in 2015 rose above $205 million, coming from almost one million donors, with the money going to almost 31,000 nonprofit organizations.[38]

The Ice Bucket Challenge (IBC) is another example of how social media can be harnessed to raise hundreds of millions of dollars for charity. This endeavor first reached viral status in July 2014 when Pete Frates and Pat Quinn, both of whom had been diagnosed with ALS (amyotrophic lateral sclerosis, also called Lou Gehrig's disease), encouraged Internet users to post videos in which they douse themselves with ice water as a way of challenging others to contribute money to research on the causes and treatment of that disease.[39] In the year since Frates and Quinn took IBC viral, it is said to have raised $250 million for a variety of charities and has attracted celebrity IBCers such as Taylor Swift, Justin Timberlake, Lady Gaga, and Robert Downey Jr.[40] James Surowiecki, writing in *The New Yorker*, expressed optimism about the potential of such initiatives as IBC. He writes as follows: "That, really, was the true accomplishment of the [ice bucket] challenge; it took tools—the selfie, the hashtag, the like button—that have typically been used for private amusement or corporate profit and turned them to the public good. The campaign's critics implied that, had people not been dumping freezing water over their heads, they would have been working to end malaria instead. But it's far more likely that they would have been watching cat videos or, now, playing Pokemon Go. The problem isn't that the Ice Bucket Challenge was a charity fad. It's that it was a charity fad that no one has figured out how to duplicate."[41]

The Internet and the social media that depend on it have facilitated countless new kinds of fundraising initiatives, including bike rides, often cosponsored with corporate donors, benefiting such illnesses as multiple sclerosis. The National Multiple Sclerosis Society has raised more than $1 billion for research since Bike MS was founded in 1980.[42] Other such events include the American Diabetes Association's Tour de Cure, which orchestrates regional, national, and local single- and multiple-day bike rides all over the United States; Juvenile Diabetes Research Foundation's JDRF Rides to Cure Juvenile Diabetes; the Arthritis Foundation's multiple-day rides; and Cystic Fibrosis's Cycle for Life, which organizes single-day rides with multiple mileage options.[43] All of these are promoted prominently on the Internet, and most have benefited mightily from the mobilizing force of social media.

Thanks to the Internet, blogs, and the countless websites of organizations and publications that deal with or depend on philanthropic dollars, the profile of thinking of all shades of opinion regarding the strengths, weaknesses, challenges, and uses of philanthropy in the United States has been raised. More than a dozen influential publications cover the nonprofit and philanthropic sector online, and many more devote a sizable share of their coverage to the civic sector. Some web-based organizations, such as Inside Philanthropy and the Charity Defense Council, are dedicated to activist roles as "watchdogs" of philanthropy and operating nonprofit organizations. They and others are also generating expanded media attention to philanthropies and nonprofits.[44]

Individuals looking for guidance on their philanthropic choices can also obtain information online from specialized organizations, such as The Life You Can Save. Founded and vigorously supported by Princeton scholar Peter Singer, it identifies what he regards as the most effective charities fighting against extreme poverty the world over. Professor Singer urges everyone to give 1 percent of their annual income to charity and encourages donors to identify the charity or charities that most appeal to them *and* that score highly on impact measures.[45] The following charities, listed on the website, met Singer's criteria in 2016:

- Against Malaria Foundation

- Development Media International

- Evidence Action

- Fistula Foundation

- Fred Hollows Foundation

- GiveDirectly

- Global Alliance for Improved Nutrition

- Innovations for Poverty Action

- Iodine Global Network

- Living Goods

- One Acre Fund

- Oxfam International

- Population Services International

- Possible

- Project Healthy Children

- Schistosomiasis Control Initiative

- Seva Foundation

The Internet and social media have also facilitated the establishment of a growing number of nonprofits that are pushing the boundaries of medical research. For example, Cure Alzheimer's Fund, founded by Jeff and Jacqui Morby, Henry McCance, and others, has given $34 million for cutting-edge basic genetic research aimed at curing this disease. The directors have committed to paying the organization's overhead so that all of the money raised can go to research.[46] The Prostate Cancer Foundation was established by Michael Milken in 1993 to speed up research on the causes of prostate cancer and to stimulate improvement in treating it. The foundation supports a network of prostate cancer biomedical scientists and physicians who specialize in prostate cancer and who agree, in exchange for such support, to meet regularly and update the other researchers on their progress. Based on the success of the Prostate Cancer Foundation in speeding up the pace of discovery about prostate cancer and its treatment, Milken next launched FasterCures, which "is dedicated to accelerating progress against all life-threatening diseases."[47]

A LOOK BACKWARD

In summary, some things in philanthropy and the civic sector remain very much the same as in 1990, but much else that has happened since then has dramatically transformed the landscape of philanthropy in America.

The American public has continued, year in and year out, to manifest its generosity by steadily increasing its charitable contributions for countless worthy causes and nonprofit organizations. But in the past quarter-century, the vehicles created or significantly strengthened to put that money to work have been enabling those contributions of wealth and time to achieve their intended results in much more effective ways than anyone in 1990 could possibly have envisioned. American philanthropy has moved from a silo, in which it did things in what now seem distinctly quaint and old-fashioned ways, into an era in which virtually all that it does seems to be state-of-the-art by the standards of business and most other institutions in 21st-century America.

The consequence is that both donors and recipients of charitable dollars in this century are now much more able to achieve results more intelligently, more purposefully, more creatively, more knowledgeably, and more effectively. While there is much more that should be done to strengthen American philanthropy's infrastructure, what has already been accomplished gives promise of succeeding in transforming the future even more. Americans are now able to put their charitable dollars to work with greater confidence of bringing about their money's worth of good than ever before. The primary question that now faces donors is how to do justice evenhandedly to both present and future needs of American society and America's civic sector at the same time, and it is to that question that this book now turns.

PART TWO

A BRIEF HISTORY OF LIMITED LIFE FOUNDATIONS AND TIME-LIMITED GIVING

chapter four

From John Stuart Mill to Julius Rosenwald

For more than a century before Andrew Carnegie penned "Wealth" in 1889—republished the following year in *The Gospel of Wealth and Other Timely Essays*[1]—an often heated discussion had taken place in England, France, and Germany over what should be the proper public policy stance regarding perpetual endowments and foundations. That debate was driven primarily by the large number of press reports about perpetual endowments whose principal purposes had been made obsolete by the changing times. A concomitant objective was to figure out how legally to alter a donor's explicit directions in order to make use of the endowment's income for public benefit in contemporary times. Julius Rosenwald's criticism of perpetuities that had become impossible of achievement may have been based in part on a belief that existing legal rules permitting modification (so-called "cy pres" or "deviation" proceedings) were inadequate, too costly, or ineffective. The simple fact that there were so many endowments that had outlived the purposes intended by their creators ultimately led to the establishment of an English Charities Commission with the authority required to modify the terms of perpetual endowments. The obsolescent endowments were typically hosted by freestanding nonprofits, which were stymied by the restrictions governing their use.

The situation is different for freestanding perpetual foundations, because, almost always, such institutions were not and are not limited to specified purposes. They tend to have broader objectives and an internal governing board with the power to allocate expenditures according to their discretion.[2]

The primary issues in the English discussion were such questions as: Should public policy permit permanent endowments of any kind? and If they are permitted, could government act to terminate them or alter their donors' express purposes if, in the judgment of state officials, current public need would be better served by such changes? The often strong, unequivocal views expressed on all sides suggest a pronounced antipathy to the very idea of foundations that could involve themselves in public-benefiting expenditures independently of the government. In France in 1757, for example, the distinguished economist, author, and public official Anne-Robert-Jacques Turgot, Baron de *l'Aulne*, launched the discussion in an article entitled *Fondations* for the *Encyclopédie*, in which he argued that perpetual foundations are inherently unable to function properly, simply because, as he put it, "the founder [of a foundation] is a man who desires to eternalize the effect of his will, and no person alive today can know what will be the needs of the public tomorrow."[3] Turgot's basic argument is that perpetual foundations and endowments should not be permitted by law and that, where they exist, the state should retain the power to amend the express wishes of the endowments' founders to any extent officials think proper. To American ears—attuned to the deeply held belief that a creator of wealth has full rights under law to dispose of it for charitable purposes of intended benefit to the public (in whatever way the donor interprets public benefit) and for as long into the future as he or she wishes—Turgot's position constitutes fighting words.

Yet, on the European continent, especially in "statist" countries such as France and Germany, the view was that many public services traditionally provided by the state, such as education and social services, were at that time essentially monopolies of the state. These functions were thus considered substantially off-limits for action by private individuals or nonprofit organizations; public policy did not, and in this view should not, permit foundations, whether perpetual or time-limited, to augment or reform them. In Germany in 1791, for example, Wilhelm von Humboldt, the distinguished philosopher and founder of Humboldt University of Berlin, took a position that is similar to Turgot's.[4]

Even in England, a less "statist" country, the discourse on this subject was vigorous, primarily because of the frequent writing and lecturing of Sir Arthur Hobhouse, an eminent lawyer who gave up legal practice to take a position as a member of the Charities Commission, in which role he energetically led the battle against charitable perpetuities. His book, *The Dead Hand*,[5] reads like a legal brief for the proposition that dispositions of private wealth for the public good must be controllable and amendable by the state at any time and, in any event, should not be created in perpetuity.

By 1880, when Hobhouse's book was published, John Stuart Mill, the widely respected public intellectual and philosopher of utilitarianism, had already entered the fray with his characteristically eloquent essays taking the theories of Turgot, von Humboldt, and Hobhouse to task.

Mill's position on "perpetuity," and on the extent to which a donor's wishes had to be respected in the use of an endowment, had been a constant in his life. In 1833, he had published an article in *Jurist*[6] detailing the same argument. Here are a few excerpts from that essay:

> If endowments are permitted, it is implied, as a necessary condition, that the State, for a time at least, shall not intermeddle with them. The property assigned must temporarily be sacred to the purposes to which it was destined by its owners. The founders of the London University would not have subscribed their money . . . if they had thought that they were merely raising a sum of money to be placed at the disposal of Parliament, or of the ministry for the time being. . . .
>
> The sacredness of the founder's assignment should continue during his own life, and for such longer period as the foresight of a prudent man may be presumed to reach, and no further. We do not pretend to fix the exact term of years; perhaps there is no necessity for its being accurately fixed: but it evidently should be but a moderate one. . . .
>
> All beyond this is to make the dead, judges of the exigencies of the living; to erect, not merely the ends, but the means, not merely the speculative opinions, but the practical expedients, of a gone-by age, into an irrevocable law for the present. . . . Under the guise of fulfilling a bequest, this is making a dead man's intentions for a single day a rule for subsequent centuries, when we know not whether he himself would have made it a rule even for the morrow.
>
> . . . If, then, it be in truth desirable that foundations should exist, which we think it clear from the foregoing and many other considerations, it would seem to follow, as a natural consequence, that the appropriation made by the founder should not be set aside, save in so far as paramount reasons of utility require; that his design should be no further departed from than he himself would probably have approved, if he had lived to the present time, and participated to a reasonable degree in its best ideas. If foundations deserve to be encouraged, it is desirable to reward the liberality of the founder by allowing to works of usefulness (though not a perpetuity) as prolonged a duration and distinguishable existence as circumstances will admit.[7]

Even though Mill was not prepared to allow England to validate donor wishes in perpetuity, he was clearly not fully comfortable with state modification of donors' specifications:

> And all that the higher principle requires is, that a term, not too distant, should be fixed . . . at the expiration of which their appropriation should come under the control of the State, to be modified, or entirely changed, at its discretion; provided that the new purpose to which they may be diverted shall be of a permanent character, to remove the temptation of laying hands on such funds for current expenses in times of financial difficulty. . . . In such case, until the expiration of the term during which testamentary directions in general may be allowed to be valid, the intention of the testator should be respected so far as it is not mischievous; the departure from it being limited to the choice of an unobjectionable mode of doing to the persons, or the sort of persons, whom he intended to benefit; as, for instance, by appropriating to a school for children what was destined for alms. The State is not entitled to consider, so long as the fixed term is unexpired, what mode of employing the money would be most useful, or whether it is more wanted for other purposes. No doubt this would often be the case; but the money was not given to the State, nor for general uses. Nothing ought to be regarded as a warrant for setting the donor's dispositions prematurely aside, but that to permit their execution would be a clear and positive public mischief. . . .
>
> What tempts people to see with complacency a testator's dispositions invalidated, is the case of what are called eccentric wills—bequests determined by motives, and destined for purposes, with which they do not sympathize. . . . But does not this genuine intolerance of the majority respecting other people's disposal of their property after death, show how great is the necessity for protection to the rights of those who do not make resemblance to the majority their rule of life? A case of bequest which has been much noticed in the newspapers . . . strikingly exemplifies this need. A person left a sum of money by will to found a hospital for the treatment of the diseases of the lower animals, particularly birds and quadrupeds. He made the mistake of appointing as trustee for the purposes of the endowment, the University of London—a body constituted for special objects, and which could not with propriety undertake a duty so remote from the ends of its appointment. But can it be pretended that an hospital such as was designed by the testator, would not be a highly useful

institution? Even if no regard were due to the animals themselves, is not the mere value of many of them to man, and the light which a better study of their physiology and pathology cannot fail to throw on the laws of animal life and the diseases of the human species, sufficient to make an institution for that study not merely useful, but important? When one thinks of this, and then considers that no such institution has ever been established in Europe; that a person willing to employ part of his *super-fluities* [emphasis mine] in that way, is not born once in several centuries; and that, now when one has been found, the use he makes of what is lawfully his own is a subject of contemptuous jeering, and an example held up to show the absurdities of testators, and the folly of endowments; can one desire a more conclusive evidence of what would happen if donations for public purposes were only valid when the purposes are consonant to the opinion of the majority? . . .

Because an endowment is a public nuisance when there is nobody to prevent its funds from being jobbed away for the gain of irresponsible administrators; because it may become worse than useless if irrevocably tied up to a destination fixed by somebody who died five hundred years [ago]; we ought not on that account to forget that endowments protected against malversation, and secured to their original purpose for no more than two or three generations, would be a precious safeguard for uncustomary modes of thought and practice, against the repression, sometimes amounting to suppression, to which they are now exposed as society in other respects grows more civilized. The fifty or hundred years of inviolability which I claim for them, would often suffice, if the opinion or practice is good, to change it from an uncustomary to a customary one, leaving the endowment fairly disposable for another use. Even when the idea embodied in the endowment is not an improvement, those who think it so are entitled to the opportunity of bringing it to a practical test.[8]

While foundations as we have come to know them today were not prevalent or even much in existence when Mill wrote, everything he says about endowments' value to society, to the virtue of philanthropic wealth in the service of facilitating change in public attitudes and governments' behavior, applies just as strongly to today's foundations and philanthropically minded individuals. Moreover, as we shall see, some of what John Stuart Mill pointed out as criticisms of perpetual endowments is plainly evident in today's ideological attacks on the roles of foundations and individual philanthropists in American society.

When I read Carnegie's *The Gospel of Wealth* and note his injunction to his fellow wealthy individuals to give away their "surplus wealth" during their lifetimes, I hear echoes of Mill's "superfluities" as quoted above, written 20 years earlier. When Carnegie writes that his overall purpose in devoting his wealth to benefit society is to foster many greater opportunities for community across class divisions that have been created by capitalism, I hear Mill's voice arguing against state prevention of private initiatives to improve the administration of such public services as education and social service.

Clearly Carnegie stood on the shoulders of John Stuart Mill. It is not likely that they met, however, since Carnegie made his first business trip to London in 1870, when he was 30; at that time Mill was 63 years old and at the peak of his fame, having just finished serving as a Liberal Party member of Parliament from City and Westminster, in which role he had been the first member in that governing body's history to call for women to be given the right to vote. Because Mill died three years later, which was well before Carnegie had become celebrated among London's "important people," a personal relationship is highly unlikely. However, because Mill's ideas on philanthropy, especially his 1869 essay on endowments, were likely the subject of conversation among those Londoners of sufficient wealth to be interested in philanthropy—and with whom Carnegie did interact during the following two decades before he published "Wealth"—it is not farfetched to conjecture that those ideas would have found their way to Carnegie. So I urge the reader to keep Mill in mind as you consider what Carnegie himself wrote and did.

IT STARTED WITH ANDREW CARNEGIE . . .

The man who dies thus rich dies disgraced.
—**Andrew Carnegie, 1889**[9]

Why are so many of the important practices in American philanthropy attributable to Andrew Carnegie? The first person who credited Carnegie with establishing the model of American giving was a famous contemporary of his—John D. Rockefeller Sr. In 1896, on the opening of the Carnegie Library in Pittsburgh, the oilman wrote a letter to steelman Carnegie that included the following sentence: "I would that more men of wealth were doing as you are doing with your money; but, be assured, your example will bear fruits, and the time will come when men of wealth will be willing to use it for the good of others."[10] On another occasion, Rockefeller allegedly wrote Carnegie, acknowledging "Everything I know about philanthropy I learned from you!"[11]

A quick scan of *The Gospel of Wealth* suggests countless examples of post-1990 nonprofit and philanthropic phenomena that are closely related to Carnegie's philanthropic practices and preferences. Think "social entrepreneurship," for example, which Carnegie personified with his frequent leadership of the institutions that he founded or supported. Think "venture philanthropy," which is what Carnegie did in establishing and initially funding what is now TIAA-CREF, one of the largest pension funds in America. Think of Carnegie's insistence on serious research in the style of Grogan's work at The Boston Foundation prior to funding, which moved him to commission Abraham Flexner's study of American medical education. That exercise involved Flexner's interviewing of virtually every faculty member in every American medical school and producing a set of findings and recommendations that literally transformed medical education from science-absent to science-based in one generation. Think of today's widespread use of the challenge (or matching-required) grant across America's civic sector and many foundations. It really is no exaggeration to attribute to Carnegie so many of the practices that dominate America's nonprofit and philanthropic life to this day.

Andrew Carnegie's essay on "Wealth"[12] embodied the first American philanthropic giant's attempt to articulate the detailed plan he had developed and applied to his own giving. As he wrote in that essay, he did so not only in the interests of transparency and self-justification but also and explicitly because he hoped to persuade other wealthy individuals to adopt his rationale for giving.

The most important point that Carnegie wished to drive home was that every wealthy individual should give away his assets during his lifetime. He reasoned that a wealthy person facing death has only three choices: to give his money to his children (if he has any), bequeath it to others (individuals or institutions) at his death, or give it away during his lifetime. He dismissed the first option by declaring that giving it all to his children would ruin them forever and asserted that the second option risked the possibility, indeed the likelihood, that after his death the recipients would not use his wealth as effectively as he himself would have done. That left only option 3, which he strongly preferred, primarily because he believed that the successful creator of wealth is best positioned to bring to bear on the wise administration of his wealth the self-same talents and skills he had used in creating it. Note that rarely in his writings is there an emphasis on the concern that dominates the thinking of some of today's would-be spenders-down, who feel driven to dispose of their philanthropic wealth before they die: that their fortunes will inevitably be wasted or frittered away if deposited in perpetual foundations. Carnegie did take note of the possibility that the donor's intentions might be thwarted, however, when he wrote the following: "The cases are not few in which the real object sought by the testator is not attained, nor are they few in which his real wishes are thwarted. In many cases the bequests are so used as to become only monuments to his folly."[13] But that observation does not appear to have been Carnegie's dominant concern. It was certainly not strong enough to deter him from leaving a sizable proportion of his wealth to a perpetual foundation, to the successor trustees of which he gave almost unlimited discretion. Carnegie's insistence on "Giving While Living," therefore, is almost wholly positive and not dominantly based on any fear about the likely future misuse of his philanthropic dollars.

Carnegie worked hard to identify the individuals who seemed most worthy of support, according to his values and philanthropic objectives, as spelled out in *The Gospel of Wealth*. His philanthropy is well known for his earliest and longest-lived "Carnegie Libraries," which he catalyzed by challenge grants scattered in cities and towns all over the United States and in parts of his native Scotland and late-adopted England. They were motivated by his reputed injunction, "You cannot push anyone up the ladder unless he is willing to climb himself."[14] Or in Carnegie's terms, "Rather than give a man a job, teach him how to read."[15] Hence the libraries, the first of which he authorized in 1880 in Dunfermline, Scotland, his birthplace, and was dedicated in 1883. The second Carnegie library, commissioned in 1886, was to be in Allegheny, Pennsylvania, where he grew up, but it was not dedicated until 1890, one year after the library he commissioned opened in Braddock, Pennsylvania, the site of one of the Carnegie Steel Corporation plants. Over the next 20 years, the number of Carnegie libraries swelled to 1,679 in the United States, with a total worldwide number of 2,509.[16]

Between the time that Carnegie began to crystallize his intention to sell Carnegie Steel Corporation—which was ultimately sold in 1901 to J. P. Morgan and became the US Steel Corporation—and 1919, when he died, Carnegie devoted most of his energies to his philanthropic giving, especially the founding and guiding of major institutions that continue to bear his name. It is worth noting the enormous scope and ambition of his grantmaking—not only because it is so impressive but because, as we shall see, it still wasn't enough to reach his goal of putting all his charitable wealth to use during his lifetime. The following are just some of his more significant contributions.

Perhaps most famous of all is Carnegie Hall in New York City, established with a gift in 1889 of $2 million. What is relevant to this book's primary focus and notable indeed is the extent to which Carnegie endowed *for perpetuity* so many of the institutions that he founded or supported. In 1893, with an initial gift of $1.12 million, Carnegie founded The Carnegie Institute in Pittsburgh, which later, with additional gifts from Carnegie, added the Carnegie Library of Pittsburgh, the Carnegie Museums of Pittsburgh, and the Carnegie Music Hall. A $2 million gift in 1900 was used to establish Carnegie Technical Schools, which was reorganized in 1912 into the Carnegie Institute of Technology and in 1967 became Carnegie-Mellon University. In 1901, Carnegie gave $10 million to establish The Carnegie Trust for the Universities of Scotland, also based in Dunfermline. That same year he established The Carnegie Institution of Washington, now known as The Carnegie Institution for Science, with an initial endowment of $10 million, followed by a total of another $12 million in subsequent gifts in 1907 and 1911. In 1903, Carnegie endowed the Carnegie Dunfermline Trust to benefit his hometown; in 1904, with an initial gift of $5 million, he established the Carnegie Hero Fund Commission to celebrate and publicize acts of lifesaving heroism by individuals in the United States and Canada, followed in subsequent years by creating funds with an identical mission in Scotland, Ireland, Northern Ireland, England, and all parts of what is now known as the United Kingdom, and thereafter additional Carnegie Hero Funds in France, the Netherlands, Germany, Norway, Sweden, Switzerland, Denmark, Belgium, and Italy. In 1905, Carnegie established the Carnegie Foundation for the Advancement of Teaching and endowed it with $10 million. That foundation originally provided pensions for retired professors, but today it seeks to improve teaching in colleges as well as in graduate and professional schools. From that original mission of supporting professors' retirements grew one of Carnegie's most notable achievements: the founding and initial funding of Teachers Insurance and Annuity Association, which has evolved into TIAA-CREF, today's retirement income provider for most university and college faculty and staff, as well as for the staff of nonprofits and foundations.

In 1910, on the occasion of Carnegie's 75th birthday, he founded the Carnegie Endowment for International Peace, first in New York but soon thereafter moved to Washington, with an initial endowment of $10 million. In 1911, he established the Carnegie Corporation of New York, initially endowing it with $25 million, to which in the following year he added another $75 million in endowment and which received still another $35 million on his death in 1919. In 1913, he established the Carnegie United Kingdom Trust, located in Dunfermline, for the benefit of the people in Great Britain and Ireland; and, finally, in 1914, he founded the Church Peace Union with a $2 million endowment given by the Carnegie Corporation of New York, which has had several different names over the years and is now known as the Carnegie Council on Ethics and International Affairs.[17]

The creation of the Carnegie Corporation of New York, which is the only general-purpose foundation among his many gifts, comes very near the end of his benefactions in their chronological order. It has often been observed that the reason for that sequence is that, although Carnegie was determined to give away all of his wealth to specific recipients during his lifetime, by the beginning of his last decade he had run out of opportunities that appealed to him as worthy of supporting. This is striking and indeed worth keeping in mind as you read this book: not only did he bestow permanent endowments on many of the institutions he created—thus extending the reach of his philanthropy many generations beyond his lifetime—but he concluded his philanthropic career by establishing a *perpetual* institution. When he could no longer meet the high standards he had set for his giving, despite a breathtaking list of achievements that were wide ranging not only in their geographic locations but also in their substantive purposes, he relented and chose as his default course of action the creation of a perpetual general-purpose foundation. That choice is virtually equivalent to the option of giving by bequest at the point of death that he rejected in *Wealth*. In a very real sense, there were no more specific purposes or institutions that commanded his interest, so he put the remainder of his assets in a perpetual foundation to be distributed by his carefully chosen associates serving as trustees of the Carnegie Corporation of New York.

Therein lies a very important precedent for those wealthy individuals who are tempted to deploy all of their philanthropic assets to purposes that are dear to them during their lifetimes. If Andrew Carnegie, among the most visionary and resourceful philanthropists in history, could not identify in his lifetime worthy recipients of all his wealth who were doing or wishing to do things that Carnegie cared about passionately, perhaps his example will be a cautionary word to those who are sure that they can achieve all the charitable impact they desire while they are alive.

To be sure, all of the recipient organizations of Carnegie's beneficence were different in kind from the intended recipients of many of today's wealthy, who often talk in terms not of creating ongoing institutions, such as Carnegie founded, but rather of solving specific, grievous global problems. Obviously, Carnegie had the humility to recognize that there were significant limits to what he could achieve in his lifetime, even with his vast wealth. He often wrote and spoke about the need for mechanisms to bring peace to Europe, calling for the creation of a "League of Peace," and later a "League of Nations." In 1903, he financed the Peace Palace in The Hague. He spent enormous amounts of time and energy in trying to persuade Theodore Roosevelt, both during and after his presidency, to bring Kaiser Wilhelm II of Germany together with Britain's King Edward VII for talks intended to prevent war. When all of his exertions failed and war broke out, Carnegie was cast into a deep depression, the worst of his life, and many speculate that it was his heartbreak over the occurrence of World War I that hastened his death one year after it ended.

So, while Carnegie cared passionately about the need for peace among nations and spent his final years trying to make it happen, he recognized that it would require many years and the continuing efforts of countless others and of resilient institutions bolstered by perpetual endowments to accomplish that elusive goal. One might well call what he did a strategy of "hedging his bets." He gave his all during his lifetime, throwing his energy and financial resources into the causes about which he cared passionately, but he was wise enough to recognize that their magnitude and complexity were beyond his powers of direct action during his lifetime. Therefore, he created and endowed institutions that would be around to enlighten and empower the leaders of subsequent generations so they could devote themselves to lasting solutions to the problems to which he devoted his life.[18]

For all his multiple successes, both in business and philanthropy, Carnegie's hope of disposing of his philanthropic wealth during his lifetime fell short—though it was a "failure" that has since bestowed a century of benefits and continues to bear philanthropic fruit. However, for one of Carnegie's successors among the great philanthropists of the early 20th century, the prospect of completing one's giving before death was not merely a hope but a cause—one that would define his life as a donor and would grow, a century later, into something of a *cause célèbre*.

JULIUS ROSENWALD PICKS UP THE "GIVING WHILE LIVING" MANTLE

The horrors that are due to race prejudice come home to the Jew more forcefully than to others of the white race, on account of the centuries of persecution which they have suffered and still suffer.
    —Julius Rosenwald, 1911[19]

Julius Rosenwald became a partner of Sears, Roebuck and Company in 1895 and was promoted to vice president the following year. SearsArchives. com gives a barebones summary of his leadership of the company:

From the moment he joined Sears, Roebuck and Co., Rosenwald's abilities meshed amazingly well with those of Richard Sears. He brought a rational management philosophy to Richard Sears' well-tuned sales instincts. From 1895 to 1907, annual sales skyrocketed from $750,000 to $50 million. In 1908, Rosenwald was named president when Richard Sears resigned. After World War I, Sears was in dire financial shape and Rosenwald brought Sears back from the brink of bankruptcy by pledging some $21 million of his personal fortune, in cash, stock and other assets to rescue the company. By 1922, Sears had regained financial stability. Rosenwald continued to serve as president until 1924, when he became chairman of the board, a position he held until his death in 1932.[20]

That summary helps to explain why Rosenwald is almost always referred to as "The Man Who Built Sears, Roebuck," which is the first half of the subtitle of his biography, written by his grandson Peter M. Ascoli.[21] While it was Rosenwald's years of running Sears, Roebuck that created his wealth, what earned him fame was his decision to devote most of his fortune to improving educational opportunities for African American children by building schoolhouses, as spelled out in the second half of the subtitle: "and Advanced the

Cause of Black Education in the American South." His gifts were structured as challenge/matching grants, in emulation of the model Andrew Carnegie employed in building his many public libraries.[22]

Initially, Rosenwald began building schools at the suggestion of Booker T. Washington. From 1912 (seven years before Andrew Carnegie died) until 1937, when the last Rosenwald school was opened in Warm Springs, Georgia, at President Franklin D. Roosevelt's personal request, close to 5,000 Rosenwald schools had been erected. The impact of those schools is clear from this brief statistic: "In 1928, Rosenwald schools accounted for one out of every five African American schools in the South, and these schools enrolled one of every three Southern African American pupils."[23] In 1915, Aviva Kempner produced a widely reviewed and admired documentary film on Rosenwald's achievements, *Rosenwald: The Remarkable Story of a Jewish Partnership with African American Communities.*[24]

Five years after starting the first school, he founded and gave $25 million to the Julius Rosenwald Fund. In 1928, four years before his death, Rosenwald contributed about 20,000 shares of Sears, Roebuck stock to the Fund and instructed his trustees as follows: "I have stipulated, therefore, that not only the income but also all of the principal of this fund *must* [emphasis Rosenwald] be expended within 25 years of my death."[25] That injunction made the Rosenwald Fund the earliest (and for decades afterward the best-known) spend-down foundation.

The limited-life model Rosenwald imposed on his own foundation became the focus of his speeches and writings aimed at persuading other wealthy individuals to follow his example. Opposition to perpetual foundations became the signature theme of Rosenwald's public pronouncements about philanthropy. He quickly became well known for the first of two articles he published in 1929, "The Burden of Wealth."[26] A second article, in the May 1929 issue of *Atlantic Monthly*, elaborated on the same points but was "far more scholarly"[27] and not as widely circulated.

Frequently, Julius Rosenwald is lumped together with the much wealthier and more prominent Andrew Carnegie, whom he did not personally know but with whom he occasionally corresponded. Rosenwald clearly revered Carnegie. The primary reason for that admiration, I think, is that he felt a kinship with most of the message that Carnegie delivered to the public in *The Gospel of Wealth*—essentially, the latter's pioneering role in advocating "giving while living." Rosenwald's overall interpretation of Carnegie's writing and speeches suggested that he and Carnegie were indeed on the same page in their views and actions regarding perpetuity in philanthropy, but clearly they were not. While there are many statements in Carnegie's *The Gospel of Wealth* with which Rosenwald undoubtedly agreed enthusiastically, none of them jibes easily with Rosenwald's determined, even relentless, opposition to perpetual foundations. Here are Rosenwald's words in *The Saturday Evening Post* article that made him famous:

> My differences are not with philanthropy, but with certain of its methods or tenets. In fact, my chief quarrel is with only one of these tenets: the principle of perpetuity endowment. I am emphatically opposed to never-ending endowments. . . . I unqualifiedly disapprove of the efforts made by certain benevolent trusts and foundations to perpetuate themselves by restricting their enterprises and expenditures to the interest on invested capital, and not only leaving the principal untouched but even adding from time to time to it from unused income.[28]

Both Carnegie and Rosenwald preached that wealthy individuals should give away all of their surplus wealth during their lifetimes and not wait until they are at death's door to dispose of it. Carnegie, however, did not oppose perpetual foundations. In fact, he established *two* of them. As we have also seen, he founded and endowed many other perpetual institutions and created perpetual endowments in many other institutions that he supported. Moreover, Carnegie was willing to allow the Tuskegee Institute, to which the Carnegie Corporation had made a gift of endowment, to modify the use that had been originally specified for it when the gift was made. Furthermore, there is good evidence that Carnegie was comfortable in allowing donors to permit the recipient institutions to spend endowment capital, as opposed to interest on capital, if they wished to do so.

Rosenwald's article in *Atlantic Monthly*, although much shorter than Carnegie's *The Gospel of Wealth*, articulated much of what Carnegie preached but, as we have noted above, was not what Carnegie actually practiced. In comparing the stances of the two men, Rosenwald's biographer acknowledges as much:

> But Carnegie did not carry his ideas far enough, for he did not, in fact, give the bulk of his fortune away in one generation. . . . By making his foundation self-liquidating, Julius Rosenwald's inspiration for the duration of his foundation came from a philosophical view that was already

rapidly diminishing in its force even in England as well as in the United States, but which led him nonetheless to try to breathe new life and blaze a new trail that significantly departed from the example set by Andrew Carnegie and John D. Rockefeller, Sr.

That new trail gained very little traction in Rosenwald's lifetime, as all but a handful of the foundations that were being born in the next half-century were created with no limit to their lives.[29]

As we shall see, however, the movement toward limiting the lives of foundations acquired new momentum from highly publicized incidents in the philanthropic world, beginning with Henry Ford II's resignation from the Board of Trustees of the Ford Foundation. Like dominoes falling, this strategy of limited spending horizon began to enjoy resurgence among the newly wealthy technology and financial industry billionaires starting in the last decade of the 20th century.

chapter five

The Dominoes Fall

Henry Ford II resigned as a trustee of the Ford Foundation in 1976, 40 years after he assumed his first role at that foundation. His decision to leave, and the way it was interpreted by the press and then popularized by ideological groups with an axe to grind, created a myth about wayward foundations and frustrated founders that continues to reverberate to this day. In a chain of events that has grown into a movement toward time-limited foundations, Ford's departure from his namesake foundation powerfully tipped over the first domino and set the others cascading into what now seems like free fall.

Edsel Ford, son of the first Henry Ford, established the Ford Foundation in 1936 with a gift of $25,000 and became the foundation's first president. Because Edsel was then also the president of the Ford Motor Company and deeply involved in running it, he brought his son Henry Ford II onto the foundation board as one of the founding trustees and left to him the many responsibilities for attending to the establishment of the institution and its grantmaking. All the evidence is that Henry II viewed his obligation as being to "advance his personal agenda, drawn from the philanthropic interests of Edsel Ford, to be identified with the resolution of the important issues of his time."[1] In 1943, Edsel died unexpectedly of cancer, and Henry II was named the second president of the foundation, as well as chairman of its board of trustees. Two years after that, in 1945, Henry II became president of the auto company as well.

In his dual roles as both foundation president and board chairman, Henry II led the planning of everything about the Ford Foundation, including conceiving in 1948 the idea of establishing "The Study Committee," which he charged with defining the mission of the foundation, and the recruitment of H. Rowan Gaither as the committee's chair. In November 1948, he wrote Mr. Gaither and the seven other "Study Committee" members as follows:

> The Foundation was established for the general purpose of advancing human welfare, but the manner of realizing this objective was left to the

Trustees. Now that the time is near when the Foundation can initiate an active program, I think that its aims should be more specifically defined.

The people of this country and mankind in general are confronted with problems which are vast in number and exceedingly disturbing in significance. While important efforts to solve these problems are being made by government, industry, foundations and other institutions, it is evident that new resources, such as those of this Foundation, if properly employed, can result in significant contributions.

We want to take stock of our existing knowledge, institutions, and techniques in order to locate the areas where the problems are most important and where additional efforts towards their solution are most needed.

You are to have complete authority and responsibility in this undertaking, and you are to have a high degree of discretion, subject, of course, to the general policy approval of the Trustees, in the means you employ and the choice of consultants and other personnel . . . We want the best thought available in the United States as to how this Foundation can most effectively and intelligently put its resources to work for human welfare.[2]

"The Report of the Study" goes on to describe the Ford Foundation trustees' reception of the Study Committee's recommendations as follows:

In the opinion of the Trustees, the conclusions and recommendations of the Committee were influenced by and responsive to the best American judgment of our times. . . . The findings of the Study Committee are, in the opinion of the Trustees, of sufficient general interest and importance to warrant the publication of the General Report in its entirety. Publication of the Report was therefore authorized by special action of the Trustees on September 6, 1950. The opinions expressed in the Report are, of course, those of the members of the Study Committee and not necessarily those of the Trustees. Action taken by the Trustees on the Report, as well as a summary of the considerations underlying that action, has already been published in the Report of September 27, 1950, by the Trustees of The Ford Foundation.

Henry Ford II
Chairman, Board of Trustees
October, 1950[3]

After the trustees' approval of the Study Committee's Report, Henry Ford II immediately set about recruiting someone to succeed him as president of the foundation and chose Paul G. Hoffman, head of the Marshall Plan in Europe, for that role. Along with many of the foundation's trustees, Ford grew steadily unhappier with Hoffman's leadership and, two years after hiring him, removed him from that role. Then, not surprisingly, he persuaded H. Rowan Gaither to become the foundation's fourth president, a position Gaither held until resigning in 1956. The board chair at that point was the distinguished lawyer, banker, and federal government official John J. McCloy, who was soon to be succeeded in that role by Julius A. Stratton, then president of the Massachusetts Institute of Technology. Together, Gaither and McCloy, in consultation with Henry Ford II, selected Henry T. Heald, then president of New York University, to become Gaither's successor as Ford's president. Heald held that office until 1965, after which he was succeeded by McGeorge Bundy, former national security adviser to Presidents Kennedy and Johnson, who served as foundation president until 1979.

In 1955, as a foundation trustee, Henry Ford II, together with his friend and fellow trustee Donald K. David, vice chairman of the Ford Trustees and of the Trustees Executive Committee, played a leading role in the first major grant program implemented by the Ford Foundation—a $500 million endeavor called "The University and College Faculty Salaries and Hospital Grants Program"—that involved making grants "to every accredited college in the United States in support of faculty salaries."[4] That grant program was made necessary by the significant increase in the value of Ford Motor Company stock and the consequent public pressure on the foundation to show evidence of benefits flowing to the public in proportion to the growing endowment. Warren Weaver, a much-admired vice president of The Rockefeller Foundation, described the allocation of those grants:

> The manner of distribution was surprisingly, and to many disappointingly, mechanical. Each of the country's 630 privately-supported liberal arts colleges received a sum equal to their 1954–1955 faculty payroll. Each of 3,400 nonprofit hospitals received a sum determined by the number of births and patient days on an average annual basis.[5]

While it was—and still is—exceedingly unusual for a professionally staffed foundation to distribute grant funds in such a "cookie cutter" fashion, and while Ford was criticized in many foundation quarters for doing so, it goes without saying that others were overjoyed:

> The program was received with great enthusiasm by the public and by the academic community but was significantly less popular within the Foundation. The program did not originate with the staff. It was instigated by the board with the endorsement of Henry Ford II and Donald K. David. . . . The staff clearly did not like the idea of trustee-directed programs that did not go through established procedures for review and evaluation.[6]

Note that the program was announced in a press release by Henry Ford II, who was then without any formal official foundation position other than that of trustee.[7]

Later on, in 1968, during the presidency of McGeorge Bundy, the foundation staff proposed investing a modest portion of the foundation's assets to help establish in a district adjacent to the foundation a "United Nations Development Corporation, to provide office space, hotel space, and other facilities . . . [to] members of the international community."[8] This was the first time the foundation had ever done anything like that, but "Henry Ford II accepted the . . . plans for the U.N. development project without a single objection or question."[9]

Henry Ford II remained on the board of trustees for 40 years. Despite relinquishing the chairmanship of the trustees in 1951, he continued to be the dominant trustee influence on the foundation's major decision-making for another 25 years. Verne S. Atwater and Evelyn C. Walsh, authors of *The Ford Foundation,* describe Henry Ford II as "the key factor that enabled the foundation to function independently of the control or direct influence of the Ford Motor Company."[10] They go on to write the following:

> Henry Ford II . . . played a critical role in organizing and selecting the leadership of the Foundation. He was also the determining factor in assuring the independence of the Foundation's Board and staff from the inevitable public disputes caused by Foundation decisions in sensitive cultural and political issues that conflicted with the interests of the family, the Ford Motor Company and its dealers.[11]

Moreover, again according to Atwater and Walsh:

The disengagement of Henry Ford II from representing the interests of the Ford family and the Motor Company, after stepping down as chairman of the Foundation, was never quite complete. He continued to play a quiet, but influential role in the management of the Foundation and in the selection and the firing of presidents. He seldom spoke in the board meetings, but, when he did, it was apparent that everyone listened. . . . Ford's influence as a board member continued in the new McGeorge Bundy administration, although on a declining basis.[12]

Nonetheless, in 1976 Ford decided that the time had come for him to resign from the foundation board. In his resignation letter written to Board Chairman Alexander Heard, he puts his reasons as follows:

I have served as a Trustee since 1943, which means that I have been involved, one way or another, in virtually every step of development from its rather informal beginnings to its present highly-structured state.

. . . As the son and grandson of the two founders, I have a uniquely special reason to want the Foundation to be an effective institution. . . . All in all, I have strongly positive feelings about my own and the family's long-standing relationship with the Foundation.

In reflecting on my recent participation as a Trustee, however, I realize that I have not been approaching the task with quite the same enthusiasm as I once did. My interest in many of the things the Foundation is doing has waned considerably. I find it increasingly difficult to make a substantive contribution either to the policy-setting process or to the deliberations that result in giving directional thrust to the organization.

I don't ascribe this sense of disengagement to any temporary set of conditions, either on my part or on the part of the Foundation. After 33 years I have come to the point where I have pretty much done all there is to do as a Trustee and have said all that there is to say. I think it is time for me to step aside and, accordingly, I wish to resign from the Board effective immediately.[13]

Ford then includes several paragraphs in his letter devoted to constructive suggestions about ways of strengthening the foundation, from "[scaling] down its activities to reflect its diminished resources"[14] and resisting its practice of long-term repetitive support to some grantees, to devoting some of its grantmaking to the recognition of the importance and strengthening of America's capitalist system and resisting the natural tendency of "large institutions" to become insular and afflicted by the "not invented here" syndrome.

Ford's primary disappointment is clearly with what he regarded as the foundation's unwillingness to deal adequately, presumably supportively, with America's capitalist system. In *A Time for Truth*, William E. Simon, former secretary of the Treasury and later president of the John M. Olin Foundation, writes:

> Those capitalists who, in the interests of "fairness," have financed the intellectual opposition have seen their foundations literally taken over. The textbook case of such infiltration was dramatized recently when Henry Ford III [*sic*] resigned from the Ford Foundation. I called Mr. Ford on reading of this in the newspapers and asked him to explain how this had happened. He answered: "I tried for 30 years to change it from within but couldn't." Of course he couldn't, not after he had allowed the Ford Foundation to become a veritable fortress of the philosophical opposition. One does not work from "within" the egalitarian world to change it; one can only work from without—and this absurd financing of one's philosophical enemies must not be tolerated in the new foundations.[15]

Ford closes his letter with the following paragraphs, which hardly seem like the words of someone vexed by his failure to change a disappointing and intransigent institution:

> The 33 years of my association with the Foundation have given me a great respect for the organization's potential for good. The Foundation already has a magnificent record of achievement. I am confident that it is capable of still more significant contributions to the world in the years ahead.
>
> My greatest satisfaction in all the years of my connection with the Foundation has been my association with the Trustees. The strength of the Institution is a true reflection of the caliber of those who have served on this Board. I have great admiration and a sense of deep appreciation for the members who gave of themselves so generously in the past, as well as those who are now serving. The future of the Foundation is in capable hands.

Although my formal role with the Foundation now comes to an end, my interest in its progress will continue for a long time to come. If I can ever at any time be of any help, I am at the service of the Trustees.

Best Regards,
Henry Ford II[16]

It is not hard to understand Ford's decision to resign from the board. Thirty-three years of building the Ford Foundation from scratch while at the same time running the Ford Motor Company and being one of America's leading businessmen are bound to have taken their toll. Less than three years after leaving the Ford trustees, Henry Ford II resigned from his post as CEO of the Ford Motor Company on October 1, 1979, and, eight years later, on September 29, 1987, he died. It is a source of wonder to me that he remained a Ford trustee for as long as he did, all the more so if he really had significant differences with the way the foundation was being run.

THE MYTH

I thought the [Gaither] Report was good then. I still think the Report was good. . . . [M]y criticism is of myself for being so stupid as a young kid, not being . . . sensible enough to realize, if you let this thing go you're going to lose control. . . . We lost control the minute we started to enlarge the Board after the Gaither Report came out.
—Henry Ford II, in an oral history interview, 1973[17]

Henry Ford II expressed the above sentiments 37 years after his father appointed him to the Ford Foundation Board of Trustees, 30 years after he assumed its presidency upon his father's death, and 3 years before he resigned from that board. They are a classic example of what many call "donor remorse." Such sentiments are often expressed by a donor when realizing that he or she made a serious error of judgment about a prior philanthropic gift—in this case, governance of an entire foundation—when little, if anything, can be done to rectify it. Ford clearly wished he had retained control of the foundation, whatever he meant by those words; even while recognizing that he had given up control, he nonetheless praised the major achievements of the foundation over the decades of his involvement, including the drafting by Gaither of what was intended to be, and actually became, the authoritative statement of the foundation's mission.

But what did "losing control" mean to Ford? Did it mean the capacity to control single-handedly everything that the foundation did or did not do? Did he regret not having a board that would say "yes" to his every whim? Did he wonder what kind of foundation the Ford Foundation could have become had he exercised that kind of control? Did he examine his feelings about what he was prevented from achieving by not "having control"? Clearly he felt frustrated to some considerable degree, but one wonders what exactly was bugging him in 1973 when he gave vent to these feelings. Did he weigh the value of whatever he felt that he had lost against the benefits gained for society and the reputation of his family? Could what he felt be accurately described as some reflection on his inability to shape the Ford Foundation even more than he did—probably with respect to a small number of actions or inactions about which he, his friends, and associates felt strongly—in other words, more precisely in his own image?

If the Ford Foundation had indeed had a board of trustees entirely in Henry Ford II's image, could it possibly have achieved anything like what his father hoped when he decided to establish the foundation? Would it have been anything like what Henry Ford II himself actually created by his active participation in shaping the foundation's accomplishments—results that he later praised as socially valuable? That is extremely unlikely. Moreover, assuming Henry Ford II was not lying when he stated his approval of most of what the Ford Foundation did during his tenure, on what grounds can anyone reasonably describe his resignation from the board as a protest against what the foundation was doing or not doing?

The wisest and most effective foundation boards have been those that combine smart, disinterested, and thoughtful individuals from varying backgrounds, each of whom has the abilities necessary to inform the others' decisions about the best courses of action for the foundation as a whole to pursue, and all of whom are willing to speak their minds in a respectful way. Such boards include a combination of nonfamily, publicly known, and admired individuals along with other members, usually scions of the founding family or close professional associates of the founding donor. The latter can serve as counterbalancers—the "sober second-thought" possessors who embody the values of the founding donor, who therefore have moral authority as representatives of donor intent by descent, and who are broadly recognized as such by the board as a whole. Such individuals can play a determinative role in decisions that effectively enable them to guide the proceedings toward better outcomes than are likely to be achieved in their absence.

If such figures are not present, some self-perpetuating foundation boards are apt to develop a lack of cohesion that causes the group to remain a collection of individuals who compete rather than cooperate with one another and who fail to serve as the institution's memory of what the donor intended. Such foundation boards tend not to focus on carefully deliberated, strategically oriented, cumulative actions that help fulfill the foundation's mission. When such moral authority–wielding individuals are members, however, they can and often do serve as unifying figures who help preserve the foundation's identity and purposefulness.

Such vehicles of moral authority don't regard themselves as "dictators." If they try to impose their will on their fellow trustees, they cannot embody moral authority effectively, because they cannot earn the required respect and inclination to deference. To the contrary, those who try to monopolize the board's authority are more likely to catalyze divisiveness in the board rather than cohesion around the foundation's mission. If they are members of the founding donor's family, their moral authority originates in the fact of their descent from the founder and, if they wield their influence in a nonpolarizing way, they can easily become the guiding influencers of the board as a whole.

Henry Ford II seems to me to have been such a figure in the first 30 years of the Ford Foundation. Despite the enlargement of the board, his views and voice dominated in the selection of the foundation's presidents and other senior officers. His assessment of prospective fellow trustees was influential if not determinative in their election. His presence on the board ensured that the Ford Foundation would persist in a state of organizational purposefulness and balance, which is a feat that some other perpetual foundation boards have too often failed to attain and preserve.

As I read the complete text of his interview for the oral history, from which a few phrases were quoted earlier, I was struck by the many more instances of endorsement of the foundation's actions than by the several negative examples cited. It's hard not to wonder exactly how the Ford Foundation's record of grantmaking might have differed had he actually retained "control" as he imagined it. In comparing what Ford said in his exit letter to Alexander Heard with his interview, I think it reasonable to conclude that the actual track record would not have been much different from what it was. If that is correct—recall that Henry Ford II was repeatedly described as *the* most influential member of the board of trustees—he could be accurately described as having had a decisive role in shaping the content of Ford's actions despite, as he put it, not having "real" control.

From his reference to the "enlargement of the Board" as the cause of his having lost control, it is reasonable to wonder whether the substantive record of the foundation's achievements, which Henry Ford II endorsed as it was evolving and praised after the fact, could have been achieved without the wisdom and governance participation brought to the board by the distinguished trustees he helped recruit but apparently later wished he had not chosen to include. Given the few disagreements he enumerates, it had to have occurred to him that the expansion of the board, while technically a loss of control to him, was a major if not *the* major contributor to the creation of the foundation record that he overwhelmingly praises. Moreover, in his oral history interview, he has words of affection and gratitude for almost all of the board members.

What then was the real cost of his loss of control? Judging from the examples he offers in his interview and his exit letter to Alexander Heard as a guide, they appear to be almost all instances of omission rather than commission. With very few exceptions, they were things he would have liked for the Ford Foundation to do but that he had not succeeded in persuading the board to undertake. One of the rare exceptions was the foundation's decision to support public interest law firms with full-time litigators who could bring suit against corporations as well as government, which apparently played a role in his calculus about whether to continue serving on the board. Of the cases in which the foundation declined to pursue something that Ford promoted, perhaps the most significant was his desire for more grantmaking in support of America's capitalist system, whatever that meant to him. Depending on the precise question, one can reasonably argue on both sides of it but, compared to the social benefit of the almost countless other foundation activities that Ford endorsed, a "support of capitalism" program would likely have been a minor addition to the foundation's large grants portfolio.

Moreover, it is not clear what "support of capitalism" can mean in the context of a foundation program. One could easily argue that efforts to rectify the failures of the capitalist market system by providing jobs, job training, educational opportunities, and affordable housing, for example, are indeed ways of supporting the continuing dominance of the capitalist system. Those and many other similar initiatives indeed were and still are the bread-and-butter of Ford Foundation programs.

It is well known that, during the Ford Foundation presidencies of Mc-George Bundy, Franklin Thomas, and Susan Berresford, Ford in fact made many grants for the purpose of correcting the negative social by-products of America's capitalist system and the shortcomings of its welfare state—and thus of strengthening and preserving both. There is Ford's major support of the founding of The Urban Institute in Washington, which is regarded by many as America's leading centrist-liberal social policy think tank. There is Ford's support in founding the Center on Budget and Policy Priorities in Washington, headed still by Robert Greenstein, a leading centrist-liberal research and advocacy organization. There is Ford's support for the founding of the Manpower Demonstration Research Corporation, which experiments with ways of making America's welfare programs more effective, and which is credited by members of Congress and most observers as having crafted and run the randomized controlled trials that generated reliable evidence of better and worse ways of moving welfare recipients to work. Those trials are now regarded as having provided the persuasive impetus to the Clinton administration's Welfare-to-Work legislation in the late 1990s as well as the establishment and growth of the Earned Income Tax Credits thereafter.

There is also Ford's leading role, especially in the Bundy years, in establishing the countrywide network of community development corporations in many major metropolitan areas as well as the Center for Community Self-Help, which obtained Ford funds to catalyze billions of dollars for minority and low-income citizens to buy homes. In addition, there is the widely celebrated recent Grand Bargain initiative by a dozen or so foundations, to which Ford gave $125 million, the largest single contribution to that effort, to help resolve Detroit's bankruptcy in 2014 (and, in the process, to rescue the Detroit Institute of Arts, to whose collection Henry's father, Edsel, had made enormous contributions that might otherwise have ended up on the auction block). At the same time, the Ford Foundation has also had other major programs and lines of grantmaking to defend civil rights, advance urban development, confront poverty, champion education, and uphold human rights. All of these major initiatives and many others are aimed precisely at helping our country perfect and, thus, defend its capitalist system. It may well have been the case that Henry Ford II was not enthusiastic about the Ford Foundation's programs aimed at correcting the socially unjust functioning of aspects of America's capitalist system, preferring instead energetic Ford Foundation efforts to defend the capitalist system against "a creeping tide of socialism." However, if correcting the socially unjust by-products of

America's capitalist system isn't what Henry Ford II had in mind, it is not at all clear from anything in the record what he *did* have in mind—and that is precisely the point. His inability or unwillingness to articulate or advocate a clear program of action may well explain why the Ford board didn't take on such initiatives and why he later expressed frustration.

Henry Ford II's resignation as a trustee of the Ford Foundation was widely reported in the press with a short, sensationalist explanation for his motives that was, at best, one-sided and, at worst, substantially misleading. (As late as 2003, a Detroit newspaper was still describing the episode, against volumes of evidence, as beginning when Henry Ford II "stormed out of a board meeting of the Ford Foundation"[18]—something that manifestly never happened.) The headlines were seized upon by critics of foundations in general, as well as of the Ford Foundation in particular, and broadcast widely to make that foundation the poster child for the great risk that donors supposedly undertake when they consider creating perpetual foundations: at some point after their deaths, allegedly, their foundations would likely depart from donor intent. That myth continues to persist despite the paucity of evidence to support it. For example, Adam Meyerson, the highly respected president of the Philanthropy Roundtable, which is the leading association of mostly conservative philanthropists and foundations, wrote recently, "The Ford Foundation is one of the best examples of donor neglect."[19]

In a March 26, 2012, Letter to the Editor of the *Wall Street Journal*, Marta Tellado, the Ford Foundation's vice president for global communications at that time, expressed disagreement with Adam Meyerson's view of Henry Ford's role at the Ford Foundation, to which Mr. Meyerson responded as follows: "When Henry Ford and his son Edsel established the Ford Foundation (Henry Ford II referred to his grandfather and father as its two founders), they left future trustees with no instructions on its purposes. The language in the charter, 'to administer funds for scientific, educational and charitable purposes, all for the public welfare,' offered no guidance about principles or priorities and would be consistent with a very broad range of philanthropic strategies."[20] If, as Mr. Meyerson says, the founders of the Ford Foundation neglected to specify their intent as to the mission of their foundation and to establish boundaries to ensure future fidelity to their intent, how can Henry Ford II's resignation from the foundation's board of trustees be accurately described as a prime example of "departure from donor intent"? That, I assume, is the reason that Mr. Meyerson decided to refer to what happened as an example not of a violation of donor intent but as an example of "donor neglect." If that is indeed the proper interpretation of Henry Ford II's role at the Ford Foundation and his decision to resign from its trustees, then it would seem hardly accurate for others to blame the Ford Foundation for any departure from donor intent since donor intent had never been established. The Ford family could have shaped the philosophical and philanthropic direction of the Ford Foundation but voluntarily chose not to do so.

Moreover, if Henry Ford II was indeed the dominant force in shaping the Ford Foundation's first 33 years of existence, surely it is a misstatement to characterize the foundation as having violated the intent of its founding donors, which has negative ethical connotations. It is of course possible and appropriate that persons of differing ideological views can rightly criticize the Ford Foundation for some of its program initiatives, but what seems clear from the foregoing is that those initiatives did not come about by means of violating donor intent!

The many examples of Henry Ford II's primary role in molding and shepherding the foundation should convince any fair-minded reader of the contrary. Similarly, any reader of his resignation letter is likely to conclude that even "donor neglect" is not an accurate description of Ford's relationship with the foundation. Were there differences between Henry Ford II and the foundation's senior staff with regard to particular policies? Of course there were. Such differences occur in all organizations and are, in healthy ones like the Ford Foundation, signs of vigor and strength rather than evidence of decline and weakness. The fact that Ford remained a trustee for so many years suggests that any differences he had with the foundation's leadership and policy were less important to him than were the foundation's many achievements. One is forced to credit to Mr. Ford those achievements and the people who created them, even if at times those accomplishments were often the result of differences among them.

Nonetheless, the myth took hold and sounded an alarm to countless wealthy individuals who were considering setting up foundations, including John M. Olin.

JOHN M. OLIN AND HIS LIMITED LIFE FOUNDATION

John M. Olin—a prominent, well-connected, and very successful businessman—happened to be visiting Cornell University, his alma mater, as a trustee, during the protests against the Vietnam War that took place in April

1969. That Saturday of Parents Weekend, students armed with guns took over Willard Straight Hall.[21] The saga ended after negotiations between the students and Cornell officials, when the students "emerged from the Straight carrying rifles and wearing bandoleers."[22] Their image, captured by Associated Press photographer Steve Starr in a Pulitzer Prize–winning photo, appeared in newspapers across the country and on the cover of *Newsweek* magazine under the headline "Universities Under the Gun."[23]

John Olin was profoundly upset both by what he saw and by what he regarded as the attitude of Cornell students, as well as students elsewhere, toward America's capitalist system. According to James Piereson, whom Mr. Olin later chose as president of the foundation he created, that experience significantly influenced the businessman:

> The incident led to some soul-searching on his part about the future of higher education and the free enterprise system in the United States. He saw clearly that the students at Cornell, like those at most major universities, were hostile to businessmen and to business enterprise, and indeed had begun to question the very ideals of the nation. He wondered if this situation could be reversed if these students, and the faculty members who encouraged them, could better understand the free enterprise system and our heritage of limited government.[24]

Olin's weekend at Cornell may well have been the catalyst for the substantive programs he chose as the focus of his foundation, but it was hardly the only significant factor that shaped his vision. In his article, Piereson mentions two others:

> He was greatly influenced by Julius Rosenwald, an early advocate of the idea that foundations should spend their assets within a generation of their donor's demise. Olin was also guided by another event that took place in 1977—Henry Ford II's highly publicized resignation from the board of the Ford Foundation. [Ford's resignation in late 1976 was not widely reported until early 1977, and many sources thus cite the later date.] . . . The lesson Olin took from this public flap was that his foundation would likely come under the sway of people who did not share his principles. If this could happen to the Ford Foundation while a member of the family still served on the board, it could certainly happen to the John M. Olin Foundation after he died.

His answer was to instruct his fellow trustees to liquidate the assets of the foundation over their working lifetimes. With the exception of Bill Simon, the trustees were John Olin's business associates; all of them understood what he was trying to accomplish. Most were roughly a generation younger than he was. The expectation was that the foundation might last for perhaps 25 years after Mr. Olin's death, just as Julius Rosenwald had recommended.

Mr. Olin had another reason for choosing to sunset his foundation: He wanted to influence contemporary thinking about economics and public policy, in the hope that the severe problems he saw could be corrected. It made little sense, in his view, to establish a perpetual foundation if these more immediate problems could not be ameliorated. His wish to end the foundation at some point has thus required the foundation to allocate the assets to current problems, rather than to those that might arise way out into the future.[25]

And "influence contemporary thinking about economics and public policy" he most assuredly did. Over the 23 years following John Olin's death in 1982 at the age of 90—which triggered the payment of his $50 million bequest to the Olin Foundation—the foundation steadily emerged as "perhaps the premier philanthropic institution supporting conservative causes during its existence."[26] It was able to achieve that impact in a comparatively short period of time because its decision to spend down its assets freed it to grant as much money as it thought necessary to achieve its goals. Its original bequest had been augmented in 1993 by another $100 million bequest by Olin that he specified would come to the foundation when his wife died, which occurred that year. Thus, according to James Piereson, in many of the years between 1993 and 2005, the year it chose to end grantmaking, the Olin Foundation was able to spend about $20 million a year, much more than the minimum annual foundation payout required by the Internal Revenue Code for a foundation with its level of assets.[27]

In essence, the Olin Foundation kickstarted a large number of organizations that became key to the intellectual and policy infrastructure that flowered in the United States, as well as in England, starting during the Reagan administration and continuing through the George W. Bush administration. Its momentum enabled it to flourish during the Clinton and Obama administrations as well. The spreading and strengthening of conservative ideas in political discourse among Republican scholars, activists, journalists, and business people undoubtedly have contributed to the creation of the dominance of conservative officeholders in the US Congress and in many of the state legislatures. That movement was accomplished substantially by the foundation's grantmaking strategy.

In a 2002 overview of the foundation's program focuses, James Piereson elaborates on the relationship between its extraordinary influence and its limited lifespan:

> Of course, we are prominent as one of the few foundations committed to developing and promoting conservative ideas. Our interests are diverse and include law, economics, foreign affairs, education, journalism, and public policy. About half of our grants go to university programs of various kinds. We have invested heavily in law and economics programs at leading law schools, in an effort to promote a deeper understanding of markets at those institutions. We have also supported programs designed to instruct federal judges in economics and economic reasoning.
>
> A large share of our funds go to leading market-oriented think tanks, such as the American Enterprise Institute, the Heritage Foundation, the Manhattan Institute, and the Hoover Institution. We support a wide range of programs and projects, including books, fellowship programs, television documentaries, opinion journals, and so forth. We have made a strong effort over the years to bring conservative ideas into the intellectual mainstream of the nation, which is what John Olin wanted to accomplish.
>
> Some friends have criticized us for spending down, likening it to suicide. We do not see it this way, but even if we did, we have no choice—it's what our donor required. Actually, the whole institution, trustees and staff, believe we are doing the right thing. Several of our most important accomplishments could only have been achieved through the kind of aggressive spending that our plan made possible. We prefer to think we are simply retiring or stepping aside, with the hope that others will step in where we have left off and continue to sustain the skillful, dedicated scholars, writers, and administrators who have used our funds to develop and communicate the ideas Mr. Olin intended to support.[28]

An excellent example of the foundation's success in finding niches that, to achieve its objective, had to be filled is the role that the foundation played in creating The Federalist Society. Steven Schindler, coauthor of *Casebook for The Foundation: A Great American Secret*,[29] describes its history as follows:

> The Olin Foundation was particularly concerned with the direction of legal education. The Foundation was fearful that liberals controlled most law schools and directed the brightest students toward careers supporting liberal ideas in public interest law firms. One of the Foundation's early grantees, the Institute for Educational Affairs, was recruited to help identify high-impact conservative projects; it agreed with this assessment.
>
> Understanding the direct concerns of the Foundation in the field of law, the Institute recognized early promise in a group of conservative law students in the early 1980s. These students were acutely aware of their minority status as conservatives at elite law schools, particularly after realizing that so few of their colleagues had supported Ronald Reagan in 1980. Despite the increasing success of the conservative law and economics movement, . . . these students felt more could be done to give conservative perspectives on legal and political issues a more prominent platform in law schools. In particular, the group wanted to bring to their law schools leaders of conservative thought to engage in dialogue on conservative issues, which they thought were woefully underrepresented. . . . The Foundation made grants to sponsor the Society's first major event, a conference which helped to jump-start the organization's visibility and recruitment capabilities.
>
> Over the next two decades, the Olin Foundation contributed more than $2 million to the Federalist Society. [As of 2007] the Society now counts among its members more than 5,000 law students at approximately 180 law schools and more than 20,000 practicing attorneys. . . .
>
> The Federalist Society's impact has stretched beyond the imagination of its early donors. Some credit the Society with effectively counterbalancing what the Federalist Society calls a shift to the left of the American Bar Association. In particular, many say the Federalist Society enabled the Bush Administration to cease the traditional practice of asking the ABA for evaluations of judicial nominees, a practice many conservatives considered detrimental to the confirmation of conservative judges. . . . Three of President George W. Bush's cabinet members in his first term, as well as Bush's solicitor general and staff members in The White House Counsel's Office, were members of The Federalist Society. In addition, members of

The Federalist Society are reported to have played central roles on President Bush's committee to propose nominees for judicial appointments. The Federalist Society's importance in advancing conservative ideas in the law became a matter of common understanding during the confirmation process of Chief Justice John Roberts; the appearance of his name on a leadership roster for the Society was a point of contention between Democratic senators and The White House.[30]

The Olin Foundation is a textbook example of the potential of philanthropy to achieve significant results. There are several relevant lessons here. The first is the importance of having a good idea whose time has come or of choosing an idea that, through one's efforts and resources, can enable its time to come. It is important to remember, however, that countless other foundations and philanthropists have spent hundreds of millions of dollars trying, in vain, to jump-start and scale ideas whose times had not come or not come yet. What is clear is that John Olin, William Simon, and James Piereson had an uncannily accurate sense of the existence of a huge gap in US socioeconomic and political discourse crying to be filled.

How did they come to this realization? Undoubtedly, the then-prevailing ethos of American foundations and philanthropists was so monochromatic in its liberal slant that, absent an initiative by them, conservative ideas had not been and would not be given a chance to be seeded, take root, and blossom. Feeling excluded, they came to believe that the marginalization of their ideas simply had to be corrected in some way. The monopoly centrist or center-left ideology of most American philanthropy demanded initiatives to try to rebalance public discourse. And as William Simon, then president of the Olin Foundation, wrote, "I felt those of us on the Right needed to learn and then do what McGeorge Bundy [the Ford Foundation President] had been doing for years on the left."

Second, they clearly understood that a carefully chiseled strategy of creating a solid intellectual foundation that would grow its own thinkers, scholars, professionals, activists, journalists, and candidates was indispensable. Simon appears to have learned very well what Bundy and other centrist or center-left leaders had been doing in focusing their leadership development initiatives on professors, students, internships, and mentorships and on the building of organizations to champion the cause. If you start with scholars who do research, publish, and teach students, then create journals to publish articles and books that disseminate the supported professors' writings, and then foster like-minded institutions (such as think tanks and conservative-leaning public interest law firms) as well as university-based conservative academic centers with jobs to fill with the graduates, then you have built a structure similar to what the Ford Foundation and other centrist foundations had been creating and supporting for several decades.

As James Piereson said, "Our strategy was to locate the best universities and think tanks to express thoughtful conservative views. Now the political climate has changed, and we think we played an important role in that change."[31]

Third, they knew that to make a lasting difference in the long run, they had to achieve scale of discourse in the short run and, by spending capital now rather than only the income on capital over the long run, they were able to build the necessary on-ramp to gain entrance and achieve scale within the "respectable center of public discourse."

Admittedly, the Olin Foundation had not been alone in pursuing this agenda. Other conservative foundations, such as those created by Richard Mellon Scaife's family and the Lynde and Harry Bradley Foundation, were working alongside and coordinating their efforts with Olin, with Olin often the leader. The Scaife family foundations and the Bradley Foundation, however, are not spend-down foundations but at this point presumably are perpetual. The fact that the Olin Foundation, working in concert with them, could achieve such impressive results definitely does not mean that other spend-down foundations can easily emulate its success. The nature of a problem to be tackled is *the* most important determinant of how long it will take a foundation with a well-designed strategy to achieve even modest success. The problem chosen by the Olin Foundation was the substantial absence of conservative thinking in the public policy realm. The lack of something is much easier to correct than if there had been people already working in a field whose opposition had to be overcome or who had to be persuaded to try new methods. Most of the intransigent social problems, such as poverty, social inequity, global warming, and stubborn illnesses, that have defied understanding and the development of cures or successful medical treatment are radically different in character and magnitude and require a different approach to solve.

THE MYTH TAKES HOLD

We have seen how Henry Ford II's resignation became widely, even if erroneously, portrayed as the paradigm example of a foundation's flagrant departure from the founding donor's intent. Permit me to say a few more words on that subject.

While it was Henry Ford, automobile manufacturer, who created the family fortune, he was never significantly involved in the Ford Foundation or the large gifts to it of Ford Motor Company stock. Besides, I think it unlikely that even the conservative critics of the foundation's actions would have liked the Ford Foundation to mirror the publicly stated anti-Jewish, antidemocratic, and generally xenophobic views of the Ford Motor Company founder.

However, it was not Henry Ford but his son, Edsel, then president of the Ford Motor Company, who founded, funded, and originally presided over the Ford Foundation until his death, and it was his views, as well as those of his son that decisively set the foundation on the course it pursued. The biographers of Henry Ford *père* and Edsel Ford make clear that, while the relationship between father and son was cordial, they had many vigorous differences of opinion on both company and public affairs. In view of Edsel Ford's presidency of the Ford Foundation from its beginning in 1936 to his death in 1943, it is safe to say that those years saw no departures from donor intent. When Edsel Ford died, his father was still alive, and it is striking to note that at that time he was not selected to become president of the foundation. Instead, that role fell to Edsel's son. It was Henry II who, from 1943 until his resignation in 1976, represented the Ford family on the foundation board—and played the critical role in selecting the officers and trustees of the foundation and in shaping the program that the board adopted and implemented.

It is clear, therefore, that the Ford Foundation's actions through 1976, when Henry Ford II resigned as a trustee, cannot accurately be described as any kind of departure from donor intent because, as we saw earlier, no donor intent had been embodied in the legal instruments that created the Ford Foundation. Moreover, Henry Ford II, while not the donor, was his son and representative on the foundation board. While his father might be tarred with the charge of neglecting to specify any founding intent in its governing documents, Henry Ford II was the de facto family representative in person on the Ford Foundation board throughout all the years that it was allegedly "departing" from his father's nonspecified intent.

In other words, there is a strange illogic in citing the Ford case—regardless of how Henry Ford II's statements are interpreted—as an argument for creating time-limited foundations that do not long outlive their founders. During the entire period of foundation activity to which Henry Ford II took exception, Ford himself was very much alive and fully present at the board table. Disagreements between Ford and the foundation board, whatever they were, had nothing to do with any absence of Ford family voice and even less to do with the life expectancy of the endowment. Henry Ford II left his family's namesake foundation by choice, not by death. Until he resigned, his was the voice of a highly influential trustee with the moral authority to prompt serious debate, if not outright changes of direction, had he so chosen. Whatever regrets he may later have felt (if "regrets" is even the right word) surely had more to do with his own failure as a trustee to promote his point of view than with the perpetuity of the Ford Foundation.

It is astonishing to me that many later potential foundation founders have bought into the myth that the Ford Foundation should be regarded as the poster child for departure from donor intent. Unquestionably, this is attributable to a significant degree to the extent to which the Philanthropy Roundtable has kept alive a questionable interpretation of Henry Ford II's role in, as well as resignation from, the Ford Foundation. Moreover, other conservative foundations and think tanks have joined the chorus in imputing departure from donor intent specifically to liberal foundations. The following is an example involving such a claim by the North Carolina–based Civitas Institute targeting the Z. Smith Reynolds Foundation of Winston-Salem, North Carolina:

> "How does it happen?" is hands-down the most-often asked question when discussing foundations that stray from their original mission and move to funding liberal organizations. In this case, the original funding organization was founded with the money from the hard work and vision of one of America's most successful free-market industrialists—R.J. Reynolds. When did it begin to cater to groups that attack free enterprise?
>
> . . . [T]he inner circle likes to point all the way back to Katherine Smith Reynolds, the wife of Reynolds Tobacco's founder, R.J. Reynolds. She encouraged better education and better housing conditions for the company's workers. However, that type of humanitarianism is a far cry from today's extreme and sometimes radical progressive activism that most groups today try to sugarcoat with benign and benevolent-sounding names.
>
> The simple answer to "How does it happen?" is that foundations' missions and philosophies change when their boards change. This phenomenon has become so prevalent that many of today's more conservative

foundations have included "sunsetting" clauses in legally binding agreements in order to protect donor intent. "Sunsetting" or a "spend down" is the act of spending down all of a foundation's assets in a set period of time. The Z. Smith Reynolds Foundation's history is a classic example of what happens when philanthropic ventures continue too long, allowing the founder's original vision to be lost.[32]

Like Civitas, the Philanthropy Roundtable has not limited itself to alleged donor drift at the Ford Foundation. In my research for this book, I have come across other examples of the Philanthropy Roundtable's imputing instances of drift away from donor intent to donors' successors in other foundations. Another such example of purported donor drift is The Pew Charitable Trusts, which was, until it converted into an operating public charity in 2004, one of the largest foundations in the United States. It is widely admired among foundation professionals, as well as among environmentalists; food safety experts; scholars of religion, public opinion and journalism; educational professionals; and countless others. Of the 13 individuals on the trusts' board of directors, seven are members of the Pew family, either direct descendants or close relatives of the four founders. In its articles on The Pew Charitable Trusts, the Philanthropy Roundtable often claims that the trusts' programs are significant departures from the intent or the views of one of the founders, J. Howard Pew. In one of Adam Meyerson's references to the Pew Trusts, in the *Wall Street Journal* article "When Philanthropy Goes Wrong," mentioned earlier, he writes:

Consider oil magnate J. Howard Pew (1882–1971). As Waldemar A. Nielsen noted in *The Golden Donors*, the charter of the J. Howard Pew Freedom Trust [one of seven trusts making up The Pew Charitable Trusts] in 1957 spelled out that Pew intended to "acquaint the American people" with "the evils of bureaucracy," "the values of a free market," and "the paralyzing effects of government controls on the lives and activities of people." Pew also wanted to "inform our people of the struggle, persecution, hardship, sacrifice and death by which freedom of the individual was won." Admirers and critics alike of Pew's recent signature initiatives—such as its crusades for campaign finance regulation, universal early childhood education, and recognition of the dangers of global climate change—can agree that in the past two decades—with the exception of its emphasis on religion in public life—J. Howard's worldview and philanthropic goals have played little role in Pew's charitable giving. The founding donors themselves are often partly to blame for any departures from their principles, thanks to open-ended statements of their philanthropic intent.[33]

In response to those words of Adam Meyerson, Rebecca Rimel, CEO of The Pew Charitable Trusts, wrote the following reply to the *Wall Street Journal*:

To the Editor:

Your recent profile of J. Howard Pew, one of the four founders of the Pew Charitable Trusts, accurately portrayed him as the successful, principled, entrepreneurial, and creative man many knew him to be. Unfortunately, through a series of omissions and a narrow reading of history, your profile went off track in claiming that the institution he helped found does not live up to his ideals. Nothing could be further from the truth.

J. Howard Pew, his brother Joseph N. Pew Jr., and their sisters Mabel Pew Myrin and Mary Ethel Pew, created seven trusts over three decades, which today provide the majority of funding to the Pew Charitable Trusts. Our founders did far more than assure the financial health of our institution—they entrusted those who succeeded them with the values that guided their remarkable lives, values that we work hard every day to honor and uphold.

The four founders were optimists who believed in the power of science, research, and practical knowledge. Today, the Pew Charitable Trusts approaches society's challenges with the same innovative and entrepreneurial spirit. We seek creative solutions that are based on independent, nonpartisan, sound data. We follow the facts where they lead us, never signing up to support a political party, ideology, or point of view.

It is therefore disappointing that by focusing on language applicable to just one of the seven trusts, your article insinuates that we are no longer living up to the goals of our founders. In fact, they personally guided our work during their lifetimes, as did Joseph N. Pew III (son of one founder and nephew to the others), who served on our board for six decades until his passing in 2011. Through his intimate, decades-long conversation with his father, uncle, and aunts about their goals and aspirations, he inculcated their expectations into our work.

Based on his guidance, and under the leadership of other Pew family members on our board, we continue to invest in areas of interest to the founders, including health, religion, and civic life. . . .

Like any institution in its seventh decade, of course, our day-to-day work has evolved. Pew was once a traditional grantmaking foundation. We are now a public charity, able to put our resources—and those of our partners—directly into projects we operate and which our research shows can inform the public, improve policy, and stimulate civic life.

Joseph N. Pew III, known affectionately as "Joe the Third," always reminded us that our founders understood that they could not anticipate the challenges our nation and the world would face as time passed. That is why they so wisely designed the institution that bears their name to respond to changing circumstances with flexibility. But with that came the responsibility to hold true to their ideals and to exercise sound judgment. "They gave us the stewardship responsibility to lead this institution as the needs of society change," he would say, "so let's exercise it wisely." We believe we do, ever mindful of those who came before us and those still to come.

Respectfully,
Rebecca W. Rimel
President
Pew Charitable Trusts[34]

Keep in mind that Howard Pew's words quoted above were included in only one of the seven trust agreements establishing the Pew Trusts. In an organization with four founders, only one of whom expressed a particular point of view on a matter, why should the six other trusts be required to adhere to the words of the founder of the seventh trust? Moreover, and of far greater import, who, then, can credibly speak of what a donor's intention was 50 years ago? Which is a more reliable reflection of a donor's views— statements of one of four trust donors taken out of context at a much earlier point in time or seven descendants or close relatives alive today representing the family of donors who together created a philanthropic institution?

What is also interesting to me is this: just as Ford's resignation letter indicates that his primary difference with his fellow trustees and the foundation's president was about initiatives that they refused to undertake, it seems that Meyerson is leveling the same kind of criticism at The Pew Charitable Trusts.

This is not, in other words, a case of a foundation taking on causes inimical to the wishes of the founder. It's simply a complaint that the founder might have preferred other initiatives or would have wished to travel down different programmatic roads that the foundation, for whatever reason, has not taken. Is that a violation of donor intent? Given the presence of the donors' heirs on both the Ford and Pew boards, and given the heirs' deep involvement in crucial decisions of both institutions, it seems to me more like two differing interpretations of what the original donor *might* have done—under circumstances that that donor never actually had the opportunity to confront.

The Philanthropy Roundtable's growing focus on what it regards as examples of the drift away from donor intent has been troubling me for some time. The more I had read about the growing number of wealth-holders deciding to shift away from presumably perpetual to specifically time-limited philanthropy, the more convinced I became that the Roundtable had strategically chosen such a course as a deliberate strategy to persuade prospective foundation-creators *not* to establish perpetual foundations. It seemed clear that the Roundtable's premise was, perhaps still is, this: because presumably perpetual foundations will inevitably outlive their founders, the Roundtable believes that such foundations are particularly vulnerable to drifting away from their founders' intent when successor trustees take charge, whether they are donors' descendants, relatives, or unrelated philanthropic professionals. Moreover, it is not just drift-away from donor intent in general but drift-away from donor intent *toward left-leaning policies and programs* that the Roundtable and many of its affiliated philanthropists fear.

To be fair in my criticism, I feel obliged to clarify that the official Roundtable position is that donors should "strongly consider" a sunset, not that this is the only way of ensuring fidelity to donor intent. Nonetheless, a reasonable reader might find it hard to encounter any defense of perpetuity whatever in the Roundtable's publications. Still it's true that the Roundtable's published material does offer guidance on ways to ensure fidelity to donor intent if he or she creates a perpetual institution—if, despite the warnings of the Roundtable, a donor is nonetheless intent on taking on that "terrible risk."

The Roundtable's assumption is that rich donors' descendants are very likely, after the death of the donors, to be significantly influenced by the changing times and the socioeconomic and political attitudes of their peers. That's possible but far from self-evident. So, in order to make its argument persuasive, the Roundtable seems to scour the landscape of philanthropy to showcase bogeymen to frighten donors away from the chance that their philanthropic heirs might become misguided, left-leaning distributors of the philanthropic wealth their right-leaning ancestor had amassed.

The Roundtable could not possibly have found a more perfect specimen on whom to try to pin this preconceived threat—the family board member departing from a founder's or ancestor's intention—than Henry Ford II. If the goal of the narrative-creation is to dissuade foundation creators from running the risk of allowing their philanthropic wealth to be deployed by left-leaning philanthropic descendants, it seems that the reality of how Ford viewed the foundation doesn't necessarily matter at all. It's the hint of salaciousness in the example that sets the target donors running, rather than the solidity of the case on which the narrative rests. As a mythic figure, Henry Ford II is just about ideal: he was a titan of his age, and the Ford Foundation (at least until the arrival of Bill and Melinda Gates) was the titan of philanthropy.

From the celebrity of Henry Ford II's example of donor "neglect"—which is the way Adam Meyerson now tends to describe Ford II's actions (rather than "drift")—to the utter noncelebrity of most of the other foundation examples that the Roundtable today cites for "drift away from donor intent," there is a very long drop. None of the other examples has grabbed public attention or, so far as I can tell, has attracted public sympathy for the anti-perpetuity cause. The Roundtable has tried to make its "drift" allegation stick with The Pew Charitable Trusts, but readers can reach their own conclusions on the success of that effort based on the exchange previously cited between Meyerson of the Roundtable and Rimel of Pew.[35]

On a related issue, it is fascinating to read Meyerson's criticism of the founders of the MacArthur Foundation and The Rockefeller Foundation for not expressing their philanthropic intent for those two foundations more narrowly. He writes:

> Of course, founding donors themselves are often partly to blame for departures from their principles. Instructions have frequently been so open-ended that future trustees have very little guidance in setting philanthropic strategy. John MacArthur gave his trustees no instructions at all. "I'll make [the money]," he told them. "You people, after I'm dead, will have to learn how to spend it." John D. Rockefeller's mission for the Rockefeller Foundation was "to improve the well-being of mankind throughout the world," a charge that could justify about any philanthropic expenditure.[36]

Meyerson does not explain here why a foundation founder should be obligated to come up with specific instructions to his philanthropic successors. From the perspective of the public good, foundations that are unconstrained as to their expenditure purposes are freer to respond to changing times. I would never criticize donors for not wishing to constrain how their philanthropic wealth is to be deployed. Instead, I would regard their decision as likely to be an intentional act of modesty, a provision for needs on which they themselves are not experts, and for a future whose problems they cannot foresee. Too often, critics who lament this sort of modesty seem to be pleading not really on behalf of the donor but on behalf of some body of ideological predilections of their own—beliefs that they are *sure* the donors would have endorsed, had they just given the matter more thought.

Really? Neither of the John D.'s—MacArthur nor Rockefeller—was known for shyness or philosophical timidity. Had they wished to create a foundation for something specific, it is hard to imagine what would have stopped them from doing so. However, if donors are concerned about hewing to a specific cause or purpose, I would advise being as precise as possible in words of instruction that bind their successors to abide by such guidance.

I do share Meyerson's indignation, and in the same intensity, when the express instructions of the donors are ignored or violated, whether those instructions are left leaning or right leaning. The case of Bill Daniels and the Daniels Fund is an excellent example of a donor whose foundation had gone astray but whose legacy of words and example provided a means by which to set the institution aright. Daniels was a thoroughly patriotic American, dedicated to the preservation of freedom, who had served for years as a navy combat pilot. He had made a fortune in cable television investments and used it in part to create a large foundation. Several years after his death, the National Air and Space Museum requested a grant from the Daniels Fund, but a program officer turned down the grant, explaining that it would be inappropriate to provide a grant featuring "instruments of war." When the museum challenged that decision, the chairman and trustees of the Daniels Fund conducted a review and decided that the fund staff needed to learn what Bill Daniels's values and interests were. That "triggered a process of recovery and restoration, of rediscovering Bill Daniels's intent for his foundation and instituting a process by which it would be protected in the future. It is a story of fidelity to a person and a principle."[37]

More concerning to me, however, is the fact that the Philanthropy Roundtable does not test its theory that perpetual foundations inevitably depart significantly from their founders' intent, much less "go left," after the deaths of their founders. Countless examples, uncited by the Roundtable, exist of perpetual foundations that have not departed from their donors' intent and have not "gone left" after the deaths of their founders, yet I could find only one of these—The Duke Endowment—widely publicized by the Roundtable.[38] Instead, its website and publications insist that egregious departures from donor intent are frequent, despite the fact that most of the high-profile examples highlighted, such as the Ford Foundation and The Pew Charitable Trusts, simply don't hold up under scrutiny.

Thousands of foundations that were founded by now-deceased donors do not appear to have wavered to any significant degree in trying to fulfill the intentions of their founders, but virtually all of them are left unheralded in the annals of the Philanthropy Roundtable. What is the reason for that omission? It would do a great deal to establish the objectivity of the Roundtable, assuming it desires to be perceived as objective, if it were to pair with every foundation alleged to have departed from donor intent another foundation that appears to have done the opposite. If the Roundtable were willing to do so, then wealthy individuals and the public could judge whether the donor "drift, neglect, or departure" problem is as real as the Roundtable contends or greatly exaggerated or, I hesitate to say, "invented" for ideological purposes. From the examples of foundations that have adhered to their donors' values and purposes over several generations, future philanthropists might then learn how simple it is to ensure the faithful use of their own philanthropic wealth in the future. But perhaps the Roundtable is not as eager to foster trust as it is to peddle fear.

Among the well-known foundations that exemplify adherence to expressed donor intent after their founders' deaths are these: the Alfred P. Sloan Foundation, founded in New York City in 1934 by the former CEO of General Motors Corporation; the George Gund Foundation, founded in Cleveland in 1952 by the president of the Cleveland Trust Company; The Kresge Foundation, founded in 1924 in Troy, Michigan, by Sebastian Kresge; The McKnight Foundation, founded in Minneapolis in 1953 by Mr. and Mrs. William McKnight (Mr. McKnight was CEO of 3M Corporation); The William and Flora Hewlett Foundation, founded in 1966 in Menlo Park, California, by William Hewlett, cofounder of Hewlett Packard Corporation, and his wife Flora; The David and Lucile Packard Foundation, founded in 1964 in Los Altos, California, by Hewlett-Packard's other cofounder and his wife; the Robert Wood Johnson Foundation, founded in

New Brunswick, New Jersey, in 1972, by Robert Wood Johnson II, CEO of Johnson & Johnson, the celebrated health products company; the Robert W. Woodruff Foundation, established as the Trebor Foundation in 1937 by the president of The Coca-Cola Company, who died in 1985; the W.K. Kellogg Foundation, founded in 1930 in Battle Creek, Michigan, by the founder of the W.K. Kellogg Company; The Andrew W. Mellon Foundation, founded in 1969 in New York City in memory of their father by Paul Mellon and his sister Ailsa Mellon Bruce, by merging the Avalon Foundation and the Old Dominion Foundation; the John S. and James L. Knight Foundation, founded in 1950 in Miami, Florida, by the cofounders of Knight Newspapers; and The Wallace Foundation, founded in 2003 by a merger of four charitable foundations created earlier by Dewitt and Lila Acheson Wallace, cofounders of the Reader's Digest Association, who died in 1981 and 1984, respectively.

Having expressed the above criticisms of the Philanthropy Roundtable, I feel obliged to say very clearly that I genuinely admire Adam Meyerson for his vision in establishing it and his leadership in taking it to the prominence it rightly enjoys today. The Philanthropy Roundtable is a vibrant, energetic, and indeed now indispensable part of America's philanthropic sector, which plays a highly effective role in protecting that sector as a whole and not only the right wing of that sector. My differences with Mr. Meyerson and the Roundtable are few compared to their many initiatives, for which I admire them and support what they are doing. I wish only that they could be more evenhanded in acknowledging the benefits that the perpetual foundation sector confers on America and less insistent in urging wealthy individuals automatically to put a spend-down clause in the governing documents of the foundations they establish.

PART THREE

IS IT BETTER TO GIVE NOW OR LATER?

If the aspiration to spend wealth now in hopes of solving or mitigating major problems facing society is the driving reason for spending assets down, why are virtually all of today's spend-down foundations continuing to make grants that are little different from what they have spent money on in prior years? If the purpose of spending down is to put large amounts of assets to work in the short run in order to achieve greater impact, why are the foundations that are committed to spending down not consistently making the "big bets" that are called for by their theory for spending down? Why are such foundations continuing to do what they've been doing but perhaps with an incrementally larger amount of money? Why are they reluctant to adopt new courses of action? Why aren't they willing to take the risks inherent in betting the farm?

In the next few chapters, we will consider some answers and examine more closely the rationales for spending everything soon rather than providing for the future. Some of those rationales, as we shall see, are based on fear—of losing control, of institutional lethargy, of mission drift—and some on aspirations, like the hope of solving an urgent present-day problem or of achieving something that pays huge future benefits to society or simply the hope of a joyful experience in helping others. All of these rationales are reasonable, to a point. But they are easily overstated and oversimplified. And when that happens, the result can be both disappointing and chastening.

chapter six

Rationales for "Giving While Living"

Andrew Carnegie's *The Gospel of Wealth* may have urged other wealthy individuals not to die rich, but, as we have seen, he didn't quite put his money where his pen was. Here was a philanthropist of great vision and irresistible passion, whose actions manifest the fact that he gained deep experience over three decades in making thousands of decisions about whether, when, and how best to give, so when he abruptly decides to change course, stops donating in the present, and instead reserves about a billion dollars in present value to benefit the future, that action should demand our attention and perhaps respect.

The choice that Andrew Carnegie faced is not different from the one confronting today's rich, many of whom are moved by the urgent needs of the present that the public and social media highlight 24/7. Many individuals have imposed limited lives on their foundations, and others have publicly declared a goal of giving their wealth away during their lifetimes or soon thereafter. As of the end of 2015, Duke University's Center for Strategic Philanthropy and Civic Society had identified some 20 donors and foundations that were in the process of giving away everything or that had just finished doing so, and more than 50 others that had spent down in years past.[1] (You'll find a list of foundations publicly committed to a limited life as of 2016 in Appendix A.) It is important to note, however, that other institutions may be spending down with no fanfare—or even without having made a firm decision to do so. As their decisions become known and as new donors and institutions make the choice, the limited-life club is certain to grow.

Let's consider some of the reasons that philanthropists are more often now choosing to deploy their philanthropic wealth during their lives or shortly thereafter.

DOES AGE MAKE A DIFFERENCE?

Why the Younger Rich May Be Inclined to Give It All Now

Those who have decided to give away their wealth now rather than later fall into two discrete groups—the younger and the older. Let's begin with the first group and turn later to the second. The younger rich are mostly in their 30s and 40s—a stage of life considerably earlier than that at which most of the great philanthropists of the past were making their mark. These young philanthropists may be eager to replicate in the civic sector the rapid, risk-taking, high-stakes quest that characterizes the still recent years of their early wealth accumulation. Some might be tempted to describe them as "cocky," but I do not—indeed, emphatically not—because the motivations to which they attribute their philanthropic spending decisions are almost always altruistic, idealistic, and, surprisingly, even marked by humility, compared with when the same youthful tycoons describe their commercial and financial successes.

That is not at all to suggest the total absence in these donors of the same competitive drive that marks their for-profit pursuits. With them, however, I am inclined to believe that they see their competitors in philanthropy not primarily as their generational peers but as the well-established multibillion-dollar endowed foundations—the ones that can expend huge amounts of money while paying out just 5 percent of their assets each year. Perhaps we should call this "the giving-while-living-David vs. the 5-percent-Goliath" phenomenon. Many of those who have announced their intention to spend their wealth during their lifetimes will likely end up spending more each year on any given initiative than all but a few of the largest foundations. Because they are spending, or planning to spend, much more than just the earnings on their capital each year, and because they sometimes concentrate their spending on just a few areas of need, their annual outlays in any given field may match or exceed those of huge institutions that preserve their capital by donating only 5 percent of it per year. The desire to make yearly contributions on this scale may well be part of those donors' motivation for concentrating their philanthropy within a limited time.

Immediate results are an assumption of this generation. Most have not known a time without personal computers, e-mail, Internet (powered at ever-increasing speeds), cell phones, social media, streaming live video, movies on demand, and overnight delivery. Perhaps this mindset, this way of life, drives their view of giving and the expectation for results.

Moreover, as most of those donors are comparatively young, they are energized by the entrepreneurial successes that have helped them achieve unprecedented wealth often at unprecedentedly youthful ages. They are almost always competitive by nature, or they would not likely have amassed so much wealth so swiftly. Spending more than many of the largest foundations would be a way for these individuals to make the statement that they belong in philanthropy's big leagues. Indeed, many of them have already chosen to become members of the Buffett–Gates Pledge, which of course none of the perpetual foundations are eligible to join, as the Pledge is exclusively for living donors, not for any foundations they or others may have chosen to create.

For all these reasons, I wonder whether the competitive drive of the start-up impresarios may be part of what is pushing them to spend now and also their decision to *announce* now that they plan to do so over a lifetime.

The Influence of Venture Capital

Most of the very wealthy young or youngish donors who are considering spending down their philanthropic assets come from the venture capital, start-up, high-tech, and/or finance arenas. It may be relevant, therefore, to think of spending down as a form of venture philanthropy and then ponder the differences between it and venture capital.

One of the most important analogies between the two fields deals with assumptions about risk. Venture capitalists report that they are successful if only one or two out of every ten investments greatly succeed. Indeed, their business model is based on that success ratio. Christine Letts, William Ryan, and Allen Grossman underscored this in their influential 1997 *Harvard Business Review* article, "Virtuous Capital: What Foundations Can Learn from Venture Capitalists." They noted that achieving the one or two successes—what they call "moon rockets"—is essential for the survival of a venture fund, and consequently the fund managers tend to take a keen interest in the management and organizational quality of the companies in which they invest. They need to make certain that the most commercially viable ideas are piloted astutely enough to help them escape gravity when their time comes to soar. Or, as the authors put it: "If a [venture capital] firm has too many project failures, future investors may be scared off and the venture capital fund itself may fail. It is in response to those risks that venture capital firms have developed many of their organization-building skills."[2]

Moreover, the moment of success for venture capitalists comes not in the very long run when an enterprise proves its full potential but at an earlier stage when the investor can reap some form of "take-out": when the emerging company can be sold to an eager acquirer, absorbed in a merger, or sold to shareholders in an initial public offering. Venture capitalists may be patient investors but with limits. They are not typically permanent owners. Thus, limited and even close-at-hand time horizons are a central part of the venture capitalist's approach to business. These and other comparisons between venture capital and philanthropy that Letts, Ryan, and Grossman described in their article suggest to me the usefulness of making a similar comparison between venture capitalists and spend-down philanthropists.

Even if a time-limited foundation does not think of itself as practicing "venture philanthropy" in the sense that that phrase has come to be understood, the foundation must nonetheless bank, like a venture capitalist, on a looming day of reckoning when the success or failure of its investment will be determined. For philanthropists, however, there is no comparable possibility of a "take-out" through an initial public offering and little chance of a successful merger with another nonprofit. (The philanthropic graveyards are full of bungled mergers; successes are the rare exception.) In addition, for most nonprofits to reach scale requires a continuous infusion of more and more philanthropic dollars; only the tiniest number ever earn enough revenue to generate their own growth capital. Finally, a take-out by the most common source of large, sustained support—government—requires strong, reliable, objective evidence of success in achieving an organization's stated purposes. Even then, the likelihood of government funding is at the mercy of political winds. Therefore, if eight or nine out of every ten "big bets" by spend-down donors fail or are left orphaned on the day the "big bettor" leaves the table, and if the successful one or two must achieve a take-out by continuous infusion of other philanthropic, government, or fee-for-service dollars, the risks inherent in such bets are very high indeed. If all the spend-down donor's dollars have been invested in a bundle of such gambles, the portfolio must be so high risk at the beginning as to discourage any but the most high-rolling donors from betting the farm on them. In other words, this approach to philanthropy calls for precisely the kind of personality on which the meteoric successes of Silicon Valley and Wall Street tend to be fueled.

The Older Rich: Taking the Short View?

The older rich, on the other hand, are more often motivated by a risk-averse fear of what might happen to their wealth after they die if they (or their hand-picked trustees) don't spend it sooner rather than later. They are more focused on avoiding the possible deployment of their hard-earned philan-thropic dollars on purposes in which they are uninterested or, worse, that they oppose. Whether said obliquely or directly, the basic message here might be construed as "If I cannot take my money with me, I am going to make sure I have chosen, and am personally attached to, every recipient who gets it!" That anxious and mistrustful attitude is quite different from what Andrew Carnegie espoused in *The Gospel of Wealth*, where he stressed the benefit of giving away one's wealth while living as enabling a donor to bring to bear in his giving the same talents and insights he had used in making his wealth in the first place. He wrote that there is "no grace" in such gifts to the public at one's death, elaborating that "men who leave vast sums in this way may fairly be thought men who would not have left it at all had they been able to take it with them."[3]

The spend-downers who are motivated primarily by such mistrust of their philanthropic successors strike me as almost as "graceless," in Carn-egie's terms, as those who hold onto their wealth until they die, while the non-spend-downers manifest a praiseworthy nobility of spirit in giving for the benefit of future generations, even if such future giving may not accord with how the donors would have preferred to see their philanthropic wealth spent. As in many other matters, Andrew Carnegie pointed the way for oth-ers to leave their wealth to perpetual foundations "gracefully," when he wrote as follows (occasionally using his idiosyncratic innovative spelling) to the trustees of the Carnegie Corporation of New York:

> My desire is that the work I hav been carrying on, or similar beneficial work, shall continue during this and future generations. Conditions upon the erth inevitably change; hence, no wise man will bind Trustees for ever to certain paths, causes or institutions. I disclaim any intention of doing so. On the contrary, I giv my trustees full authority to change policy or

causes hitherto aided, from time to time, when this, in their opinion, has become necessary or desirable. They shall best conform to my wishes by using their own judgment.[4]

On the other hand, the mistrust of successors that some "giving while living" donors exhibit is the result not of inadvertent gracelessness but rather of stubbornness. It may arise out of the deeply rooted, experience-based belief that "Over my long number of years, I have learned best how to tackle the social problems I care most about, and I sincerely resist having others, who don't have the benefits of my experience, substitute their judgment for mine in distributing my philanthropic assets." In this instance, I am tempted to applaud these donors' stubbornness in wanting to benefit society as they see fit, based on their lifetime of experience, rather than risk the possibility that the wealth that they have amassed might be spent in ways that they regard as ineffective or wasteful.

Zalman Bernstein, the principal founder of what is now the investment management firm AllianceBernstein, is an exemplar of such views, and they clearly influenced him when he established the AVI CHAI Foundation. His devotion to the strengthening of traditional Judaism led him to choose as the foundation's trustees several distinguished and deeply trusted friends whom he knew to share his values. Like others who have followed the same course, he had often expressed views echoing those of John Olin who, as we saw earlier, had been profoundly influenced by his understanding of what occurred with Henry Ford II and the Ford Foundation. According to at least one of Bernstein's associates, it was not the Henry Ford II example that troubled him the most, however, but the example of the trustees of the Buck Trust, which was in the news at the time Bernstein was creating his foundation. In that case, trustees pressed a California court to allow them to depart from the express conditions of Beryl Buck's will, arguing that changed circumstances had made it imprudent to follow the deceased widow's instructions to the letter. The court agreed to a change in terms but imposed its own solution, different from both the will and the plan recommended by trustees.[5]

Nonetheless, while Bernstein, during his lifetime, may have considered the possibility of spending his foundation down for such reasons, he himself made no decision to do so. As Bernstein was known to be strong willed, his reluctance to specify spend-down as the course of his foundation may well suggest that he was genuinely ambivalent about taking such a course of action, perhaps because he believed that the cohesion and harmony of the

Jewish people that he hoped for was not something that could be ensured in a few decades. We know only, however, that he did not make the decision to spend down the AVI CHAI Foundation while he was alive nor did he make an express decision to keep it perpetual but left that question to his trustees. After he died in 1999, they made the decision and announced in 2005 that the AVI CHAI Foundation would go out of existence at a date certain, first specified as the end of 2027, the 100th-anniversary year of Mr. Bernstein's birth, but subsequently fixed to be December 31, 2019. It is worth noting that the 20-year window of AVI CHAI's spend-down from Mr. Bernstein's death in 1999 to his foundation's end of grantmaking in 2019 has recently become the window of choice for other donors, including Bernard Marcus's foundation (originally to be given 30 years of life after his death) as well as the giant Bill and Melinda Gates Foundation (which recently reduced its window of life from 50 years after the death of the survivor of Bill and Melinda to 20 years thereafter).

While Zalman Bernstein did not formally limit the life of his foundation, most foundation creators who were known to have deep concerns about the likelihood that their philanthropic successors would be faithful to their wishes have not hesitated to make the decision to spend down. One of those is Bernard Marcus, the cofounder of The Home Depot, who established The Marcus Foundation, based in Atlanta. Marcus is a visionary philanthropist with varied interests, which has enabled The Marcus Foundation to create an impressive track record in a number of fields. The Marcus Foundation gives away about two-thirds of its annual budget for biomedical research, prominently including research and advocacy on autism. Another important institution founded by Marcus is the Israel Democracy Institute, which the foundation has supported for 25 years. A final example is the breathtaking Atlanta Aquarium, which Bernard Marcus both envisioned and supervised the process of building. At some point after establishing his foundation, he decided that it would last for only 30 years after his death, then he later changed that to 20 years. He took the added step of developing a statement of guidance for his successor trustees, who include his wife and two of their children as well as close friends and professional associates, in which he specified not only what he intended the foundation to support during the years remaining after his death but also the objectives that he instructed the trustees *not* to support. He made the spend-down decision because he wanted to ensure that his wealth would not go for initiatives that he didn't care about.

FEAR OF LATER REGRET: VIOLATIONS OF DONOR INTENT VERSUS DONOR REMORSE

Like Zalman Bernstein and Bernard Marcus, many donors choose to limit the life of their foundations not only because they believe their lives and experience have given them a unique purchase on how to pursue their philanthropy but also because they believe that future trustees could put their funds to use in ways that would disappoint them. There are two different ways in which this disappointment might play out: (a) through misunderstanding, carelessness, or poor memory, future trustees may come to misinterpret or ignore a donor's wishes; or (b) donors may, during their lifetimes, find themselves regretting their *own* choices about the way their wishes were formulated and conveyed, or the way their successor trustees were chosen. These are not mutually exclusive; both circumstances might well occur at the same foundation. But the two are separate problems, too often lumped together.

It is important to distinguish between the understandable human reluctance to "lose control" over one's philanthropy or foundation, along with the accompanying remorse for having done so, and an actual drift away from donor intent. One can simultaneously regret losing control and nonetheless agree with the substance of what one's foundation has done. For example, in my interview with Lord Jacob Rothschild for this book, he recalled a meeting with David Rockefeller Sr. some years ago, in which Rockefeller described the decisions by his grandfather John D. Rockefeller Sr. and his descendants to give up control of the governance of The Rockefeller Foundation as a "great mistake for both the family and the Foundation." Yet he said that he nonetheless substantially agreed with the foundation's record of activity.[6]

A quite different example of donor remorse is vividly described in Conor O'Clery's biography of Charles Feeney, *The Billionaire Who Wasn't*.[7] In the founder, donor, and long-time trustee of The Atlantic Philanthropies, one can find a widely admired major foundation creator, then still a trustee of the foundations he created, who was not satisfied by simply expressing "donor remorse" over having let go of his philanthropies but acted vigorously to retake the reins and force his foundations to change course. At the peak of his dissatisfaction, he asserted vehement opposition to some of what his foundations were doing and relentlessly acted to force out the then CEO of the foundation as well as some of the trustees who were supporting that CEO. The fact that he had once personally endorsed the selection of the CEO and trustees in question may well have added to his feelings of remorse.

The attitude of Henry Ford II, as noted earlier in Part Two, Chapter 5, is midway on the spectrum between that of the Rockefellers and that of Charles Feeney. In Ford II's oral history interview commissioned by the Ford Foundation in 1973, referred to in Part Two, three years before he resigned from the Ford Foundation Board of Trustees, he simultaneously manifested "donor's descendant's remorse" and endorsed almost all of the major initiatives that the foundation board and presidents had undertaken.

For the purposes of this discussion, the significant thing about these "donor's remorse" cases is that the life expectancy of the foundation played no role in either the problem or its possible solutions. Neither the perpetuity of the Rockefeller and Ford Foundations nor the limited life of Feeney's Atlantic Philanthropies prevented the founders from regretting a forfeiture of control over the institutions they or their forebears had created. The solution, in their cases, would have lain not in lengthening or shortening the lifespan of their foundations but in taking better care to clarify their wishes and to preserve their own role in seeing those wishes implemented.

UNWILLINGNESS TO BURDEN CHILDREN

In my interviews for this book, as well as in numerous conversations with parents with sons and daughters under 30 years of age, I often heard many wealthy donors express reluctance about imposing the burden of philanthropic wealth deployment upon their children. In an interview in 2015, the founders of a family foundation described it to me this way: "If one's children are young, their parents fear burdening them with the responsibility of deploying philanthropic dollars. If they are older, parents tell us that their children are not interested in what their parents are doing with their philanthropic dollars."[8]

Parents often spoke to me of finding their children resistant to their encouragement to devote time and energy to their parents' foundations. Other parents have told me that their children's lack of interest in participating with their parents in allocating philanthropic dollars had convinced them to divide up their funds into separate foundations for each of their children. Usually, they concluded that their children simply did not share the philanthropic commitment to the same objectives as their parents and that it would be a waste of precious charitable dollars to give part of their wealth to their progeny under those circumstances.

My impression is, however, that such uninterested or philanthropically resistant children are outliers rather than the norm. Parents with multiple children who have systematically sought to engage some or all of their children with them from an early age in their family foundations and/or informal philanthropic giving have often succeeded in developing enthusiasm for philanthropy in their children along with the skills to give carefully and wisely. The key to success is philanthropic involvement of children with parents from an early age, so that the children can personally experience the greater joy of giving to others that their parents feel before they themselves become obsessed with and addicted to the countless, dare I say "selfish," digital and other distractions that attract young people to pour their time into other diversions.

Over the years, the Duke students who have taken my course on philanthropy report that their earliest involvement in charitable giving took place alongside their parents, who personally cooked or served food in soup kitchens, delivered gifts to poor families at holiday times, or were engaged in varying service activities of their churches, synagogues, mosques, and community organizations to which they regularly volunteered time. It is also the case that parents who prime the philanthropic interests of their children by encouraging them regularly to give away part of their allowances or earnings to the needy succeed in hooking their children with the inherent satisfaction of having done something good for others. The most important thing that parents can do for their children is to model, themselves, the behavior in which they desire their children to engage.

Once again, the choice of whether a foundation should be time limited or perpetual is a poor proxy for the more intimate choice of whether to involve one's children in philanthropy or not. If children are reared in a philanthropic life, then taking their place as adults in an ongoing foundation will be a privilege for them, not a burden. If they are not, then watching their parents draw their family foundation to a close could merely reinforce the impression that giving is somehow an antiquated undertaking, the preoccupation of the old, a vestige of an era whose time has passed. Either way, the key choice is about how the children are introduced to philanthropy, not about the life expectancy of the foundation.

FEAR OF BUREAUCRACY AND STAGNATION

The executive directors of most major private foundations, endowments and other nonprofit institutions are dedicated, first and foremost, to preserving the resources and reputations of the

institutions they run. This is achieved by creating layers of bureaucracy to oversee the resources of the institution and prevent it from taking on too much risk. As a result, many large private foundations become slow, conservative and saddled with layers of permanent bureaucracy, essentially taking on the worst characteristics of government. Hacker philanthropists must resist the urge to institutionalize and must never stop making big bets.
—Sean Parker, "Philanthropy for Hackers"[9]

These words by Sean Parker, which sound like echoes of similar charges made almost a century ago by Julius Rosenwald, embrace the conventional wisdom expressed about perpetual foundations by their countless critics, and, like much conventional wisdom, it is mostly, indeed cynically, wrong. Moreover, it is often motivated by ideological differences with the kinds of programs supported by particular perpetual foundations rather than with the idea of perpetuity itself. Are there any foundations the behavior of which jibes with Parker's description? Of course there are. In *The Foundation: A Great American Secret*,[10] I devoted a chapter to discussing the pathology he describes, but the rest of that book explored the countervailing fact that the overwhelming number of perpetual foundations are distinguished by their willingness to take risks, by their embrace of the very kind of "big bets" Parker espouses, and by the countless successes in serving the public interest they already have achieved to their great credit.

I have no doubt that Sean Parker is speaking out of ignorance of what those foundations have achieved and is parroting what he has heard from his contemporaries and friends. His quotation suggests that he is motivated primarily by an undiscriminating anti-institutional ideology. Nonetheless, he is not the only person who expresses those views. They clearly underlie much of the criticism that the Philanthropy Roundtable regularly levels against perpetual foundations. But that doesn't make such criticism credible, because the conservative ideological lens through which the Philanthropy Roundtable views most perpetual foundation initiatives on today's social policies is well known. Its logic is pretty simple: most perpetual foundations tend to support liberal social policy initiatives. Therefore, we and our fellow conservatives are justified in disparaging perpetual foundations and discouraging donors from creating them.

While it is certainly true that perpetual foundations are not subject to any significant external accountability-enforcing discipline, it is equally true that instances of perpetual foundations being "slow, conservative, and saddled with layers of permanent bureaucracy"[11] are rarely uncovered. This is all the more surprising in an age of ever-increasing transparency, given the plethora of blogs, social media, and other forms of digital communication. Moreover, virtually all of the largest perpetual foundations steadily and regularly achieve impressive results in their grantmaking, and many of the midsized and smaller foundations do so as well in their substantive focuses or geographical catchment areas.

It is also important to note that the overwhelming proportion of perpetual foundations have no staff members. They are trustee-led and trustee-administered. By definition, a staff-less foundation may well be stodgy or conservative but, being without any bureaucracy, logically cannot be called bureaucratized. Moreover, even the largest foundations vary widely in the number of staff they have. The Robert Woodruff Foundation in Atlanta, for example, shares a common administrative staff with several other foundations. Together, the Woodruff, Whitehead and Evans Foundations possess assets of $10.1 billion and make $400 million in grants a year with only 12 staff members. That does not fit any reasonable definition of bureaucratization.

However, no one can deny that, once a founding donor is no longer present on a perpetual foundation board, such foundations' lack of any effective accountability enforcement does inevitably leave them vulnerable to the possibility of laziness and the lack of urgency. But being vulnerable to laziness or a lack of urgency is hardly the same thing as being lazy or actually lacking urgency. The serious mission commitment of most foundation program officers, most trustees and directors, and most foundation CEOs; the much greater transparency of most foundations today; and the most extensive utilization of social media sites by foundations and their staffs to engage in interactions with foundation stakeholders—all of those factors—tend to mitigate any tendency toward laziness and lack of urgency. Moreover, as I have underscored earlier in this book, the fact that many foundations today, especially perpetual ones, are increasingly engaging in active partnerships with large and small grantees and are routinely involved in significant continuing collaborations with multiple other foundations unquestionably ties them closely to continuing stimulation from the outside, which is bound to counter any tendency toward passivity. Finally, the fact that virtually all of the large perpetual foundations continually produce results that receive acclaim by countless objective outsiders and observers speaks much more loudly than does the mere possibility that such foundations *might* be vulnerable to laziness and other bureaucratic behavior.

FEAR OF OBSOLESCENCE

Another variation on the fear that a lasting endowment will eventually come to no good is the belief that, sooner or later, either the original intent of the funds will be abandoned or that intent will itself become obsolete as times change. Julius Rosenwald expressed the sum of these fears in 1929: "The history of endowments abounds in illustrations of the paradoxical axiom that while charity tends to do good, perpetual charities tend to do evil."[12] We have already encountered, in earlier sections, the fear that donors' wishes will somehow be violated sooner or later and that institutions will, over time, become hidebound and inept. But what about obsolescence? Isn't a perpetual endowment bound to become irrelevant in some distant future?

Once upon a time, especially in 19th-century England and early 20th-century America, newspaper editors seemed to have relished writing articles about the existence of permanent endowments established to further purposes that were made obsolescent by changing times. One sees those articles rarely today, although legal proceedings do occur from time to time aimed at rectifying any obsolescences.

Rosenwald also bemoaned the purported absence in US law of any avenues for repurposing an obsolescent endowment:

> No such legal safeguards to keep vested benefactions from degenerating into a dead loss exist in the United States. It is almost impossible by law to change a benevolent program planned by a person long dead, even though its obsolescence is unquestioned. Our courts have again and again refused the applications of trustees to revise the purposes of a useless endowment in order to meet a current need. The charters of foundations are considered as contracts with the states that granted them, and the attempt to change any provision of a foundation is usually construed as an abridgement of a contractual obligation, which is prohibited by the Federal Constitution.[13]

Again, this is simply not true. There is a long line of cases in the federal and state courts affirming the capacity of *Cy Pres* to be used by judges in repurposing charitable foundations and other endowments when their original purposes become obsolete. (*Cy Pres*, pronounced "see-pray," is the legal doctrine by which courts may amend the terms of a trust when the testator's original purpose is no longer possible or practicable.)

Such endowments, both in England and the United States, can today be easily cured by asking a court for a ruling to modify their purpose under the doctrine of *Cy Pres*. For a century or more, it has also been possible in England for the Charities Commission to repurpose such endowments. Rosenwald seems to be generalizing from what was, and may still be, true regarding some perpetual endowments that are administered as endowed funds within the endowments of universities, colleges, hospitals, and other freestanding nonprofit entities. However, I know of no freestanding perpetual philanthropic foundations in the United States that have been alleged to constitute "a disheartening chronicle of misuse, disuse, and abuse as to give a man pause before he contemplates founding one."[14] While Rosenwald's purple oratory rings poetically, its reasoning resounds pathetically false, indeed totally uninformed by existing law.

WEARINESS OF TRUSTEES

Some foundations that have chosen to spend down are doing so not because they cannot figure out how to allocate their assets for the public good but because their trustees have become weary of spending the time to put those quasi-public resources to effective use. One sees this phenomenon clearly in many of the smaller family foundations, where, plainly put, the family members have lost interest in devoting their limited time and energy to distributing wisely a limited quantity of charitable resources.

In some of these cases, one is tempted to believe that the foundation simply has the wrong trustees and that recruiting more astutely would soon reinvigorate the board's flagging energies. However, it must be acknowledged that in some families, as the generations pass and the family grows too large or too widely dispersed to share any common interest, the hope of administering a coherent foundation may genuinely be fading.

In 2013, philanthropy advisor Alice Buhl reported on the case of the Irwin Sweeney Miller Foundation, whose third-generation family trustees decided to expend their full $25 million endowment and bring the foundation to a close. Their main reason was that the foundation was dedicated to their grandparents' small hometown of Columbus, Indiana (population 50,000), and only one of the grandchildren still lived there; none of the others had any expertise in its local affairs. Nor were all the grandchildren especially close to one another, geographically or, in some cases, even emotionally. Disputes among board members were becoming more common, and the endowment was not large enough to command the diligence and imagination of the family members. Though weary of the effort, they wanted to ensure that the money was put to a use that fully respected their grandparents' intent, so they made a number of very significant, creative final grants for economic and cultural development projects in Columbus and then went their separate ways.[15]

This was a responsible solution to a genuine problem. The alternative would have been to perpetuate a grudging, desultory, perhaps even divisive administration of what was meant to be an energetic and visionary enterprise. However, as Alice Buhl notes in her conclusion, the problem was not inevitable. Although the previous generations had been careful to instill the values of giving and volunteering among their children, members of the third generation had not actually been "involved in significant ways in the foundation. . . . When the time came for their leadership in the foundation, the siblings had very little experience at working together."[16] A more concerted effort to build the foundation into the routine of family life might have preserved it for another generation or more.

FEAR OF TIMIDITY

It is conventional wisdom that, in principle even if not a widespread practice, one of the cardinal obligations of both perpetual and life-limited foundations is to pioneer solutions to public problems that government itself would be loath to undertake because of their inherent risks. Indeed, that assumption is one of the primary rationales offered by wealthy individuals, foundations, and observers of philanthropy for giving-while-living and spend-down foundations. The hope is that an intense, short-term burst of philanthropy in some field of need would lead to pioneering experiments that reveal what works and what doesn't work, thereby reducing the risk to government in implementing a solution to the problem being focused upon.

In the case of limited-life foundations in which the donor/founder is still active, his or her gutsiness might well set a low bar (or a large appetite) for risk, and the donor/founder will then be around to enjoy the applause if the experiment works out well and can take the heat if it doesn't. But after the donor/founder has left the scene, which is eventually the case with perpetual foundations, choosing a high-risk course of action becomes more difficult, as there may then be no obvious trustee around at crunch time who is sturdy enough to take the fall.

That suggests that when the donor of a perpetual foundation dies, whatever possibility there might have been for high-risk grantmaking will likely be diminished. That point has been eloquently made by Bernie Marcus of The Home Depot and The Marcus Foundation: "As a living donor/chairman of a foundation, I can and do take significant risks in my philanthropy. After I die, my foundation will likely be unable to emulate my risk-taking approach to philanthropy because boards of trustees without living donors usually don't have anyone with the same degree of moral and legal authority necessary to take big risks."[17]

It is impossible to disagree in principle with Marcus's point. Clearly, a foundation with living donors, if they are truly inclined to make big bets on high-risk grants, has a much freer hand to take on significant risk. But it is not a foreordained conclusion that successor trustees will not follow in the donor's footsteps. If the successor trustees are carefully chosen, as were those of Andrew Carnegie, Alfred P. Sloan, and Robert Wood Johnson, and if the founder has blazed a trail for high-risk grantmaking that can set an example for those who come after, the tolerance for high-risk grants need not diminish. Long after Carnegie died, his successor trustees made the decision to try to create a Public Broadcasting System and a National Public Radio for the United States. Decades after the death of General Johnson, the Robert Wood Johnson trustees decided to establish a grantmaking program to diminish teenage pregnancies, to discourage teenage smoking, and to develop strategies for diminishing obesity—all of which are about as high risk as any foundation's efforts anywhere. And 50 years after the death of Alfred P. Sloan, his successor trustees decided to seed the academic discipline of bioinformatics, as well as to underwrite all-encompassing inventories of all the stars in the heavens and all the creatures that inhabit the seas.

The fact that there was no living donor among the trustees—and therefore no one "to the manor born" who would have to bear the blame if those initiatives did not pan out—did not deter those respective foundation boards from taking the high risks involved. Each founder had chosen trustees who understood well what a risk-taking culture demands, and the founder's absence on the board of trustees did not deter the successor trustees from embracing high-risk bets at the outset. To create a bold institution with high risk tolerance, it is only necessary to choose astute risk-takers to govern it. Foundations are no different from other organizations in that respect. Goldman Sachs is no less agile in embracing and managing risk today than it was 145 years ago, even without Marcus Goldman and Samuel Sachs to stiffen its spine. Why should the Johnson or Sloan Foundations or any well-governed perpetual foundation be any different?

Indeed, as I assess the risk-tolerance of the largest American perpetual foundations with no living donor involved, I do not see evidence of significant risk-aversion in any of them. And that *must* be the result of the risk-tolerant culture bred into such foundations by their donors.

Moreover, as discussed in Part One, the ability of a growing number of community foundations, which do not have individual founder/donors on their boards of trustees, to undertake high-risk, controversial initiatives is also relevant here. While it is true that many of those community foundations were not known for taking big risks in the past, in recent years they have been able, because of vigorous boards and chief executives with energy and courage, to strike out in bold new ways and to do so without any obvious trustee present to take the blame for bad judgment or bad fortune.

THE FEAR OF DWINDLING VALUE

There is yet one more fear to consider, of real practical concern as well as perhaps more urgency than the other fears discussed—the challenge of how to meet the continuing need for cash with which to make grants, coupled with the equally challenging strategy to generate sufficient growth in foundation endowment value to preserve the foundation's purchasing power over the long run of a presumably perpetual foundation. As things stand now, there are only two ways to compensate for the lack of the cash income that formerly came from interest on debt instruments. One is to sell endowment assets in bond holdings that no longer generate interest, thereby generating the short-term cash needed, and the other is to sell equities, which, while providing cash in the short run for grants and operating expenses, simultaneously diminishes the equity base that would otherwise be available to grow the foundation's assets for future needs.

Long gone are the days when investment officers were able to calculate their endowment asset allocations at 40 percent debt instruments and 60 percent equity investments. With such a predictable flow of income from interest on debt instruments to backstop cash needs for grantmaking and other expenses, and with reasonable growth prospects likely in a carefully chosen mix of equity investments, cash shortfalls could be supplied by selling some equities and the remaining increased endowment value would likely guarantee the foundation's financial strength for the future. Therefore, neither inadequate liquidity nor inadequate growth was likely. As long as interest rates on cash and debt investments remain close to or below zero, however, foundation investment officers will be forced to continue to struggle to generate earnings on their endowments sufficient both to provide the liquidity needed for payments on grants to satisfy the 5 percent minimum annual distributions required by the Internal Revenue Code for foundations and to generate enough asset growth over and above the minimum distribution requirement to ensure the preservation of the foundation's purchasing power.

James Shulman, Senior Fellow at the Andrew Mellon Foundation, concisely sums up the challenge now faced by foundation investment professionals and foundation trustees:

> This [current low-interest environment on debt investments] makes it harder to get the 5 percent return, but since all endowments practice "total return" strategies (whereby the payout is garnered by planned harvesting of assets that have grown, rather than by depending much on interest or dividends), they already don't really depend on the fixed-income part of their endowment for funds in the way that they used to. But with both lower income from such investments and lower projected growth throughout the worlds' economies ("the new normal"), endowments are driven to more aggressive strategies (90 percent equities in one form or another) in order to get the "juice" that they need. This can mean more volatility in the short run as they seek the growth they need to outpace inflation, cover their expenses, and achieve their payout target. Those charged with managing endowments are anxious about how hard it will be for them to get returns that enable them to keep growing for the near future.[18]

The returns on university endowments for the year ending June 30, 2016, underscore the problem faced by all endowments, including those of foundations. Yale University reported a year-over-year increase in its endowment of 3.4 percent, but Harvard reported a year-over-year decline in its endowment of 2 percent, and Duke reported a year-over-year decline in its long term capital pool of 2.6 percent.[19]

If the current interest rate environment persists for much longer, the likelihood that a foundation's assets will erode in value over time would certainly constitute a logical reason to decide to spend them to achieve greater social impact in the near term (more assets available now than later, therefore more impact), rather than watch endowment values sink little by little, until spending down is virtually a fait accompli.

Fortunately, for donors and foundation managers struggling to understand their options while satisfying their obligations, Bill Meehan and his colleagues Kim Jonker and Joanna Pratt have developed an online tool to help philanthropists "face future uncertainties by informing various payout-related decisions." This guidance is available at their website: www.engineofimpact.org. Here is Meehan's list of some of the questions the website can help answer:

- If we want to remain perpetual, what is the highest payout amount we should target?

- If we hope to remain perpetual and select a payout level accordingly, what are the odds that—due to market volatility—we will not achieve our goal of remaining perpetual and instead will run out of funds?

- If we want to operate for a certain number of years and then terminate, what level of annual payout should we target?

- What impact do market returns have on the longevity of our endowment, at a given payout level? Will we run out of funds if real market returns are 6 percent? 5 percent? When will we run out of funds? What payout level would we need to target in order to not run out of funds?

- If market returns are lower than they have been historically, can we still meet the 5 percent minimum federal payout requirement and remain perpetual?

"Using the Foundation Payout Tool," Meehan explains, "philanthropists can input simple variables such as real return expectation, volatility of real returns, payout level, and then receive helpful outputs such as the expected termination year, the probability of perpetuity, the odds of running out of funds a given year, expected payout level to achieve perpetuity, the odds of achieving perpetuity at various payout level, etc."[20]

In the sluggish financial markets of the early 21st century, the fear of an unintended spend-down—of watching an endowment erode relentlessly despite all efforts to maintain it in perpetuity—is not an unreasonable one. But neither is it necessarily an argument for a deliberate spend-down. Each path presents multiple options, with different combinations of investment and payout policies. Resources like the Meehan-Jonker-Pratt model can help donors and managers think through their choices realistically and find the best route to the goals they hope to achieve.

THE FIERCELY URGENT NEEDS OF TODAY

We are now faced with the fact that tomorrow is today. We are confronted with the fierce urgency of now.
    —Martin Luther King, August 28, 1963[21]

In "Burden of Wealth," Julius Rosenwald writes:

[T]here is a growing total of uncounted billions in prospect for the purposes of organized public welfare. It is the consensus of opinion among students of our social order that unless this money is quickly used for contemporary philanthropic needs, it is almost certain to stagnate within a comparatively short period. I hold to this opinion.[22]

The most frequently mentioned positive reason offered by those who have decided to spend all their philanthropic dollars at the present time is the urgency of the many problems being faced by society today. Usually, those who give that explanation also couple it with a statement that tomorrow's social problems should be tackled by the wealthy of the future rather than by those of today. Their tacit assumption is that at least the same level of wealth-creation that we are experiencing at present will continue through tomorrow, whenever that turns out to be. Moreover, almost every major field of philanthropic concern is likely to be in need of as much support as possible now.

Indeed, the present existence of an unlimited range of severe socioeconomic problems, countless environmental threats arising from global warming, and the many still uncured and often untreatable diseases, for example, make them real and palpable to us in a way that problems likely to exist some years from now can never be. Moreover, we know that almost all of those problems as well as many others, if left unattended, are bound to grow even worse by the time the future gets here, so that dealing with them now is of the essence if we are to have a chance to be successful in dealing with anything in the future. Unlike the problems we imagine society facing in the future, today's can be grappled with now. So it is no surprise that such problems are gaining traction in the hearts of many people today, wealthy or not. As Chuck Feeney, founder of The Atlantic Philanthropies, has written, "I see little reason to delay giving when so much good can be achieved through supporting worthwhile causes today."[23]

The major problems facing humankind today that are susceptible to being mitigated by voluntary philanthropy fall into three major baskets: the purely charitable; the complex problems for which solutions, long-run or short-run, are known or suspected; and the complex problems that first require a great deal of rigorous research in order to understand their causes and only then the possible ways of mitigating or solving them. The most immediately pressing need is the one that biblical and philosophical imperatives have historically enjoined human beings to tackle: charity, which is derived from the Latin *caritas*, meaning a godly love for fellow human beings who are suffering in one way or another. The longer-term, more intellectually challenging problems involve understanding and solving the underlying causes of that human suffering—the "root causes," as Andrew Carnegie, John D. Rockefeller Sr., and other devotees of scientific, strategic philanthropy described them. These are the contents of the second and third baskets.

The purely charitable problems, those that serve an immediate summons on the conscience, are simultaneously the easiest to deal with, at least to some degree, but yet the most difficult to persuade large philanthropic donors to part with enough of their wealth to solve or to mitigate significantly. Foremost in this category are urgent life-or-death needs such as adequate food, preferably healthy and nutritious; safe and sanitary housing; and effective health care. As this is written in 2016, the massive flow of refugees from Syria comes to mind. Wealth given to help those refugees will save lives, but many donors appear to be reluctant to give enough of their philanthropic dollars for that purpose, partly because they instinctively prefer to pursue causes that are "higher and better"—meaning longer term, more complex, less tangible—than common charity. Many of us try to do both, which is certainly better than doing nothing, but, to put it plainly, we tend to aspire to get a bigger bang for our philanthropic bucks than to spend them to feed the hungry, house the homeless, heal the ailing, support the frail and elderly, and save the alien refugees. One must wonder, however, what could possibly achieve a bigger bang?

On the other hand, purely charitable needs can be met immediately, with nearly instant knowledge of the good each dollar has done. That is no doubt an important part of their appeal to some individual givers and to those who are not focused on making strategic or systemic changes with their contributions. However, most of us—and certainly most large donors and foundations—tend to disdain providing mere "Band-Aids" for basic needs, because we have been taught to put our philanthropic wealth into solutions at the root of problems and not to apply band-aids to them.

And that, too, is where the philosophical forbears of modern philanthropy point the thoughtful giver. Maimonides, the 12th-century physician and philosopher, urged others, "Give a man a fish and you feed him for a day; teach a man to fish and you feed him for a lifetime."[24] Carnegie captured this idea when he wrote, "Teach a man to be a good citizen and you have solved the problem of life."[25] That was the underlying reason that Carnegie built 2,509 libraries—to help indigent men and women learn how to read.

This quest for focusing philanthropy on avoiding band-aids in order to focus on root causes goes back to the founding of America's first foundations. Kenneth Prewitt, Carnegie Professor of Public Affairs at Columbia University, referring to Carnegie and John D. Rockefeller Sr., puts it this way: "The gift that matters is not to the individual beggar but to the situation represented by the beggar. To attend to the situation rather than the symptom was an idea that permanently and fundamentally altered the relationship between private wealth and public purpose."[26]

With rare exception, however, the search for root causes leads to the second and third baskets: the complex problems for which the solutions are either known or suspected, yet still elusive in practice, and those for which the solutions are yet to be discovered. The various diseases suffered by human beings are the most comprehensible examples of what are found in the second and third baskets. At present, diseases in the second basket—where the nature of the problem is understood—tend to attract more of the available public dollars than those in the third, where the nature of the problem is not understood. Think of the former as requiring applied biomedical research and a large number of clinical trials and the latter as calling for basic biomedical research. In fact, only rarely has government been willing to make significant public funds available for basic research.

While most of those who have decided to spend down their philanthropic dollars explain that they are doing so to engage in "urgent social problem-solving," they are in fact rarely focused on the immediate demands of charity, for all the reasons just described, but on problems whose urgency derives at least partly from the elusiveness of their solutions—in other words, those in the second and third baskets. These have a tendency to stir the imagination and to inspire the kind of boldness and optimism that prompts the thought "With enough effort (or money or leadership or entrepreneurship), I can solve this one!" That is, one suspects, the kind of enthusiasm behind Mark Zuckerberg's impulsive $100 million grant in 2010 for school reform in Newark, New Jersey. As often happens, the result of that exercise, while not quite as disastrous as some press accounts suggested, were chastening at best. The grant and the reforms it was meant to support ran into considerable opposition, proved tricky to implement, and ultimately led to the election of a mayor with decidedly different ideas about how to improve the schools. The lesson was that even the problems that appear to be in the second basket—those with seemingly clear solutions that need only a means of effective implementation—may actually be less clear and their solutions much harder to carry out than they seemed at first.

Sometimes, the bold venture pays off, and the fierce urgency of a need really is met by a fierce, urgent, and successful drive for a solution. That was the happy experience of the Aaron Diamond Foundation, a time-limited institution that concentrated on medical research, minority education, and culture. (A fuller description is available in Appendix A.) When the spread of AIDS threatened to overwhelm hospitals nationwide in the 1980s and early 1990s, the foundation injected enormous resources into AIDS research—a field that was then still struggling to organize and amass the necessary capacity to tackle a still-mysterious, universally deadly disease. It was, at that point, unquestionably a third-basket challenge and a long shot for a foundation that intended to wrap up its work within a decade. Undeterred, the foundation created the Aaron Diamond AIDS Research Center in 1989, which, a few years later, pioneered the combination of antiretroviral drugs (commonly referred to as the "AIDS cocktail") that ended the death sentence for people infected with HIV. With that and other achievements to its enduring credit, the foundation put the last of its $200 million to use and closed its doors in 1996.[27]

And it must be noted that the challenge of developing a vaccine to prevent AIDS—a third-basket task—is still with us, even after many foundations and philanthropists, as well as governments, have poured cumulative billions of dollars into discovering one that is effective! One must thank God that the Aaron Diamond Foundation had the vision and the courage to deploy its wealth 30 years ago to develop an effective life-preserving treatment despite society's inability to prevent AIDS in the first place. If there is a lesson from this example, it is that a small foundation, free to act on its own, may have sufficient wealth to take a big bite out of the consequences of a problem even if it has nowhere near the wealth to solve the problem at its root.

Still, such stories are as rare as they are thrilling. More often, when dealing with problems in baskets two and three, the fierce and urgent drive for a solution ends up becoming a long slog, marked by progress and discovery but also by setbacks, and perhaps eventually rewarded with at least some partial breakthroughs—but rarely distinguished by dramatic and punctual obedience to a preordained timetable. Donors and foundations for whom such a timetable is critical may therefore understandably choose to focus on the least mysterious contents of basket two, preferring the relative predictability of success over an objective judgment about which problems are the gravest or most critical.

COMPOUNDING SOCIAL RETURNS

Those who analyze philanthropy in the language of investment sometimes present an argument for time-limited giving that focuses not so much on the urgency of the need as on the magnitude of the benefit. A philanthropic accomplishment today, they argue, will produce ripples of social return that will compound at high rates over time, aggregating far more value than if smaller amounts were invested piecemeal year by year. Or, to quote Chuck Feeney again, "Intelligent philanthropic support and positive interventions can have greater value and impact today than if they are delayed."[28]

This may be a reasonable belief, but it is not always easy to pin down why someone subscribes to it. In some cases, it may be just a sophisticated-sounding way of privileging the present over the future, just because the people who share the planet with us today seem more important to us than people not yet born. But that would be a poor reason to inflate the value of accomplishments today compared with those of tomorrow. As Stanford professor Michael Klausner wrote in an influential 2003 article about present and future philanthropy, "[A]s a matter of analysis, we need to recognize that current charity comes at the expense of future charity, and that the mere timing of a generation's presence on this planet is not relevant to the social value of charity provided to that generation. Moreover, because charity deferred to the future earns a return in the foundation's investment portfolio, a dollar withheld from the current generation can be expected to yield more dollars of charity for future generations."[29]

Nor is it necessarily true that placing all one's chips on a present-day effort—even one that would pay gigantic social dividends if successful—is necessarily the best way to maximize benefits for society. If, for example, all the experts on a rare disease are already at work seeking a cure, is it necessarily true that flooding their labs with more cash today will do more to produce a breakthrough than providing a steady stream of support, and gradually training new and larger generations of researchers, over a much longer time? Are there good reasons to believe that the music world will be much better off if a dozen more orchestras perform today than if new generations of musicians and audiences are nurtured and sustained over a longer period?

The concept of fast-compounding social return is beguiling—every donor and foundation executive wants to envision billows of expanding social benefit ballooning from their grants like cosmic expansion from the Big Bang. But to make this argument persuasive, one needs to have some idea of the kind and quantity of social return likely to be "earned" by one's philanthropic investment and what would make that initial return compound in value later on. These calculations then need to be discounted for the risk of failure and for the likelihood that the effects of any success will probably diminish as time marches on (even the Big Bang cooled after a while). It is rare to hear these complexities spelled out, but there are surely circumstances in which it would make sense to do so.

For example, perhaps not enough experts are productively employed in fighting a fast-spreading disease, and their labs and equipment are inadequate, but with greater effort a breakthrough does seem tantalizingly plausible. Then, to be sure, it would be reasonable to believe (as the Aaron Diamond Foundation did with antiretroviral research) that a great, present-day commitment to an all-out effort will save many more lives than a slower, steadier approach. There, the human reward—plus the compounding economic value of saved, productive lives and the stanched flow of health care dollars no longer needed for treatment—adds up to a significant payoff that starts big and grows even bigger. True, the researchers might fail; the tantalizing breakthrough might prove chimerical. Not everything ends as happily as the Aaron Diamond program. But, if the risk of failure seems small enough, it is easy to imagine a smart investor—philanthropic or otherwise—who would consider this a solid bet.

Similarly, if one could provide enough schools, teachers, and textbooks to educate an entire generation of girls in a place where they now have little or no chance at education, think how quickly the benefits of their longer, happier, and more productive lives would compound—for them, for their communities, and for the world. Surely that opportunity would cry out for a no-holds-barred effort, right away, without hesitation. But one would need to be fairly certain that the schools would be built and maintained, the teachers well trained and dedicated, and the girls' families and communities prepared to send them to the schools and to support their education. The money spent today will not be available later to see that all those critical factors persist. Without a proper discounting for present and future risk, the impressive image of compounding returns is misleading. Meanwhile, the all-out quest for an expensive Big Bang may leave nothing for later, when it comes time to deal with a long, slow disappointment.

The more closely one looks at this calculation, the clearer it becomes how many critical factors need to line up just right—high initial returns, high likely rates of compounding, low performance risk, low rates at which future value erodes—or else it is not so clear why "interventions can have greater value and impact today than if they are delayed."[30] Sometimes hesitation is the very thing that can reduce the risks and raise the return. Investors who leap into the markets dreaming only of profit and underestimating the risk of delay, surprise, or loss tend to part with their money in short order, sadder but wiser. The same may be true in the market for social improvement.

THE JOY OF GIVING

I think that giving away money is a pleasurable thing thing [shares David Rubenstein], and my observation is that so do most people who give away their wealth. Rarely do people say, "I hate myself. I gave away money and I don't really feel good about it. I really wish I hadn't helped those people." People don't say that. They say, "I feel better about myself." So if you feel better about yourself for giving away the money, why not give away more of it while you're alive, so you can feel better about yourself more than before? . . . And I would like to give it away because I want to see it while I'm alive, and I'm not as confident that in the afterlife, I will actually be able to see it.[31]

Of all the rationales for giving during one's lifetime, surely the most incontrovertible is that doing so is deeply satisfying, in a way that providing for an unseen future simply cannot match. Donors who are motivated, partly or entirely, by the joy of seeing their wealth do good in the world have an understandable impulse to want to use everything they have now, while they are still present to witness the results. Of course, it is possible—and, on the logical left side of the brain, I would argue that it is reasonable—to want to do both: to devote some resources to the joyful present and some to a beckoning future (when new problems will vex unborn generations) and when entirely new kinds of solutions will cry out to be nurtured.

After all, the joy of present giving is not solely an emotional treat for the donor; it is a source of energy and inspiration that can enliven whole institutions. Living donors can, through their passion and talent for giving, make a distinctive contribution to the foundations they establish. Because of the moral authority that stems from their generosity, if they so will it, their fellow board members will almost invariably defer to their judgments about initiatives to undertake and will help them translate their ideas and inspirations into working programs that carry on after they are gone. For example, the major achievements of Carnegie and Rockefeller during their lifetimes—including Carnegie's libraries and TIAA-CREF and John D. Rockefeller Sr.'s Rockefeller Institute of Medical Research (now Rockefeller University) and the University of Chicago, both of which he founded—were followed by equally pioneering initiatives undertaken by their foundations' trustees after the founders were no longer alive. John D. Rockefeller Sr. died in 1937, yet The Rockefeller Foundation's Norman Borlaug won a Nobel Prize in 1970 for developing new food grains that, according to demographers, saved 1.5 billion lives. Andrew Carnegie's successor trustees were instrumental in the creation by Congress and President Lyndon Johnson of the Public Broadcasting System and National Public Radio in 1967 and the establishment by Congress and President Johnson in 1972 of the Pell Grants for higher education scholarships, which are now the primary source of scholarship support for students in need. The billions of lives saved by the post-Rockefeller Rockefeller Foundation, the uncounted millions of Americans who rely on NPR for their daily news, and the 30 million young people who are able to attend college because of Pell Grants are certainly equal in public benefits to the pioneering philanthropies of those two foundations' founders.

Nonetheless, I acknowledge the difference between the "personal" philanthropy of hands-on living donors and the "institutional" philanthropy of foundations created by now-deceased founders. Of all those whom I interviewed for this book, perhaps the words of the hedge fund pioneer Michael Steinhardt, cofounder of Taglit Birthright Israel, which sponsors trips to Israel for Jewish young adults living in other countries, underscore this distinction most precisely: "I do think that I wouldn't derive such pleasure, such joy, as one should from this activity, if I set up a foundation and knew that the board of trustees was going to revolve over a period of time and it would become more and more impersonal."[32]

Steinhardt made it clear that he does not intend his comments to disparage the achievements of perpetual foundations but only that he is not willing to forego the satisfaction of doing his giving himself. Other than leaving significant inheritances to his children and grandchildren, he intends to make virtually all of his philanthropic giving during his lifetime.

I have great respect for the way Steinhardt sees philanthropy and wish that there were many more wealthy individuals who instinctively love the act of giving as he does. It must be said, however, that Steinhardt's passion does not lead him to act indiscriminately. Just as powerful as that love of giving is his insistence on achieving the greatest possible impact with his dollars. The joy that he derives is based on having helped make something happen that, but for his efforts, would not have come to pass. Like so many other successful philanthropists, Steinhardt is an excellent finder of niches that can be filled by employing his wealth and that of others who are inspired by his example and who share his passions.

A CAUTIONARY WORD: WISHFUL THINKING VERSUS THE REALITY OF TIME LIMITS

There is not the slightest doubt that donors who decide to "give while living" will be able to spend more money in the short run. That is the major positive purpose that animates such donors, and it is based on their assumption that greater impact can be achieved by spending ever larger amounts of money. But that assumption is untested as a general rule, and the accuracy of the assumption clearly depends on the problem that is being targeted. If it is a large, amorphous issue—such as decreasing inequality in America—most experts would agree that the problem itself is so big and so complex that

it likely cannot be solved or even significantly mitigated by the limited resources any philanthropist can bring to the table and cannot likely be solved
during anyone's lifetime. Of course, philanthropically supported initiatives
may be able to make a dent in it. One good example of such an initiative is
the National Employment Law Project, mentioned in the section on foundation advocacy, which has been credited with bringing about the increase in
the minimum wage in some cities and states to $15 an hour.[33]

Although this is a welcome step forward, on its own this will not "solve"
the problem of inequality in America. In truth, it is just one small step toward rectifying only one of the many problems that together create inequality and that make it so difficult to solve. Obviously, philanthropic resources
alone are substantially inadequate to address the issues. Inequality can be
solved only by the disproportionately large resources available primarily to
government itself. In the United States, the only successful course that will
yield results is to advocate for changing public policy with regard to such
issues as the minimum wage, the tax code (now written usually to favor the
haves over the have-nots), and the reluctance of state legislatures and Congress to provide more substantial income, food, housing, educational, and
health benefits to America's poor and near-poor. In addition, achieving these
goals requires changing the minds of many Americans so that they would be
willing to elect public officials who are committed to supporting major—
and costly—public policies that would in fact require tax increases to fund
them. Changing minds (and behaviors) invariably requires a great deal of
time—meaning decades, not years.

If the past behavior of "giving while living" philanthropic donors is any
indication of their future willingness to put their "end-of-life" dollars into
such advocacy efforts, I don't have much hope that the many advocacy initiatives required to solve the inequality problem will come from them. They
seem to prefer high-visibility "big bets" that will pay off in the short run
rather than many years in the future. As pointed out earlier, virtually all of
the support for the National Employment Law Project has come from perpetual foundations.

Global warming is a comparable if oft-cited example. It, too, is a large,
amorphous problem that can be solved, if at all, only by changing the attitudes of citizens around the world. Therefore, it is not surprising that present
global warming efforts bear another similarity to the existing efforts to address inequality in this country: virtually all of the substantial philanthropic
support now being deployed to tackle this problem is provided by perpetual

foundations. Here too the "spend-down" foundations and individual philanthropists are aiming for greater impact in the short run.

One of the major factors that deter "giving while living" philanthropists from deploying sizable amounts of money to remedy large, intractable problems is that the existing nonprofit organizations that might be considered as grantees, or any new organizations that the donors might establish to address those problems, simply cannot absorb and put to good use so many dollars over a short period of time. As my colleague Tony Proscio elaborates, "There may not be enough manpower in the field, the ideas for possible successful solutions often aren't ripe enough, and the tractable targets of opportunity may simply be too few. As anyone who has worked in foundations for any length of time will realize, many cash-hungry nonprofits simply cannot absorb a great deal of cash to be spent over a short time span. Only so many experts capable of researching cures for a given disease are available. There are only so many advocacy organizations capable of rallying major climate-change forces. You simply cannot, in a brief period, multiply the kind of highly trained talent needed for advanced-level work by flooding the field with money."[34]

As I stressed above, such problems cannot be solved with quick fixes. Deploying large amounts of money in the present, when the funds cannot possibly yield the desired results—regardless of how large the sum—virtually guarantees that such precious resources will be wasted. What is required are institutions with long enough lives to make the financial resources available when the acute, complex problems are ripe for solution and the resources can productively be put to use. That means perpetual foundations or perpetual universities or perpetual think tanks. Note the repetition of the word "perpetual."

Increasing experience with strategies that stretch over decades has enabled foundations and researchers who work with foundations to understand how long it takes to implement and achieve success in bringing about changes to intractable social problems.[35] Indeed, ask research scientists in pharmaceutical companies how many years—and how many billions—it takes to create and test a new drug and how often the pursuit after many years ends in a "dry hole" with the money already gone. Solving or even significantly mitigating difficult, complex problems requires collaboration among many stakeholders, and success often depends on retaining involvement and commitment over many years. Bridgespan consultants Willa Seldon and Meera Chary, writing in *The Chronicle of Philanthropy*, reported in 2015 that "On average, the collaborations we studied have been operating for a dozen years. We initially picked this group of programs because they had produced measurable improvements in communities, and most continue to get results. . . . Getting key players to the table and keeping them there"[36] is among the great challenges. This research underscores why all the money in the world applied to such problems over the short run cannot hasten reaching the solutions.

If you care deeply about curing any one of the various kinds of cancer or other diseases, spending down your philanthropic resources over your lifetime is not likely to be an appropriate way to proceed. In general, it is usually difficult if not impossible to speed important breakthroughs in understanding, treating, or preventing disease by pouring massive amounts of money into research in the short run. What is required instead is maintaining a constant flow of smaller amounts of money targeting a problem over what can be a very long time. For example, the recent discovery by Drs. Henry Friedman and Matthias Gromeier and their Duke Medical Center associates of a new way to disarm a brain tumor's shield against the body's immune system's activity, thereby permitting a patient's immune system to destroy a glioblastoma tumor, occurred thanks to the steady, sustained flow of modest amounts of money over some 25 years.[37]

However, you can certainly spend significant amounts of money in the short run to provide funding for an endowment or for facilities and equipment or otherwise to support researchers and infrastructure at a research center full of first-rate biomedical scientists who will devote many years to attacking the disease that you care about—as long as you understand that the results you seek will likely occur well into the future. Depending on the difficulty of the problem, you may not see the results during your lifetime. To feel comfortable making such a large amount of money available with little likelihood of personally witnessing the results requires great patience and trust in the institution and its researchers whom you are supporting. Alas, that is the only sure way to cure, prevent, or improve the treatment of a disease. This is exactly the approach used by the tech billionaire Sean Parker in 2016 when his foundation donated $250 million to establish The Parker Institute for Cancer Immunotherapy, bringing together in one virtual network 300 scientists working in a dozen or so major medical research centers in 40 different laboratories with a goal of advancing the use of immunotherapy in treating cancer.[38] The Atlantic Philanthropies, which is fast closing in on its sundown at the end of 2019, used that same strategy for a grant of $177 million to launch the Global Brain Health Institute, a partnership between the University of California at San Francisco Medical Center and Trinity College Dublin, to advance the prevention, diagnosis, and treatment of dementia.[39] Many of the global health initiatives supported by the Bill and Melinda Gates Foundation (see the details in Appendix A) are premised on the same strategy of spending significant dollars in the present in order to cure specific diseases long into the future.

There is a big difference between giving away your wealth while living and achieving impact from your wealth while living. Achieving impact from one's wealth is every bit as hard as giving away one's wealth is easy. The former is filled with challenges at every step, as the path of philanthropy is lined with people and institutions eager to receive support.

chapter seven

How Time-Limited Foundations Achieve Results

Pick Battles Big Enough to Matter and Small Enough to Win
—Jonathan Kozol, author of *Savage Inequalities: Children in America's Schools*[1]

A spend-down foundation's capacity to achieve impact in a fixed period of time varies inversely both with the size of the problem it aims to solve and with the scope of the community or geographic area on which it focuses. A foundation's decision to focus on a narrowly defined place, field, or group of people significantly improves the odds. But that is not all that is needed; being relentlessly strategic in attacking a problem or set of problems is also necessary.

A good example of this generalization is the Brainerd Foundation's concentration on land conservation in the Pacific Northwestern United States and in British Columbia. (A fuller description of the Brainerd Foundation is in Appendix A.) It chose a specific problem on which to focus in a constrained geographical area, which increases the likelihood of achieving impact. In this case, it was also helpful that the purchase and protection of land constitute discrete activities that can often be accomplished in a relatively predictable period of time—an essential factor for a foundation facing a time limit. ClearWay Minnesota, a foundation created from the proceeds of the 1998 settlement of a lawsuit against tobacco companies, also benefited from a clear geographic and strategic focus. It has targeted the reduction of tobacco use and secondhand smoke in its home state.[2] The Hagedorn Foundation had a similar advantage in focusing on social equity on Long Island, New York.[3]

Then there is the Gill Foundation, which focused part of its philanthropy on enriching education in science, technology, engineering, and math (the so-called STEM disciplines) in Colorado. On the national level, that

171

foundation has been perhaps the nation's most strategically focused foundation advocating on behalf of lesbian, gay, bisexual, and transgender Americans. Its efforts are widely regarded as having paved the way for the change in American attitudes on same-sex marriage that led to the 2015 US Supreme Court decision in *Obergefell v. Hodges*, which invalidated state restrictions against such marriage—21 years after the foundation launched its crusade.[4]

A narrow substantive, rather than geographical, focus can be equally effective in conducing greater impact achievement. The AVI CHAI Foundation's strategy in North America is an impressive example of such a focus. As noted above, that foundation's overall mission is to strengthen traditional Judaism, which conceivably could be accomplished in many different ways. The trustees of AVI CHAI, however, carefully honed strategies in its North America Program for achieving that mission by focusing only on two narrowly defined program areas—national infrastructure for Jewish day schools of virtually all Jewish denominations and overnight Jewish camping. Those two fields were selected because careful research findings suggested that, of all possible experiences influencing young people's choices of religious observance and affiliation, the two most influential are Jewish day school attendance and summer experiences in overnight Jewish camps. By relentlessly focusing on those two avenues of strengthening the likelihood of Jewish continuity from generation to generation, the AVI CHAI Foundation achieved far more than it would likely have done had it spread its financial support over a wider variety of interventions. Carefully selected focus unquestionably increases the likelihood of greater impact.

BEYOND FOCUS: TECHNIQUES FOR MAXIMIZING EFFECTIVENESS IN A LIMITED TIME

Beyond hewing to a tight focus on a particular community or place, limited-life foundations are striving to achieve impact in several other ways, which we should consider one by one.

Filling a Void in a Strategically Important Field

Foundations facing a time limit often identify a gap in fields to which they are committed or in which they have some special expertise and then set about investing in things that will fill the gap. The Julius Rosenwald Fund provided good schools for African American children where there were none.[5] As we noted in the preceding chapter, the Aaron Diamond Foundation changed the standard treatment for a deadly pandemic.[6] ClearWay Minnesota developed a science-based program, called "Quitplan," to help people who had little or no source of information, medical care, and peer support in their battle against nicotine addiction. More than 100,000 Minnesotans have since used the plan's free services.[7] The John M. Olin Foundation determined that the emerging American conservative movement lacked a national infrastructure of economic, legal, political, and social policy thinking to inform public discourse, and the foundation set about with a few key partners to build one.[8]

As this book was being prepared for publication, the Edna McConnell Clark Foundation became the latest institution to declare that it would expend its full endowment—in this case, close to $1 billion—over the coming decade. It will focus squarely on a field of work in which it has developed a national reputation over the previous 15 years: strengthening top-performing organizations so they can manage better, accomplish more, and use data to monitor and improve the quality of what they achieve. The major part of this effort has been devoted specifically to organizations serving children and youth, a field hobbled by undercapitalized, thinly staffed organizations and a desperate need for better data and performance-measurement to guide their decisions. The foundation has been attracting capital from across the philanthropic world to fill this gap, most recently through its creation of Blue Meridian Partners, discussed at greater length in Chapter 2 of this book. Now, with its strategic eye trained squarely on this one specific need in a narrowly defined field of interest, the Clark board has chosen, in the words of Hays Clark, one of its founders, to "bet the farm" on a compelling idea that it considers worthy of a final, all-out effort.[9]

Ensuring That Critical Efforts Can Survive the Foundation's Departure

The Andrea and Charles Bronfman Philanthropies, which funds organizations in North America and Israel, devoted much of its effort in its final years to strengthening the fundraising and management of its grantees in order to ensure, as the foundation's leaders put it, "that the missions of the organizations that the ACBP has incubated will continue."[10] In the same spirit, the

Jacobs Family Foundation of San Diego set out to create what it calls "social and economic enterprises that will pass into community ownership"[11] after the foundation is gone.

Similarly, The Atlantic Philanthropies, in its final round of grants, established a number of organizations that will continue to serve different aspects of the foundation's mission after its sunset. One of them, the Social Change Initiative, has been funded with about $15 million and will continue identifying and nurturing high-quality leadership for social justice nonprofits after Atlantic ceases grantmaking. Another one, the Civic Participation Action Fund, with $50 million, has been charged with "supporting advocacy aimed at diversifying democratic voices that inform and influence public policy."[12] In these and several other final initiatives, Atlantic aims at fortifying "strong, sustainable institutions" to continue promoting its priorities, improving co-ordination among organizations in the field, funding "communications to confront biased narratives," and building a network of new leaders to guide the next generation of reform.[13]

Among many efforts to strengthen its grantees and ensure their continuity, the AVI CHAI Foundation took steps to combine into one organization five national infrastructure support organizations for Jewish day schools that the foundation had been supporting separately for about 10 years. These five organizations offered programs and services for heads of school, board members, development directors, teachers, curriculum developers, and others key to day school success. Given that many of these efforts had relied heavily on the foundation's support for their expansion during this time, AVI CHAI's impending sunset means that some consolidation in the field would be all but inevitable. The foundation therefore sought to play a constructive role in that development before it left the scene and succeeded in attracting other philanthropies to partner with it in that effort. A year of intensive work among AVI CHAI staff and the board members and professional leaders of the five organizations generated a consolidated organization, now known as PRIZMAH: Center for Jewish Day Schools. What is especially significant about AVI CHAI's achievement in catalyzing PRIZMAH is that the consolidated organization serves day schools serving all of the Jewish denominations—Orthodox, Conservative, Reform, and Community day schools. If it succeeds in achieving its mission, PRIZMAH may help greatly to ease the cross-denominational tensions and facilitate more extensive cross-denominational collaboration.

Finally, the S.D. Bechtel Jr. Foundation expressed a major commitment to strengthening grantees' infrastructure by creating an Organizational

Effectiveness team to work with all significant grantees in enhancing their effectiveness and resiliency.

Designating One or More Successor Organizations to Carry on the Work

Before ceasing their operations, some foundations have created spin-offs or supported existing organizations to continue all or part of the foundation's mission, or to recruit, train, and motivate leaders who will fortify the field in the years ahead. Atlantic has done this with organizations such as the ones described above, and AVI CHAI plans to continue supporting a prominent cultural and educational center in Jerusalem called Beit AVI CHAI. Such successor organizations are, in a sense, a midpoint between perpetuity and spending down: they prolong at least some of a foundation's activities, even after the foundation itself has ceased to exist as a grantmaking institution.

Creating Strong and Effective Advocacy Organizations

The Beldon Fund, created by John Hunting, heir to the Steelcase office-furniture fortune, devoted much of its 10-year life to strengthening organizations promoting stronger environmental and conservation policy. The foundation also devoted considerable energy and resources in drawing these organizations into stronger alliances for greater impact.[14] The Hagedorn Foundation, created from the Miracle-Gro plant food fortune, has funded highly regarded efforts to defuse tensions over immigration in the suburban counties of Long Island, New York, and to make it an immigrant-friendly region.[15]

Promoting Government Action to Advance the Foundation's Goals

In one of its four programs, the John Merck Fund, based in Boston, has supported efforts "to promote the development of a clean-energy economy in the six-state New England region, and to enable that region to become coal-free within ten years."[16] To that end, its advocacy initiatives include calling for "state and regional policies aimed at reducing greenhouse gas emissions and dramatically increasing investments in energy efficiency and clean energy."[17] The Brainerd Foundation was instrumental in bringing about the North Fork Watershed Protection Act in December 2014, the Rocky Mountain Front Heritage Act in December 2014, and the decision of the Yukon Supreme Court overturning a Yukon government ruling that would have opened up the 17-million-acre Peel River Watershed to mining and resource development.[18] ClearWay Minnesota has supported the development of a Minnesota state law that ensures a smoke-free environment for the nearly 8,000 children in Minnesota's foster care system. The same foundation "led a coalition that successfully supported keeping tobacco prices high in Minnesota after a cigarette tax increase in 2013 as an effective way to deter youth smoking."[19]

Investing in Enterprises That Can Then Attract More Capital

Foundations can use some of their capital assets as well as income earned to invest in companies that contribute to a foundation's causes—such as enterprises that produce clean energy or otherwise contribute to a more sustainable environment, or those that improve agriculture in poor countries or deliver health or education to remote areas. Foundations that are spending down are, by definition, using their capital as well as earnings each year; some of them have chosen to do so with investments as well as grants. For example, The Eleos Foundation, a small, $7 million foundation based in California, spent a few years making modest grants to local nonprofits before deciding that it could be much more effective as an investor than as a grantmaker. With relatively modest amounts, the foundation has provided early-stage risk capital to companies with market-based solutions to extreme poverty in East Africa and Central America. By seeding the field in this way, it has helped those enterprises attract other investors with greater resources, thus multiplying its dollars and extending its impact well beyond its planned sunset in 2020.[20]

LESSONS FROM THE LARGEST TIME-LIMITED FOUNDATIONS

The techniques described above suggest that it is possible to spend down a foundation and still ensure that its work does not cease with its last grant. But they also provide excellent cautions about the indispensability of narrow focus, right-sizing one's ambition to align with the availability of one's re-sources, and the imperative of patience. The foundations mentioned as examples were all careful to adopt these techniques years before they spent down (although several of them wish they had started even earlier) and to keep a clear and persistent focus as they moved toward concluding their work.

Moreover, with the exception of the largest of the above foundations, such as Atlantic Philanthropies, AVI CHAI, Bronfman, and Olin, the small size of the rest of them in relation to their chosen mission and goals suggests a particular rationale for spending down in their case: the smaller the amount of financial resources available to achieve any substantial goal, the less likely it is that a foundation can achieve significant impact while preserving its capital in perpetuity. The income on its limited assets will almost certainly be insufficient to support any results-producing grantmaking over the long run. The only realistic option for such foundations is to choose a modest focus and pour their assets into achieving impact in the one area about which it cares the most.

By contrast, the larger institutions mentioned in the previous section, such as Olin, Bronfman, Atlantic Philanthropies, and AVI CHAI, would have a realistic possibility of achieving significant impact as a perpetual foundation, even if that choice would have required cutting back the amount of their annual expenditures. In their case, a limited life is not a necessity, dictated by a fear of having too little to spend. It is a strategic option, presumably chosen for reasons that go well beyond simply enlarging the annual grants budget. It may be helpful, therefore, to take a closer look at the largest two foundations to declare a limited life thus far and see what their experience can teach us.

Lessons from the Gates Foundation

The Bill and Melinda Gates Foundation is the wealthiest grantmaking foundation in history, both in endowment size and in annual grantmaking awards. Paying out at the 5 percent minimum annual spending rate prescribed by federal law, the foundation endowment, recently valued at approximately $42 billion, generates about $2 billion a year, a spending rate of $5.5 million *per day*, including weekends. In addition to those earnings on its own endowment, it receives another $1.25 billion to $2.15 billion annually in Berkshire Hathaway stock. These are payments on Warren Buffett's 2006 pledge of $32 billion, which carry the stipulation that the proceeds from the sale of such shares must be spent within a year of their receipt. As a result of these combined sources of funds, the Gates Foundation's annual required grantmaking came to about $3.9 billion in 2015—more than the total grantmaking of the dozen next wealthiest foundations in the United States combined. Between its inception in 2000 and the end of 2015, the foundation has awarded approximately $34.5 billion in grants.[21]

When the Gates Foundation was first established, it was declared to have an intended life that would terminate 50 years after the death of the survivor of Bill and Melinda Gates—he was born in 1955, and she was born in 1964. In 2012, the foundation announced that it had reduced that expectation to 20 years after the death of the second of the founders to die. It is thus not only the largest grantmaking foundation in history but also will be the largest foundation to have deliberately spent itself out of existence.

Absent serious financial market downturns, at its current spending level it is unlikely any time soon that the Gates Foundation endowment profile will begin to show decline in value caused by spending from its endowment. Therefore, the size of its spending pattern for the foreseeable future will continue to look much like that of the legacy perpetual foundations, which characteristically remain close to the 5 percent minimum payout required by federal law. Of course, if Bill and Melinda Gates wish to start spending from the foundation's endowment, there is nothing to prevent them from doing so. The fact that the foundation chooses not to spend more than the combination of what the law requires and what Warren Buffett's annual gifts stipulate is likely attributable to several facts. First, $3.9 billion is a great deal of money to spend well annually, and many critics have questioned whether any foundation could spend that much money efficiently and effectively. The jury is still out on that question, although most close observers of the US foundation scene express admiration for the Gates Foundation's gutsiness and persistence in reaching for solutions to very large and significant problems, as well as its apparent success in doing so expertly. Its one large self-described failure—the initiative to create small high schools that succeeded in outperforming larger schools—is an early exception. However, even in this case, many of the schools it created succeeded in outperforming larger schools, with promising implications for future variations on the model. But it was indeed an expensive experiment, in which the foundation invested nearly $1 billion before declaring its disappointment and ending the program.

Second, on at least one recent occasion, Bill Gates was quoted as having remarked that the foundation is having trouble identifying more objectives of high priority to it. In a *New York Times* article published on May 25, 2014, the reporter noted that Gates had slowed the pace of his contributions to the foundation's endowment, largely because its size "has tested its ability to give away money at the pace required both by law and by the fast-rising contributions of another donor, Warren E. Buffett. John Pinette, a spokesman for Mr. Gates, declined to address specific reasons for the change of pace in his giving, but he did point to the challenges of distributing large amounts of money where it can be most effective."[22]

The Gates Foundation looks like a perpetual foundation, not only in the size of its grantmaking relative to its endowment value but also in the substantive style of its grants. In the approximately 15 years since it began spending massive amounts of money annually, it has set forth goals and strategies to solve complex problems, which, if ameliorated significantly, would be large enough to constitute a quantum leap in benefiting many millions of human beings, and which promise to lend themselves to measurable, incremental change that seems likely to cumulate if steadily tackled with well-financed, focused strategies that aim toward true solutions.

The Gates Foundation has already built an impressive track record commensurate with both the magnitude of the problems it has chosen and the financial resources it has been able to deploy over a comparatively short period of time. The case study of that foundation in Appendix A includes a brief description of some of the foundation's significant achievements, from eradicating polio in most nations to combating malaria. Yet, despite having spent $3.5 billion to nearly $4 billion a year for most of the past 10 years, one can reasonably ask whether the foundation's track record in solving significant problems is commensurate with the amount of money it has spent on those problems. There is not the slightest doubt that the Gates Foundation has done a great deal of good, but remember that the rationale offered to justify spending down by foundations is the felt imperative of solving critical problems by spending a great deal of one's capital over a short period of time. The Gates Foundation's experience doesn't lend support to the realism of that rationale. On the other hand, by the standards of impact achieved by perpetual foundations, to which the Gates Foundation's grantmaking practices seem similar, the Gates Foundation appears to be among the most impactful of all of them.

In short, despite massive expenditures, a decade and a half of effort, and considerable impact along the way, the foundation's work is nowhere near completion. On balance, Gates's experience so far should serve as a caution to donors who have much less money to deploy but are nonetheless choosing to give it all away in the belief that they can solve a pressing social problem by the time their money runs out.

The bottom line is that the above accomplishments are sufficiently persuasive that the Gates Foundation can be sincerely lauded for achieving significant impact. One cannot fail to admire the determination of Bill and Melinda Gates to use their wealth to make a major difference in the world, but it seems clear that it will take many more years and many more dollars before they will have solved any of the complex problems that they have chosen as their targets.

If I am correct in that judgment, then the Gates Foundation should be viewed at this point not as a foundation that has a limited life but as very much like the foundations that are presumably perpetual. They exist to work on solving big problems over many years, step-by-step, in an iterative way that allows them to fine-tune what they are doing based on what they are learning about their progress by trial and error. A long life and deep pockets give them the opportunity to learn how to adjust when they make mistakes and otherwise stay the course until they find the silver bullet that solves the problem.

With problems as large, daunting, and intractable as those that the Gates Foundation is tackling, there simply is no other way to solve them, barring one or more divine miracles. One might conclude, therefore, that, for those wealth-holders who wish to solve a problem, they have to right-size their choice of problem to fit the assets they have in their power to deploy. Otherwise, they should accept the fact that the best they can do is to contribute to achieving a better understanding of a problem they care about, which will pave the way for others to succeed in solving it after much trial and error.

Moreover, having a long runway before the lights-out date provides an indispensable learning period for foundations that plan to give away sizable amounts of money before they close up shop. If the Gates Foundation sticks with its declared intention and schedule of spending down, the knowledge it will have gained about the strengths and weaknesses of those working around the world on its chosen problems, especially their likely capacity to deliver on their commitments, will be indispensable when the foundation begins to make its ultimate spend-down grants.

Of course, it is also possible that, after a reasonable period of time, Bill or Melinda Gates may decide to change his or her mind about the desirability of spending down. Given the ambitious and venturesome reach that characterizes their selection of problems, and given the likelihood that there will be no end to the comparable or related problems requiring solution, I would bet that there will be at least as insistent a need for the expertise and financial resources of the Gates Foundation over the indefinite future as there is today. Speaking only for myself, I hope that its founders will keep their minds open to the possibility of ultimately transforming their institution into a perpetuity.

As for those wealthy and impatient philanthropists who want to tackle comparably complex and difficult problems as fast as they can, the risk of failure and loss is exceedingly high if they have not had the advantage of educating themselves by means of a trial period of philanthropic giving that is not buffeted by the urgencies of the moment. Moreover, they must also recognize that, to solve their problems of choice, they will need significant financial reserves to be able to make use of what they have learned during their early years. The Beldon Fund's challenges in going from birth to death as a spend-down foundation in 10 years, seeking to make a difference in the complex world of environmental policy, should be a strong cautionary lesson. It found that it had to reset its objectives twice within its 10-year life in order to achieve any desired impact. (The Beldon Fund's experience is described more fully in Appendix A.)

Lessons from The Atlantic Philanthropies

With Atlantic—the largest foundation yet to give away all of its assets and come to a close, decades before the envisioned end of the Gates Foundation— the lesson is the same as from Gates. So far as I can discern, the grants that The Atlantic Philanthropies is making during the last two years of its grant-making life are thematically similar to, or at least build upon the foundation of, most of the grants it made during its earlier years. Its grants are focused on institution-building and leadership development in the program areas the foundation cares about—building capacity in human rights, in biomedical knowledge, and the like. Grants during the period of active spending down of its assets are much larger than had been typical in prior years, but even these greater amounts could have been distributed year by year while the foundation continued to exist, learn, and adjust course as needed. It is hard to discern anything about these final grants that benefited from the disappearance of their source of funds.

If that is true, then what is the great advantage gained for society by spending all of one's assets over one's lifetime? If Atlantic Philanthropies, in its concluding years, is doing more or less what it was doing during its earlier 20 years—or in any case, continuing the values and aspirations that motivated all those years of work—and by all accounts doing it well, why should it assume that spending its entire endowment and going out of business can create greater social benefit than continuing its grantmaking indefinitely?

THE TRADE-OFFS SPEND-DOWN DONORS SOMETIMES MAKE

If donors are determined, like Atlantic's Chuck Feeney, to spend all of their philanthropic dollars during their lifetimes, that may lead them or their successor trustees to feel obliged to make a substantially counterproductive decision—a decision to spend down—that actually prevents or hinders their foundations from achieving their philanthropic intentions. Let me reiterate that I would not question founding donors' or their successor trustees' decision about whether or not to spend-down in principle. I believe that such donors' and trustees' choices about whether or not to spend down should be respected in virtually all cases, depending on their motivation for spending down. The one exception on which I do feel free to criticize their choice to spend down is when two conditions are met: their decision to spend down is motivated by their fear that the successor trustees whom they select cannot be trusted to be faithful to the founder's vision and values, and the founder's and/or trustees' mission for the foundation seems unlikely, after their foundation sunsets, to attract the support of other foundations or philanthropists necessary to continue serving the mission for which their founder created the foundation. I characterize such a combination of factors as one in which the founder and his or her present trustees permit the *fear* that successor trustees will be unfaithful to the founder's mission for the foundation to trump the *likely need* for the foundation's time-unlimited existence in order to be alive to continue to further the donor's chosen mission of the foundation in the probable absence of other sources of financial support for it. Among the spend-down foundations discussed in Appendix A, such a counterproductive decision seems to me to characterize one in particular—the AVI CHAI Foundation.

Zalman Bernstein's strong commitments to Judaism, Jewish literacy, traditional Jewish observance, and the continuity of the Jewish people motivated his decision to create the AVI CHAI Foundation. Once established, it became one of the tiny handful of national foundations in the United States that support the vital national infrastructure of Jewish day school education and one of the larger handful of national foundations that support Jewish overnight camping. The reason that Bernstein, the program staff, and the trustees chose those objectives is that attendance at Jewish day schools and participation in overnight summer camps were found to be the most important predictors of continued meaningful affiliation over time with the Jewish religion and involvement with Jewish institutions.

With perhaps one exception, no other foundation at the time of this writing is so significantly supporting, at the national level, efforts to strengthen the infrastructure of Jewish day schools in North America, and at this point no other foundations are on the horizon to do so. AVI CHAI has devoted much time and energy over almost a decade in specific efforts to recruit other foundations and philanthropists to join it in supporting some of the Jewish day school infrastructure organizations that it has been supporting, with only a few successes to show for the effort. When AVI CHAI ends its grantmaking after December 31, 2019, it seems unlikely, therefore, that there will be any other significant sources to which day schools can turn to fill the gap left by this foundation's demise as a grantmaker.

Of course, that conclusion is a conjecture that may yet prove to be incorrect, just as is the fear that successor trustees may be unfaithful to the vision and mission that Zalman Bernstein bred into AVI CHAI. However, the present absence of like-minded prospective donors open to supporting national infrastructure for Jewish day schools is a fact, not a conjecture, and perhaps, in weighing *fear* against *likely need*, is therefore worthy of being given greater weight than the conjecture that successor trustees will be unfaithful stewards of Zalman Bernstein's philanthropic legacy.

The funding environment for overnight Jewish camping, on the other hand, is much different. More than a few philanthropies have been attracted to that program area, primarily because overnight Jewish camps are seen as a less expensive means of reaching Jewish youngsters than are the day schools. Indeed, AVI CHAI has found several large national funding partners with whom it has worked closely for the past decade or more and that are likely to continue to provide support for overnight camping after AVI CHAI sunsets. The quality of overnight Jewish camping and the camper participation numbers have grown steadily over the past decade.

By contrast, virtually all North American Jewish day schools are struggling financially, and some of them are being forced to close for financial reasons. Because the commitment to send children to day schools differs among the various denominations of Judaism, so far the closures have been primarily among schools serving children from Conservative and Reform backgrounds, whose families tend to regard a day school education as optional, and schools in shrinking Jewish communities. Among most Orthodox families, Jewish education continues to be virtually mandatory, and those parents will do what it takes to dedicate the funds necessary to cover tuition.

Virtually all of the philanthropic support for individual day schools is provided by generous individuals, foundations, and Jewish federations within the local communities served by particular day schools, but despite strenuous efforts by AVI CHAI to persuade some of them to help shoulder the burden of the national infrastructure that trains teachers and administrators and develops curriculum for such local schools, very little support has proved to be forthcoming. The result is that AVI CHAI has been forced to provide the lion's share of support for the national day school infrastructure organizations, and the likely consequence of AVI CHAI's spend-down is that North American Jewish day schools will suffer the loss of at least some of the benefits now provided by that infrastructure.

Is that the outcome that Zalman Bernstein would have been comfortable in bringing about? I have no doubt that some, if not all, of the AVI CHAI trustees would insist that Mr. Bernstein would not only be comfortable with that outcome but indeed would regard it as far preferable to even the remote possibility that was his greatest fear—that his philanthropy would be corrupted by the decisions of unfaithful successor trustees and administrators.

As will be clear from what I have written in this book, I respectfully disagree.

As many founders of perpetual foundations have succeeded in proving, foundation founders can, with foresight, meticulous care, and good legal advice, protect the future integrity and fidelity of their vision and mission even after they have passed away. In Chapters 8 and 9, I have listed a large number of such foundations, and the evidence they provide is that wise foundation founders who are troubled by fears about the future alignment of their foundations with their own values and vision need not, for that reason alone, feel forced to opt for the spend-down route simply because of such uncertainty about future trustee fidelity.

In discussions about this point with some of the AVI CHAI Foundation leaders, they have insisted that the likely effects of AVI CHAI's closure on its field of focus are little different from the likely effects of the end of grant-making by other life-limited foundations such as the Bill and Melinda Gates Foundation or the Marcus Foundation of Atlanta. In such discussions, they acknowledge that the causes and grantees that they have been supporting will suffer the loss of funding, but that other philanthropies will come along to cushion the loss and perhaps fill the gap.

Of course that is entirely possible, and, indeed with respect to both the Gates Foundation and the Marcus Foundation, that outcome is in fact probable because many other foundations and individual philanthropists in the United States and abroad are even now backing many of the same kinds of initiatives that those two foundations have been supporting. As I have noted above, however, that fact is starkly different from AVI CHAI's position relative to the field of national infrastructure of North American Jewish day school education. While AVI CHAI is not entirely alone in that field, it is virtually alone!

Let me underscore how greatly I admire Zalman Bernstein's devotion to his heritage and his determination to do all within his means to help perpetuate it. The leadership of AVI CHAI—Arthur Fried, Mem Bernstein, and their fellow trustees, as well as the highly talented program officers and program executive directors for North America, Israel, and the Former Soviet Union—continue to do all within their power to strengthen the future of the Jewish people in their respective locations. The trustees have been determined to be faithful to Zalman Bernstein's vision for the Jewish people and have done all things possible to increase the likelihood that the foundation's grantees will be able to continue their good work after AVI CHAI closes down.

I congratulate them for exerting themselves mightily to that end but remain convinced that, given the particular mission for which Bernstein created the AVI CHAI Foundation, a wiser course of action would have been to encourage his trustees to allow AVI CHAI to continue its grantmaking for as long as possible. In following its founder's apparent preferences, the foundation is in essence short-circuiting its ability to achieve its mission, primarily because of his and their fears about the likely fidelity of their successors.

LIMITED LIFETIME OR MISSION: WHICH COMES FIRST?

The AVI CHAI Foundation is a clear example of a founder's trustees "choosing lifetime first," but it is not alone in this regard. Consider The Atlantic Philanthropies, which is another, much larger example of the same scenario. A strong argument can be made that, despite the quite different missions to which each has been dedicated—religion and cultural heritage in one case, advanced research and social change in the other—both of them, in my estimation, could likely achieve greater results in their fields by not spending down and continuing their grantmaking as they had been doing theretofore.

The Whitaker Foundation, created from the fortune of Uncas A. Whitaker, founder of AMP Incorporated, is a good example of "choosing mission first" and tailoring its life so as to achieve significant results by spending down. Journalist Deanne Stone, an astute observer of family philanthropy, ably describes its story:

> The Foundation was a pioneer in funding biomedical engineering. After years of slow growth, the field was finally poised to take off. Technological advances in the 1980s had created new opportunities, but few universities had departments of biomedical engineering. In 1991, the Whitaker Foundation board set aside time to rethink its grantmaking strategy. At the time, the Whitaker Foundation was adhering to the legal minimum of a 5 percent payout. It determined that funding just one new biomedical engineering department would have cost several million dollars and would have consumed much of the foundation's entire annual grants budget at the time. Doubling the annual payout to 10 percent wouldn't have provided enough money to make a significant difference in the biomedical engineering field. If the field were to develop, the Whitaker board decided, several departments would have to be created simultaneously. After a year of discussion and consultations with top researchers, the board concurred that the foundation could make a bigger impact on its chosen field by spending out than by continuing in perpetuity. It worked out a plan to distribute the foundation's entire assets—at the time $350 million, and later to grow to $450 million—in 14 years.[23]

The lesson of the Whitaker Foundation's sunset is that sometimes a short, intensive burst of large-scale grantmaking—of a size that requires a foundation to spend out everything it has—does make sense as the best route to achieving a particular mission. In this case, three conditions were essential for reaching that conclusion: The foundation determined, first, that it needed to fund a great deal of activity at once—in this case, the simultaneous creation of several centers of research and development—or else the changes it was seeking would be unlikely to take root. Second, the foundation's consultations in the field led it to believe, with reasonable confidence, that such a "Big Bang" would in fact set the desired ripples of new activity in motion. And finally, the price tag for this great, catalytic first step was both small enough to fit within the foundation's means and large enough to demand *all* of those means in a fixed period of time. With those factors firmly established, the decision to spend everything on a large, present-tense goal made sense for the foundation *because of its mission*—and doing otherwise would not have set as clear a course to the foundation's goal line. That is not a common set of circumstances, but when the stars align in just this way, the best decision may well be to spend down. A similar bet was made by the Franklin Olin Foundation in deciding, after years of supporting engineering programs across dozens of colleges and universities, to dedicate the foundation's entire corpus to building a new engineering college, focused on an innovative engineering curriculum. In investment terms, the trade-off of diversification for one big "swing for the fences" represents the zenith of "high risk, high reward."

chapter eight

Stories of Impact—Time-Limited and Perpetual

Based on what you have already read in this book, you can safely conclude that, while I admire the quest of wealthy individuals to put their money to work in trying to solve pressing social problems during their lifetimes, I have great concern about the likelihood that spending even the vast wealth they promise to deploy over a comparatively short period of time can achieve their ambition for impact on the scale to which they aspire. Nothing that I have written in this book, however, should be interpreted as intended to discourage individuals from spending great amounts of money in their lifetimes on a problem they wish to address, as long as the amount of resources available is aligned with the scale of the problem to be solved and a reasonable time frame within which to solve it. To the contrary, the phenomenon of individual philanthropists' success is an important strand in the remarkable history of American philanthropy, beginning with Andrew Carnegie and continuing to the present day. Their choices about when to give in the present and what to put aside for giving in the future quite properly arise from their experience, their judgment, and their passions for particular kinds of public benefit. Fortunately, the world of philanthropy is rich with examples of significant achievement flowing from both kinds of decisions. This chapter will give examples of these, first from donors committed to completing their giving during their lifetimes and then from perpetual ones.

"GIVING WHILE LIVING" PHILANTHROPISTS

Samuel J. Heyman, The Partnership for Public Service, Washington, D.C.

The Partnership for Public Service, founded in 2001, is the only nonprofit organization in the United States that is exclusively focused on trying to enable America's national government to recruit and retain talented individuals. In 1963, after attending Harvard Law School, Samuel J. Heyman went to work for Attorney General Robert Kennedy in the US Department of Justice. He then began to watch, with growing dismay, the steadily declining percentage of law school and college graduates who were choosing to work for the federal government. While, according to his recollections, almost half of his Harvard Law class went into government service, by the mid-1990s the percentage had dropped to below 5 percent. He resolved to try to do something about this decline.

After taking over his family's real estate business in Connecticut upon the death of his father and gradually creating a great deal of wealth, he initiated the Heyman Fellowship Program at Harvard Law School. Subsequently, he did the same at Yale Law School, Columbia Law School, and Seton Hall Law School for students who would agree to work for the federal government after finishing their legal education. As the number of Heyman Fellows working in Washington increased, he and his wife Ronnie organized annual gatherings of those alumni in the nation's capital, also attended by important government officials. In the late 1990s, Heyman decided to reach out more widely in order to counter the negative perception of government among college and law school students that, according to many opinion surveys, was clearly discouraging them from considering federal employment. He organized conferences in Boston, New York, and Washington to seek advice from experts on government employment, recruitment, and retention, which eventually led him to create a nonpartisan, nonprofit organization called The Partnership for Public Service. He recruited Max Stier, a Stanford Law School graduate, former clerk to Supreme Court Justice David Souter, and former deputy general counsel of the US Department of Housing and Urban Development, as CEO. Heyman then constituted a board of trustees, of which he served as chairman, and agreed to donate $45 million over 10 years as seed money to prime the work of the partnership. Stier has succeeded in growing the partnership to the point that 80 percent of its budget—$17 million in fiscal year 2017—is now provided by fees for services rendered, mainly for training of government officials, and by foundations and corporations committed to enabling the federal government to recruit and retain talented young people devoted to the ideal of public service.

Over its first 15 years, which spanned both Republican and Democratic administrations, the Partnership for Public Service has become the most respected, successful, and influential champion of effective government. Alas, Mr. Heyman died in 2009, but, before his death, he had the satisfaction of seeing how well his vision was being implemented. The organization's signature accomplishments include the following:

- Creating the Best Places to Work in the Federal Government® rankings—the most comprehensive examination of federal employee satisfaction and commitment. The rankings, based on detailed surveys of several hundred thousand federal government employees, provide government with the means to assess and rectify barriers to its own health and performance. Now agency heads and higher-ups in the executive branch and Congress have reliable, external quantitative performance data. It is not surprising that, after the first Best Places report was released, Congress mandated that the survey be repeated every year.

- Informing changes to laws, policies, and procedures by which our federal agencies must operate. The Partnership's advocacy efforts have resulted in the enactment of more than 30 pieces of legislation that remove barriers to effective federal management and improve outdated government systems and regulations.

- Engaging annually more than 5,000 career and politically appointed leaders with high-quality, high-impact training and other services. Improving the leadership capability of these individuals has a multiplying effect across the two-million-person federal workforce. As their numbers increase and their networks expand, the examples of their dedication to improving the functioning of the federal government cumulates.

- Building the "Call to Serve" network of more than 1,000 colleges and universities and 80 federal agencies that work together to inspire and educate a new generation about public service careers and advance the federal government's ability to recruit mission-critical talent.

Michael Steinhardt, Taglit Birthright Israel, New York, New York

Taglit Birthright Israel is the largest organizer and funder of experiential and educational tours to Israel, which are available without cost to young Jewish men and women from all over the world.[1] Similar to the understanding Samuel Heyman had that there was a need for an organization to encourage young people to pursue careers in public service, Michael Steinhardt, together with Charles Bronfman, had the vision to see how a new initiative might slow down or even reverse young Jewish people's drift away from the religion and culture into which they had been born. Reliable social science research suggested that three discrete experiences make a substantial difference in strengthening young people's Jewish identity: Jewish day school attendance, participation in Jewish overnight summer camps, and a period of time spent in Israel. The last of those three seemed to require the least amount of time for its influence to stick, so Steinhardt and Bronfman chose to focus their efforts on creating a program that would bring young people to Israel.

The two men led the way in priming the effort with their own funds, then persuaded many other Jewish philanthropists and foundations to participate, and ultimately convinced many Jewish federations in the United States and Jewish communities in other countries, as well as the State of Israel and the leaders of the Jewish Agency for Israel, to support what is called Birthright Israel. That organization began offering prepaid, well-organized 10-day tours for any Jewish high school graduate between the ages of 18 and 26 who has not already had an educational experience in Israel. The trips began in the winter of 1999, and since then more than 500,000 young people from 64 countries have participated, 80 percent of whom are from the United States and Canada. Approximately 40,000 people a year participate in Birthright trips, for which there is a much larger demand than can be satisfied because of the limited availability of funding.

Systematic research, conducted by independent scholars at Brandeis University, demonstrates that the impact of Birthright Israel is life changing. Participants, compared with similar non-participants, are significantly more likely to marry Jewish spouses, raise Jewish children, and be involved in the Jewish community.[2]

Bernard Marcus, The Marcus Foundation, Atlanta, Georgia

We encountered Bernie Marcus, cofounder of The Home Depot, earlier in this book, in Chapter 6, in which he explained his reluctance to turn his philanthropy over to a future generation of trustees. His preference for using his charitable assets during his lifetime has led to a number of impressive achievements. In the 1990s, Marcus created the Marcus Autism Center at Emory University to study the causes of and possible cures for autism and to provide clinical services to young people who had been diagnosed with this disease. He continues to support that center and also provides autism research support to other universities, including Duke University. After 10 years of involvement in the field, he concluded that a public advocacy organization was needed to create greater awareness of the disease and to spotlight the lack of adequate public and private funds required to conquer autism eventually. Marcus persuaded Robert Wright, then the CEO of NBC, along with his late wife Suzanne, to take on the leadership of Autism Speaks, which Marcus launched with a $25 million grant in 2005. In the years since its founding, Autism Speaks has become the dominant autism advocacy organization in the United States. Marcus continues to serve as a member of its board of directors.

PERPETUAL FOUNDATIONS

In addition to the achievements of these three philanthropists, two of whom are still actively "giving while living" as this book is written, we have also touched on the accomplishments of many spend-down foundations of the past, including the creation of 5,000 schoolhouses catalyzed by the Julius Rosenwald Fund, the pioneering AIDS cocktail that came about with funding from the Aaron Diamond Foundation, and the John M. Olin Foundation's creation of an influential conservative public policy intellectual infrastructure. Perhaps there are others of comparable importance but, as of now, additional examples are hard to come by.

Equally significant results have been achieved, and much more frequently, by perpetual foundations. This should make prospective limited-life foundation founders think twice about making the spend-down choice. What's more, perpetual foundations that have achieved such outcomes have been remarkably successful in doing so while undertaking acceptable levels of risk.

By balancing more-risky with less-risky initiatives, they have demonstrated a remarkable ability to achieve significant impact while maintaining the purchasing power of their capital and without suffering significant financial loss. Almost 100 cases detailing such perpetual foundation achievements are included in *Casebook for The Foundation*.[3] Here is just a small but representative sampling of them: The Rockefeller Foundation's efforts to produce a vaccine that prevents yellow fever, which earned Max Theiler, the foundation's scientist, a Nobel Prize in Physiology or Medicine in 1951; the Robert Wood Johnson Foundation's state-by-state initiatives to encourage clean-indoor-air laws and increase taxes on cigarettes, which significantly reduced teenage smoking; the Doerr Foundation's pioneering collaboration with the New York and Connecticut Highway Departments to experiment with the creation of white lines on the borders of highways, which has reduced traffic accidents, saved many lives, and become the model for such highway lines nationally; George Soros's Open Society Foundations' funding of civil society organizations in Communist Eastern and Central Europe, which substantially contributed to the collapse of Communism there; and the Carnegie Corporation's establishment of the National Board for Professional Teacher Certification, which created, for the first time, a national market credentialing public school teachers so that they could easily move to jobs in most other states.

In addition to the work of large foundations like these, numerous midsized and small perpetual foundations, many of them family foundations—and all of them focused primarily on a narrow geographical catchment area—are playing indispensable roles in their communities. The next chapter will look more closely at the ability of many family foundations to carry on generation after generation, maintaining both fidelity to their founders' wishes and the philanthropic engagement of each new generation of family members. In today's often heated ideological discussions about the social utility and/or fidelity to donor intent of perpetual foundations, the consistent performance of foundations such as these is almost always overlooked. Most of them are critical to solving or mitigating the problems that face their communities, and they often operate in close partnerships with community foundations.

It is also worth noting here that the decision to spend down a foundation is not necessarily irrevocable, and a few donors have found good reason to reconsider. For example, George Soros originally intended, and indeed announced, that his Open Society Foundations would be spent down in his lifetime but in 2011 made known that he had changed his mind. Following is what he wrote by way of explanation:

> When I established the Open Society Foundations, I did not want them to survive me. The fate of other institutions has taught me that they tend to stray very far from the founder's intentions. But as the Open Society Foundations took on a more substantial form, I changed my mind. I came to realize that terminating the foundations' network at the time of my death would be an act of excessive selfishness, the equivalent of an Indian maharajah's wives being burned on his funeral pyre. A number of very capable people are devoting their lives to the work of the Open Society Foundations; I have no right to pull the rug from under them. More importantly, we have identified a sphere of activity that needs to be carried on beyond my lifetime, and whose execution does not really require either Aryeh [Neier]'s presence [former president of Soros's foundations] or mine. That niche consists in empowering civil society to hold government accountable.[4]

In my interview with Christopher Stone, Aryeh Neier's successor as president and CEO of the Open Society Foundations, he elaborated on the plan for Soros's continuing philanthropy:

> We're thinking of it now as an "indefinite foundation." That is to say, it doesn't have a spend-down plan. Its regular spending will be at a level that, given reasonable, prudent rates of return on the endowment, would allow it to go on indefinitely. But [Soros] is eager to have a budgeting process that allows us to respond with outsized spending when opportunities present themselves. He is not expecting the foundation to go. It's not like Gates, where the Foundation has announced its plan to spend down twenty years after the death of the survivor of Bill and Melinda Gates. There's nothing like that, but there is a desire . . . simply to allow it to continue for as long as that's reasonable, given the opportunities presented by the circumstances.[5]

Meanwhile, other perpetual foundations are continually being created, including the Margaret A. Cargill Philanthropies. Cargill was one of the eight heirs to the Cargill grain corporation. When she died in 2006, she bequeathed the overwhelming bulk of her assets to a group of foundations she had earlier established. When her estate was settled in 2011, the value of the assets of the Margaret A. Cargill Philanthropies was estimated to be about $9 billion, placing her foundation among the wealthiest US foundations after Gates and Ford.[6] Her instructions made clear that it was to be a presumably perpetual foundation, with a broad mandate to "address unmet needs; give individuals and communities the tools to become self-sufficient; [fund work] that will be sustainable after our support ends; and . . . build on and strengthen strong relationships within communities."[7]

chapter nine

The Unique Role of Family Foundations

The rewards on a family investment in philanthropy are—or can be—extremely high. . . . Family members report an excitement and fulfillment going far beyond what they had known simply being blooded (often bloodied) members of a tribe. . . . There is something distinctive and precious about family foundations that suggests they should remain as they are: a unique opportunity for families to make and leave their mark on the society around them, to share with others the fortune they have enjoyed and the creative energies they so often possess.

—the late Paul Ylvisaker, former Program Officer in Charge of the Social Development Program, the Ford Foundation[1]

Among the most effective and successful foundations over generations are family foundations. Where the genes and values of founding individuals or families are strong enough, families not only can endure but can blossom in pursuing a kind of philanthropy that adapts well to changing times while preserving the essential focus of their founders. Many family foundations, large and small, operating nationally as well as locally, have distinguished themselves over the course of three to six or more generations by their achievements for the public good as well as by their adherence to the values of the matriarchs and patriarchs who founded them. These institutions offer a strong rebuttal to the belief that family foundations eventually suffer from the passage of time, the growing size and diversity of new generations, and the increasing distance from the spirit of the founders. On the contrary— here are just a few examples.

THE SURDNA FOUNDATION

The Surdna Foundation will be 100 years old in 2017, and its professionalism has earned it a seat alongside some of the largest private foundations in the nation. It describes itself as a "national family foundation,"[2] and over its history it has developed a systematic plan whereby descendants of its founder, John Andrus, elect both family and nonfamily members in roughly equal numbers (12 in total) to serve as trustees. Within the past decade, the foundation's endowment reached about $1 billion in value. As of the end of 2014, its annual grantmaking was about $47 million.

THE WILLIAM AND FLORA HEWLETT FOUNDATION

William and Flora Hewlett established the private foundation named for them in 1966, and that foundation is now among the 25 wealthiest private foundations in the United States. In 1998, following the death of Flora Hewlett, William Hewlett along with other members of his family created the Flora Family Foundation as a memorial to his wife, in which successive generations of their family could participate in significant philanthropic initiatives. The Flora Family Foundation has a two-tier structure, consisting of the Family Council, of which the five children and 12 grandchildren of William and Flora are members, as well as the spouses of those offspring, and a board of directors made up of some of the Hewletts' children and grandchildren, usually six or seven of them, plus two nonfamily members, each serving one- or two-year terms.[3] Since the Flora Family Foundation was established, family members chosen to be directors of the William and Flora Hewlett Foundation have come from among those family members who have had the prior experience of serving as directors of the Flora Family Foundation. The bylaws of the William and Flora Hewlett Foundation require that, at any given time, four members of the Hewlett family be serving as directors of the William and Flora Hewlett Foundation.[4] These arrangements for involving successive generations are widely regarded as among the most effective ways of achieving intergenerational family participation. They permit Hewlett family members to acquire experience and demonstrate their abilities in a small pond and thereby create a track record on the basis of which other family members can make a reliable judgment as to who should be elevated to the board of the William and Flora Hewlett Foundation.

THE DAVID AND LUCILE PACKARD FOUNDATION

The David and Lucile Packard Foundation is another of America's largest family foundations that has remained faithful to the values and program commitments that its founders cherished, while at the same time adapting those commitments to changing times. The three daughters of the founders—Julie, Nancy, and Susan—as well as their respective spouses and their children, play an influential role in foundation decisions on the 15-person board of trustees, aided by distinguished outsiders. Packard is one of America's leading donors to the effort to diminish global warming and its consequences, having committed in 2008, along with the Hewlett Foundation, $500 million each over seven years to establish and support ClimateWorks, the philanthropic collaborative dedicated to battling climate change. In addition, in 2015, the Packard Foundation made a new commitment of $350 million over seven years. Packard is also a leading national foundation in early childhood education, marine biology, and other fields in which the founders pioneered.

THE ROCKEFELLER BROTHERS FUND

The Rockefeller Brothers Fund, created in 1940 by the five sons of John D. Rockefeller Jr., and joined in 1954 by their sister Abby Rockefeller Mauze, has distinguished itself not only by its consistent devotion to the forward-looking values and interests of its founders but also by its example of how well a large and ever-growing family can consistently manage to overcome differences among its members in order to achieve consistent congenial collaboration in philanthropy at its most impressive.

THE ANNENBERG FOUNDATION

The Annenberg Foundation was established by Ambassador Walter H. Annenberg in 1989, and he presided over it until his death in 2002, at which point his widow, Leonore (Lee) Annenberg, succeeded him. When she passed away seven years later, her daughter, Wallis Annenberg, became the chairman, president, and CEO, and three of her children—Lauren Bon, Charles Annenberg Weingarten, and Gregory Annenberg Weingarten—became vice presidents and directors. The foundation is director driven; each of the four directors leads a program of his or her own, though all of the directors make the final funding decisions together, assisted by a small program staff. As the Annenberg Foundation has been in existence through only three generations so far, it is not possible to know how its governance might evolve in the future.

THE SALL FAMILY FOUNDATION

Every family that has a family foundation struggles with how best to involve their progeny in their philanthropy, and there is no one right way to do so. It depends on the values that the parents have transmitted to their children, how well the offspring get along with one another, and the extent to which they are interested in the substantive kinds of philanthropic objectives on which the founders have chosen to focus. The Hewlett family's way makes a great deal of sense if one has a sufficiently large pool of philanthropic dollars and a large number of children and grandchildren, but other less highly structured arrangements can work well too. The Sall Family Foundation, which was created in 1993 by John and Ginger Sall—subscribers to the Buffett–Gates Giving Pledge—uses a less formal structure. John and Ginger Sall have elected their five children, the children's spouses, and several of their children's peers and friends to a young persons' committee of the Board of the Sall Family Foundation. Their plan is to add their grandchildren to the board when they reach 18 years of age. (They have only one grandchild at present, and he has 18 years to go before becoming eligible, as of the writing of this book.) They have now established a $1 million annual budget, which their children use for grantmaking without the need for their parents' approval. Ginger Sall expresses their reasons for doing so:

> One is to have some of their peers on the board. [Our children] don't want to be slackers or uninterested when their peers are on the board. Among those in their late 20s, early 30s, there are plenty of promising, enthusiastic people who would love to have access to some capital to do good in the world or to work and serve . . . as an experience builder for themselves. Maybe they're all future board members of the Ford Foundation or something like that. The other incentive . . . is . . . to have [our children] . . . learn by doing. . . .

That came about, at the first foundation meeting with our expanded board. We sat down in our dining room, looked around the table at our kids and their very smart, energetic, enthusiastic peers . . . [and] . . . I thought, "Oh, my goodness, we've got to give these people something meaningful to do. They just don't want to read reports and proposals from our large, complex grantee or would-be grantee organizations. They want to get their hands into this and talk to people and network." Some of them were quite accomplished networkers at that time already. It would have been a shame not to use those networks. We realized that they were interested in small start-ups—what we call sports-car, hot-rod organizations— the kind where you can figure out what they do when you read their annual report. . . . I have to say, the committee that volunteered for this work really surprised us. They didn't just go out and find organizations they liked. They studied the field. They talked to people for whom it was their professional job to invest in these sorts of organizations. They used their networks and asked around. They understood the fund, gained some understanding of the funding life cycles of these organizations and decided what part of the life cycle they thought we should invest in. . . . They figured out, relative to the budget of the organization, what the right percent would be for our grant and that these were going to be unrestricted grants. . . . The first year, we allocated a total of $300,000 for this committee to grant. The second year, it was $500,000 and in our third year, we're at $700,000. . . . And they're enjoying [the process].[5]

* * *

In all of my interviews for this book, I questioned perpetual foundation presidents about whether their boards had ever discussed the possibility of spending down. Many of them responded that their boards had talked about the possibility but concluded that they would do so only if they could identify an initiative of the highest priority to their mission and donor intent in which there was great likelihood of success in achieving the desired impact. The views they expressed were not different in substance from those quoted above from George Soros and Chris Stone.

In other interviews, the foundation leaders were emphatic in their intention to exist in perpetuity. Most of those were heads of family foundations, and their views seemed implicitly premised on the continuing commitment of their progeny to the mission of the respective foundations. For example, Lester

Crown, the chairman of Crown Family Philanthropies in Chicago, a second-generation leader, strongly asserted, "We are not spending down; instead we are spending *up*. As far as we're concerned, the continuation and building up of the charity funds is part and parcel of keeping the family together."[6]

Lynn Schusterman, founder and cochair of the Charles and Lynn Schusterman Family Foundation, another subscriber to the Buffett–Gates Pledge, expressed a similar view. She referred to a Talmudic tale called "Honi and the Carob Tree," which goes as follows:

> One day, Honi the Circle Maker was walking on the road and saw a man planting a carob tree. Honi asked the man, "How long will it take for this tree to bear fruit?"
>
> The man replied, "Seventy years."
>
> Honi then asked the man, "And do you think you will live another seventy years and eat the fruit of this tree?"
>
> The man answered, "Perhaps not. However, when I was born into this world, I found many carob trees planted by my father and grandfather. Just as they planted trees for me, I am planting trees for my children and grandchildren so they will be able to eat the fruit of these trees."

Ms. Schusterman then noted that a carob tree adorned by a quotation from that tale is the logo of the Charles and Lynn Schusterman Foundation, and continued:

> One of the things I love most about the Honi story is the way it exemplifies how so many Jewish teachings have become universal values. As a proud Jew, I believe we all benefit from the lives of those who came before us, and each of us has a responsibility to try to make tomorrow brighter for future generations. And while I don't know what may lie ahead, I am committed to doing whatever I can to provide those who share my belief in the fundamental goodness of people the opportunity to repair the world and make it a better place.
>
> I started the foundation with my late husband, Charlie. He was a wildcatter and was not afraid to take risks. Although he knew he would sometimes drill a dry hole, he never let the fear of failure stop him from pushing ahead. I want to give people the same kind of confidence so they, too, can take the chances necessary to succeed in their efforts to make positive change.

I believe the future is full of promise for everyone, and I am committed to making it possible for those who will be around long after I am gone to help the Jewish people and all humanity achieve their full potential.[7]

What more is there to say?

The Rothschild Foundation

The Rothschild Foundation is based in London, where Jacob Rothschild has long lived, and it is now in its eighth generation as a family foundation. Its focus is primarily on the State of Israel, where it operates under the Hebrew name "Yad Hanadiv," which means "hand of the willing giver." For many years, the Rothschild Foundation has been among the largest, perhaps *the* largest, philanthropic foundation first in Palestine and now in Israel. According to Lord Rothschild, on several occasions his relatives have thought seriously about spending the foundation down, but his relative by marriage, Mrs. James Rothschild, who led the foundation prior to him, said, "Well, that would be a pity. We have a long history in Israel, and I'd like to go on." "So," Lord Rothschild added, "she devoted quite a bit of her resources toward doing just that."[8]

Lord Rothschild feels precisely the same way.[9] He told me, in his characteristically understated way:

For us, because it's sort of important to Israel, the foundation, sentimentally, and historically, because the Rothschild family were there from the very beginnings, because we've done some notable things in terms of the institutions of Israel, like building the Knesset, building the Supreme Court, building the Israel National Library. So, if I look ahead [I would] say, after my lifetime [it should continue because] I've got a daughter, Hannah, who is very interested in the Foundation and is a trustee, and would want to carry on this work even though she's not religious.

But what I've done is . . . [to create] a balance of power between the family and the other trustees, who are a distinguished group of people [and who are strongly committed to working in Israel]. We have a powerful executive, so even if my family weren't taking an interest, it would go on. They are, however, involved, and I'm confident that they will want to remain involved. In addition to me, there are two family members who are Trustees of Hanadiv. . . . Is it tempting to do a spend-down foundation, or do the historical arguments dictate that this thing should go on, because, as I say, we are inextricably involved with the history of Israel. My feeling is that we shouldn't have a spend-down foundation. . . . Even if there isn't a member of my family who wants to get involved, I think it should go on, and I hope there always will be one who will pop up, do you see?[10]

He then added: "In an ideal world, we should have a Rothschild as a chairman, but you don't have to have one if there isn't a suitable one. So, there is a sort of balance of power between the non-Rothschilds and the Rothschilds."[11]

The Jack, Joseph and Morton Mandel Foundation

Morton Mandel and his two brothers founded the Premier Industrial Corporation, which in 1996 merged with Farnell Electronics PLC, a British company, at which time Morton Mandel became vice chairman of Premier Farnell, the merged company. He served in that role until 2002. Morton Mandel has long headed the three brothers' foundation. In my conversations with him, he vigorously argued against spending down, insisting that there would always be worthwhile initiatives to undertake in the primary areas of the Mandel Foundation's priorities—mainly Jewish education, nonprofit leadership, the humanities, and social service in the United States and Israel—and that he continues to have confidence in the faithfulness of his philanthropic successors in deploying the foundation's resources in consonance with his family's intentions. He has a board of trustees whom he trusts, and he has named Jehuda Reinharz, formerly president of Brandeis University, as president of the foundation and his designated successor as chair.

THE IMPORTANCE OF NONFAMILY BOARD MEMBERS

All happy families are alike; each unhappy family is unhappy in its own way.
   —Leo Tolstoy, *Anna Karenina*

The first half of Tolstoy's aphorism may be correct in general. When it comes to family philanthropies, however, the fact that a family is otherwise happy does not automatically mean it will function happily and congenially as a family foundation board. Even otherwise compatible family foundation trustees may hold different opinions regarding the programs their foundation should fund, and sibling rivalry is hardly unknown in these boardrooms. Still, a generally happy family brings trust, respect, and, yes, love to the table, which makes the resolution of differences much easier. Countless parents have told me that the early and continuing involvement of their children in their families' philanthropic decision-making has created strong bonds between parent and child and among the children themselves.

On the other hand, many parents seek to solve their intrafamily disagreements by engaging their progeny in philanthropic grantmaking decisions; not only does this rarely succeed, but it often adds to the areas in which family members can vehemently disagree. Family foundation participation is definitely not a cure-all for family pathology.

It is also true that leavening family foundation boards with a limited number of carefully chosen nonfamily members can be of enormous help to either close or contentious families engaging in philanthropic giving. Not only can outsiders mediate family disagreements and bring independent perspectives to bear, but they can also enable close families to be even more collaboratively productive. As Ginger Sall observed, "Having non-family members on a family foundation board is a very useful way of motivating all family members to behave properly and to work hard."[12]

Similarly, placing a founder's business associates on the board can help maintain the foundation's vitality and fidelity to the founder's intent over time. The history and track record of both the Robert Wood Johnson Foundation (RWJF) and the Alfred P. Sloan Foundation testify to the effectiveness of that practice.

When General Johnson established his foundation in 1972, he stipulated that virtually all of the trustees would come from among the senior officials of Johnson & Johnson, the corporation that he founded and led. His view was that the foundation board members would be a combination of "church and state," with those with business expertise as "the state" and those well versed in health care constituting the program staff, "the church." The trustees chose as the first president of the foundation David Rogers, who had been appointed dean of Johns Hopkins University Medical School in 1968 at the tender age of 42. Dr. Rogers recruited a staff of young stars in the world of health and health care, virtually all of whom made names for themselves as well as for the foundation under Rogers's leadership. The often tension-filled collaboration between church and state produced a foundation that not only adhered to the values and intent of General Johnson in supporting important initiatives but that set perhaps the highest standards of accountability and transparency for large American foundations. Even with more foundations today following in its transparency and accountability footsteps, RWJF continues to set the pace qualitatively and also publishes an annual compilation of evidence-based reports on its programmatic initiatives. Its 17-person board has nine current members with careers in business, five of whom are former senior officers of Johnson & Johnson.

The history of the Alfred P. Sloan Foundation is similar in this respect. When Alfred P. Sloan retired as chairman of General Motors Corporation in 1956, after working there for 33 years, he took on the role of presiding over his namesake foundation, based in New York, which he had founded in 1934 and gradually endowed over the years. Until his death ten years later, Mr. Sloan chaired and created the foundation's program, which remains substantially in effect to this very day. From the beginning, its central focuses were on business education, science, engineering, and economics, and it has been one of the few foundations to dedicate itself to facilitating the development of new methods and fields of scientific knowledge, such as genomics, bioinformatics, STEM (science, technology, engineering, and mathematics) research and education, and digital information technology applied especially to scientific research. It is likely that Mr. Sloan established the pattern of board governance starting in 1956 that General Johnson emulated when he founded his foundation in 1972. Some of the Alfred P. Sloan Foundation's original trustees came from General Motors, some had backgrounds in other corporations, and some came from the world of teaching science and economics. At present, of its 14 trustees, six are distinguished professors in the biological sciences, economics, or social sciences, three are present or former heads of universities, and five are from the corporate and finance sectors, one of whom was formerly president and CEO of GM. Like RWJF, the Alfred P. Sloan Foundation has a reputation both for identifying and supporting initiatives of very high quality and for manifesting meticulous loyalty to the values and intent of its founder-donor.

While one cannot prove causation and should be wary of generalizations, I am convinced that the quality with which both of these foundations have served the missions and visions established by their donors can be attributed in a significant degree to the continuing presence on their boards of a substantial group of trustees both from the corporate world and with the highest level of achievement in science.

chapter ten

A Case for Endurance: Causes That Plead for Long-Lasting Philanthropy

At their best, perpetual foundations, especially the large and midsized ones, are institutions that embody enduring, time-tested values that are worth preserving for future generations. Of course such foundations evolve steadily, but that evolution consists of applying their respective donors' instructions to the changing circumstances of society. The same passion that animated General Johnson's desire to improve US health and health care is as strong and focused today as it was when the Robert Wood Johnson Foundation began functioning in 1972. The same passion that moved John D. Rockefeller Sr. to aim to stamp out yellow fever 100 years ago showed itself when his philanthropic successors at The Rockefeller Foundation plunged into financing the planning of New Orleans's urgent response to Hurricane Katrina.

Like the great research universities, the great foundations have a similar social function of collecting, testing, and refining the knowledge relevant to their respective missions, preserving and enhancing the utility of that knowledge, and passing it along to future generations. If we were to cease creating such perpetual foundations, a vital link in the chain of knowledge in the service of society would be broken apart. Perpetual foundations operate in ways and fill critical needs that no other institutions are able to do. That is because, unlike universities, they are endowed with uncommitted financial resources that can be deployed any time as they see fit. They are unencumbered with the same sort of long-term commitments (extensive physical plant; significant staff or faculty commitments; financial aid or other public programs that hospitals, universities, or public charities have committed to) that constrain their directional changes. This flexibility—which leaves them exposed to the risk (real or imagined) of unaccountability, donor neglect, or even whimsy—is what also enables them to adapt to current needs in a way that no other public charity or government agency is capable of doing. To use the investment terminology, they are not constrained from opportunistic approaches to making big differences.

If American wealth-holders cease creating new perpetual foundations, they will deprive our society of the constant flow of support that in the past has left a century-long legacy of pioneering impact of immense benefit to society. America desperately needs the constancy of such social capital finance institutions to ensure the continuing regeneration of our country. As I have observed earlier in this book, perpetual foundations have been the primary route of first resort for talented Americans wishing to launch new civic-sector organizations in virtually every field of civic-sector endeavor, and I will not again list here the wide range of fields in which perpetual foundations have seeded new organizations. In this chapter, however, I wish to suggest a few areas of activity in America that are not likely to be focused on by spend-down foundations or "giving while living" donors, which therefore could benefit greatly from support by existing and new perpetual foundations. The following seem to me to be some fields in which perpetual foundations, if they continue to be created, could be of crucial help in tackling significant existing problems of today that otherwise seem likely not to be adequately attended to.

All but a few of the following are countercyclical initiatives aimed at correcting or diminishing the individual, social, or cultural effects produced by the now hyperactive malfunctioning and ever-more-widely reaching of our free market economy that prizes eyeballs more than vision, that (like sugar consumption) gives a momentary high followed by depressing lows, and that provides no genuine, healthy nutrients. The few that don't fall within that category are recurring conditions affecting society that donors of years past found attractive but that recent donors have tended to neglect. None of these initiatives is likely to find support among donors or foundations that are spending down in pursuit of high-profile, large topical problems and big public bangs for their bucks. These are not the sorts of causes that offer a hope of achieving some sudden breakthrough and garnering massive press attention. Donors who care about preserving healthy traditional values should be attracted to all of these as offering possible candidates for perpetual foundations. Each of the following threats is a continuing challenge to the kind of society that most thinking individuals would like to live in, and none of them is likely to be solved in the space of anyone's lifetime.

DOCTORING

Everybody needs a doctor at some time or other; as our population ages, more people will need to see doctors more frequently. One of today's neglected issues in the field of health and medicine is the by-product of America's system of managed care, which insistently rations doctors' time available for talking to patients. This urgent problem was powerfully called to my attention by Dr. Linda Celeste Robb-Nicholson, a primary care physician at Massachusetts General Hospital, who was the founding editor of the *Harvard Women's Health Watch*. In an era when doctors now routinely spend only 15 minutes in examining each of their patients, she says that it is of supreme importance that medical students be trained to devote adequate time to listening to their patients, so that when they become practicing physicians they will do such listening with special attentiveness. Donors and foundations that care about the quality of health care delivery should focus their advocacy and experiment-devising initiatives on ways to enrich the training of physicians so as to foster more effective communication between patients and their physicians.

RELIGION

The combination of insistently growing secularism, hand in hand with the distraction of 24/7 media and a great deal of salacious, seductive entertainment trash, is steadily undermining the individual and social norms that grew out of the teachings of most religions as well as secular humanism and moral philosophy—norms that constitute the foundations of most civilized societies. As the authority of organized religions has grown weaker, the effects of religion's waning influence on human behavior dramatically show themselves in various forms of destructive individual and social behavior. Many think that religion itself should be strengthened. Many others think that secular substitutes—moral philosophy, character education, ethics, psychology, humanitarianism, humanism, to name but a few—should be somehow strengthened in order to compensate for religion's decline. Perhaps many remedies should be tried. There is a great need for experimentation in new ways of establishing and strengthening social norms of civilized behavior. Perpetual foundations that long have had programs focused on religion in American life include The Pew Charitable Trusts[1] and the Lilly Endowment,[2] but the need for other philanthropic dollars to deal with this problem has never been greater.

POLITICS

The dysfunction of democratic governments around the world, and the polarization of politics especially in the United States, will demand a great deal of work to understand how to overcome polarization with collaboration. Solutions can come about only by identifying, recruiting, and supporting leaders who resist the steady hardening of differences among us and instead seek respectful, civilized consensus on how to solve society's most urgent problems collaboratively. That can be done only through the facilitation of leaders whom we know well enough to trust and who appeal to our better angels rather than our ever-present and ever-more-insistent internal devils nourished by today's secular culture. Our democracy has an absolutely desperate need for such leaders, for men and women of all ethnic, gender, racial, and religious backgrounds who are animated by ethical and moral norms that guide their behavior in all things. As noted previously, a group of perpetual foundations under the leadership of the Hewlett Foundation has formed a multimillion-dollar collaborative effort called The Madison Initiative to strive for a better understanding of the reasons for the extreme political polarization in America and also to experiment with practical ways of diminishing such polarization.[3]

This problem is so pervasive that there is plenty of room for other foundations to seek to remedy it. Its origins and seemingly ever-greater severity are likely the result of the increasingly large amount of dollars being poured by wealthy individuals, cash-rich corporations and their related foundations, and nonprofit organizations into narrowly based radical-right positions that demand adherence to the "one true way" and resistance to any compromise or negotiation with those who disagree with them.[4]

CHARACTER-BUILDING

For many Americans, democracy has increasingly come to mean raw and unbridled self-expression and self-serving of all kinds with few or no social restraints, whether by words or by guns or knives. Schools and colleges have gradually abdicated any responsibility for teaching their students self-discipline and for trying to enable their students to discriminate between better and worse behaviors. The uncouth language and uncivilized behavior rampant in popular culture have legitimated the use and spread of what were formerly regarded as four-letter obscenities disdained by civilized peoples. What to do to stem this cheapening of culture—and indeed of human life itself—is a subject that only a perpetual foundation is likely to explore. The long-run perspective and a devotion to long-lived values are particular virtues of long-lived institutions.

POETRY AND LITERATURE

"It is difficult to get the news from poems," William Carlos Williams wrote in his 1955 poem "Asphodel, That Greeny Flower," "yet men die miserably every day for lack of what is found there." Likewise, philanthropy has often had more of a taste for responding to the events of the day than for tending to the deeper stirrings of the mind and spirit expressed in poetry. Yet institutions devoted to promoting human well-being could scarcely do better than to help supply the "lack of what is found there."

There were countless audible gasps in November 2002 when Ruth Lilly pledged $100 million to *Poetry* magazine, which was thereby transformed into the Poetry Foundation. By the time the pledge was paid the following year, it had grown substantially, closer to $200 million according to some estimates. That munificent gift was but one in a sequence of gifts she made to support *Poetry* magazine and The Poetry Foundation starting in 1996. Many perpetual foundations continuously support literature and the arts but only a few spend-down foundations do so. Judging from the social problem-solving preferences expressed by "giving while living" donors, one would be very surprised to see them supporting poetry and/or the arts—though one could make a strong case for their doing so.

CLASSICAL MUSIC AND OTHER PERFORMING ARTS

A similar case can be made for the performing arts. It is rare that time-limited donors pursue these more timeless endeavors, though some perpetual foundations do take an ongoing interest in them. While the Ford Foundation, for example, no longer has a separate Arts and Humanities Program, which it did have in the 1960s and 1970s, it continues to support arts institutions through its new program on Creativity and Free Expression. The Ford Foundation was among the first foundations to make grants to classical and modern dance companies in the United States.[5] Moreover, it made one of the foundation sector's all-time historic grants for the arts in its 1965 gift of $85 million to American symphony orchestras. The purpose of that grant, which was part of a matching campaign, was to raise over $160 million to improve the salaries and extend the seasons of the recipient orchestras' musicians.[6]

Furthermore, many other perpetual foundations support important performing arts institutions that benefit the communities that they serve. For example, the William and Flora Hewlett Foundation's Program on the Performing Arts supports institutions in the San Francisco Bay Area. As is the case with virtually all of the Hewlett Foundation's grantmaking programs, the foundation traces its commitment to the performing arts directly to the support given by its founders William and Flora Hewlett during their lifetimes.[7] Also in the Bay Area, the David and Lucile Packard Foundation likewise makes grants to visual and performing arts organizations in the five nearby California counties that it defines as its local grantmaking area, as well as in Pueblo, Colorado, where its founder David Packard was born.[8] Other perpetual foundations that support arts and culture are the Surdna Foundation[9] and the Doris Duke Charitable Foundation.[10] There are many others, too.

As in many other fields, perpetual foundations' missions include grantmaking that is countercyclical to any given period of time. Sustaining and furthering the values of the fine arts is therefore a mission especially appropriate to foundations with unlimited lives. If no new perpetual foundations are created, where will the funds come from to ensure a thriving arts culture in America?

FOUNDATION–GOVERNMENT COLLABORATION

In years past, many large perpetual foundations frequently collaborated with federal government agencies in piloting new initiatives, often combining their funds with those of the federal and/or state government. For example, the Ford Foundation's community development program of the 1970s became a blueprint for the Carter administration's urban development policy. Later, the Local Initiatives Support Corporation (LISC) was established by the Ford Foundation as a purely private-sector initiative but soon attracted the cooperation of several federal agencies. LISC's initial purpose was to ascertain the creditworthiness of low-income borrowers and community organizations seeking capital from financial institutions, foundations, and government with which to buy or build homes or start businesses. With an initial $10 million from Ford and five other private funders, LISC went on to leverage about $4 billion from financial institutions, other foundations, and the federal government to finance LISC offices in more than 40 metropolitan areas across the United States. As of 2016, it has been in existence over 35 years, has leveraged about $48.5 billion in funds for community revitalization nationwide, and has continued to exert considerable influence on federal, state, and local policy toward struggling urban and rural communities. LISC is only one of many such influential organizations that were catalyzed by initial foundation grants.

The Ford Foundation's one-time focus on forming partnerships with the federal government reflected the era's belief that change—including turning around declining cities—must begin in Washington. Today, many funders take a more bottom-up approach. Bloomberg Philanthropies has put cities, not the federal government, at the center of its work, seeing city halls as laboratories of change. While the Gates Foundation, especially during the Obama administration, has collaborated with the US Department of Education in such initiatives as the Race to the Top school reform program, few other national foundations have the substantial record of collaborating with the federal government that the Ford Foundation had during the 1960s, 1970s, and 1980s. Since Darren Walker has become president of the Ford Foundation, that foundation has begun to resume collaborating with the federal government in a modest way, but the need for foundations to open themselves to such entrepreneurial initiatives today—with all levels of government—is greater than ever.

MAJOR RESEARCH AND ADVOCACY

It was the Carnegie Corporation that financed Gunnar Myrdal's pioneering research and searing critique of race relations in the United States, published in 1944 as *An American Dilemma: The Negro Problem and Modern Democracy*. It quickly became an intellectual platform of the Civil Rights movement and influenced the struggle for racial equality from the grassroots all the way to the Supreme Court, which cited Myrdal's work in its 1954 ruling against segregation in *Brown v. Board of Education*. Many other perpetual foundations have financed similar reports with wide-ranging consequences. Moreover, perpetual foundations have been increasingly ready to mount advocacy efforts on behalf of problems that were documented in research funded by others. The problem of global warming has enjoyed significant perpetual foundation support to document the problem and advocate action to help mitigate it. One wishes that foundations would make support available to advocate public action to remedy such problems as the vulnerability of America's electric grid, as documented in *Lights Out* by Ted Koppel. Jeff Skoll's support for widely viewed films on major problems, such as *An Inconvenient Truth* on global warming and *Waiting for Superman* on education reform, illustrate what many other foundations could do to help generate some action on the part of the public to address lingering, simmering national or state problems.

PUBLIC INFRASTRUCTURE IN A DIGITAL AGE

The backbone of the Internet was created by various government agencies to support the work of the defense department and scientific research. It has subsequently become the dominant frontier for commercial ventures, and in doing so has created great wealth and dramatically altered how people live, shop, and communicate. But many bridges between nodes of this still emerging network will not be supported by the market. Access to the Internet is considered to be essential for individual progress' but affordable access to the web (within the United States and around the world) is far from guaranteed; standards of conduct and evolving norms of behavior and laws need to be derived in ways that are not entirely driven by the market. Organizations such as the World Wide Web Consortium, Creative Commons, National Information Standards Organization (NISO), and the Berkman Klein Center for the Internet & Society are working to derive solutions for the long-term infrastructure, access, data permanence, and civil society questions that the digital age cannot afford to leave only to market players to resolve.

THE BOTTOM LINE

Perpetual foundations have played an indispensable role for at least a century in seeding and nurturing countless civic-sector advocacy organizations in virtually every field, as well as in supporting an enormous number of organizations serving other important continuing social needs. Through those organizations, foundations have played perhaps *the* critical role in facilitating peaceful, nonviolent, major social change in the United States. Perpetual foundations are there when needed with discretionary capital to start new organizations, to help them grow and, when successful, to help them scale to optimum size. America's perpetual foundations typically support undertakings that "giving while living" donors and foundations may not be interested in helping and ones that require more patience and more interplay with existing institutional players than many new spend-down foundations will tolerate. It is no exaggeration to think of perpetual foundations as constituting America's social sector investment banks. You do not want to have to create such a bank when an unexpected social problem arises; you want these institutions to be in existence to be drawn upon when needed.

In many metropolitan areas, private perpetual foundations, usually family foundations, are primary collaborative partners of community foundations and, together with them, have been principal forces for civic improvement and reform in virtually every field of social policy. As we have seen, these well-established cooperative models combine the donors' ongoing dedication to their home communities with the foundations' ability to research, test, and refine solutions to local problems. Likewise, in many states, perpetual foundations are the bulwark of civic-sector organizations and universities.

Perpetual foundations are the primary engines of peaceful social change in America's civic sector. They provide a continuing stream of fuel to start and nurture initiatives by public-interest-motivated individuals seeking to change society for the better. Without that fuel, America's social engine is bound to slow down.

chapter eleven

Advice to Donors: Creating Foundations for Today and Tomorrow

Thus far, this book has taken a critical look at the growing popularity of time limits and "giving while living" and their effects on the future of American philanthropy and compared those approaches with the long and fruitful tradition of perpetual foundations. Still, for all its reservations and cautions about the limited-life model, this book is not a polemic against spending down. On the contrary, it should be clear by now that I consider the rich diversity of forms, purposes, methods—and, yes, of time horizons—in American philanthropy to be among its greatest strengths. For any donor, the key to a right decision in deploying your philanthropic assets is to align carefully the duration of your philanthropic vehicle with the amount of resources at your disposal and the nature of the values and goals that matter to you.

In this chapter, I offer some thoughts on how to approach that challenge of alignment. Although it is written to give guidance to donors, it is in reality a broader meditation on the way foundations should be structured, the trade-offs that any funder must make, and the kind of good that various kinds of institutions can aspire to do in the world—whether in a short time or across a distant horizon.

SPENDING DOWN: ACHIEVING IMPACT IN A LIMITED TIME

Select New Recipients Carefully

Start by consulting with others who have significant knowledge of the areas in which you wish to achieve impact and who have already demonstrated success. Choose highly credible advisors and partners from among them, even if they have not manifested the ability to do exactly what you hope to do. They may well be able to help you avoid pitfalls that could otherwise waste your philanthropic assets. Leverage the experience and knowledge of highly regarded institutions in the field of your interests. The earlier you get to know the successful players in your chosen field, the more likely you will be to make informed choices about the most productive way to proceed.

Don't try to reinvent the wheel; instead, support or endow an experienced, gifted wheelmaker! Virtually always, donors must accomplish their goals through others—usually nonprofit organizations, universities, think thanks, hospitals, or scientific research centers. Undertake rigorous due diligence about which organizations and, even more important, which individual leaders are committed to the mission you envision and have a reputation for doing the best work.

If you are blessed with a superabundance of philanthropic wealth, as are the billionaires in the tech and finance worlds, consider establishing an entity similar to the Howard Hughes Medical Institute. The visionary Hughes was determined to make possible path-breaking basic biomedical research that would lead to new understandings about the molecular processes in human beings. That Institute, founded in 1953, is now the single largest source of biomedical research support for the life sciences in this country, with assets of over $18 billion and more than half a billion dollars in grants awarded annually. It achieves its mission primarily by identifying talented biomedical researchers—both individuals and teams of scientists—in universities and research institutes, designating them as Howard Hughes Investigators, and giving them the freedom to pursue their research ideas. The Institute describes its mission as being "to advance biomedical research and science education for the benefit of humanity. We empower exceptional scientists and students to pursue fundamental questions about living systems."[1] The Institute has become the seedbed of many scientific innovators of great distinction, including many Nobel Prize winners. The Atlantic Philanthropies' Global Brain Health Institute, discussed in Chapter 6, is another example of a major effort by a time-limited foundation to create a center of support and networking for the best minds in a field—in this case, the prevention and treatment of dementia.

The initiatives of Sean Parker, some of which have been described earlier, follow the same practice of identifying individuals and institutions with talent and experience and partnering with them. As mentioned, he, too, has determined to spend most of his philanthropic assets during his lifetime. Along with countless others, Parker suffers from allergies to nuts and shellfish, so it should be no surprise that he decided to finance research to improve the lives of other such sufferers. In 2014, he made a $24 million pledge over two years to Stanford Medical School to create the Sean N. Parker Center for Allergy & Asthma Research, which Stanford describes as the first interdisciplinary center in the world to focus on the wide variety of allergies affecting millions of adults and children. The mission of the Parker Center is to "focus on understanding the mechanisms of the immune system, the dysfunctions of which result in allergic reactions."[2] In 2015, he established The Parker Foundation with a gift of $600 million, announcing that its focuses would be on the life sciences, global public health, and civic engagement. In June 2015, Parker gave $4.5 million to the University of California at San Francisco (UCSF) to support research on ending malaria. In November 2015, he announced a $10 million gift to UCSF to establish the Sean N. Parker Auto-Immune Research Laboratory, which will be headed by Jeffery A. Bluestone, described by UCSF as "one of the world's leading immunologists."[3] And in April 2016, he announced a gift of $250 million to create the Parker Institute for Cancer Immunotherapy, which *Fortune* magazine described as "an unprecedented cancer research effort."[4] The goal of the Parker Institute is to speed up the development of immunotherapy treatment of various cancers by facilitating the collaboration of about 40 very highly regarded laboratories, including the six most celebrated cancer centers in the United States, and more than 300 researchers. The *Fortune* article spells out how the Institute will work: "It plans to do that by coordinating research across the field's top laboratories and pushing those findings quickly into clinical trials. The Parker Institute will not only provide comprehensive funding, clinical resources, and technology to each location, [but] it will also create a central repository for intellectual property. This will allow researchers across the six cancer centers to quickly access a broad swath of core discoveries, further speeding other research avenues."[5]

What Parker plans to do through the Parker Institute is similar to the initiative that financier Michael Milken undertook about two decades ago in creating the Prostate Cancer Foundation.[6] Milken identified and promised annual funding to prostate cancer biomedical researchers, conditioned on their coming together twice a year to share their findings with the other grantees. In 1994, the foundation received 200 applications for support, and by 1996 it was receiving 600. Dr. Patrick Walsh, the head of prostate cancer research and treatment at Johns Hopkins University, the scientist who invented the prostatectomy treatment for that disease, declared that "Mike's done more for prostate cancer research than anyone in America."[7]

Another variant of the biomedical scientist group research model is that used by the Christopher & Dana Reeve Foundation, which, in its prior incarnation as the American Paralysis Association, created a worldwide network of neuroscientists who specialize in treating spinal cord injuries and in doing research on innovative ways of understanding and remedying such injuries. That network convened periodically for report-sharing among the participants, some of whom were responsible for identifying a protein that could facilitate the growth of new spinal cord tissue.

In many ways, all of the above examples reprise a theme we examined early in Chapter 7: the virtue of identifying a gap and seeking ways to fill it. Having the vision to spot a niche and a willingness to deploy energy and financial resources to supply what is missing are the two crucial ingredients to success in such efforts. On a much smaller scale and in an entirely different field, you might emulate Duke University's Center for Documentary Studies, which was founded in 1984 initially as the Center for Documentary Photography by Alex Harris, a visionary documentary photographer and faculty member of what is now the Duke University Sanford School of Public Policy. Harris's overriding desire was then, and still is now, to enable bright students who are planning careers in government, nonprofits, foundations, and politics to augment their economics, political science, and statistics courses with knowledge of the human condition of individuals who are intended as the beneficiaries of public policies but who are all too often instead their victims. Harris began his documentary career by studying the often sordid housing conditions for migrant workers all over North Carolina. His vision for the center attracted a generous donor, Jack Lupton, who had a similar vision, also shared by the trustees and executive director of the Lyndhurst Foundation, which he founded. That confluence of ideas led the Lyndhurst Foundation to create on the Duke campus what is still the only endowed center focusing on documentary studies on any university campus in the United States. Informed by Harris's and Lupton's beliefs, the center is dedicated to social justice and to documenting the lives of America's less well-off through the work of professionals and students in the fields of photography, film, history, and literature. The Center for Documentary Studies is the parent of the Full Frame Documentary Film Festival, one of the nation's leading film festivals specializing in documentary films.

Most donors, including life-limited philanthropists and spend-down foundations, think first of partnering with institutions they care about, such as universities and colleges they attended and hospitals and physicians that treated them. The same is true for the Pritzker Family Foundation's 2015 $100 million gift to Northwestern University Law School for scholarships and for the support of social justice centers, including the Center on Wrongful Convictions. J. B. Pritzker is an alumnus of that law school, one of the top 15 in the country. As a result of his foundation's gift, Northwestern University Law School was renamed the Northwestern Pritzker School of Law, and its Entrepreneurship Law Center was renamed the Donald Pritzker Entrepreneurship Law Center in memory of J. B.'s father. The younger Pritzker's devotion to human rights and civil liberties is reflected not only in his involvement in such nonprofits but also in his philanthropic giving.

What should you do if no one with the requisite distinction or specialization is identifiable as a possible funding recipient for an initiative that is dear to your heart? Emulate Herbert and the late Marion Sandler of San Francisco's Sandler Foundation. They were concerned about the lack of significant progress in understanding the causes and treatment of asthma over more than 50 years and decided to try to catalyze discovery and innovation in asthma research. As virtually all of the sources of support from government and other foundations are focused on helping those with a track record of research on a particular disease or biomedical process, there was little funding for talented scientists who wished to tackle something that they had never worked on before. This is still the prevailing situation, despite the caution implied in the profound observation by Arthur Koestler: "All decisive advances in the history of scientific thought can be described in terms of mental cross-fertilization between different disciplines."[8]

The Sandlers decided to make funds available for a number of highly talented biomedical scientists who had never before studied asthma, and they funded the creation in 1999 of the American Asthma Foundation to administer and oversee the grants for that purpose. The AAF is based in the Sandler Asthma Basic Research Center at UCSF. Guided by the Sandlers, the AAF created a Scientific Review Board, consisting of an interdisciplinary group of distinguished research scientists; and an entirely new cadre of promising scientists has been created, most of whom are continuing to probe asthma's causes and experiment with new treatments and possible cures. As of 2014, AAF has supported 169 grantees, two-thirds of whom continue to focus on asthma after the years of their support. Their work has yielded 527 articles from 124 grantees published in peer-reviewed journals. AAF grant recipients have received $107 million in grants from other funders, more than the $100 million provided by AAF. And five drugs developed by AAF grantees were in Phase I or II clinical trials in 2014.[9]

Another possible course of action is to scour the landscape of successes in the past and to take on the challenge of updating them through the use of newly available technology. For example, the 911 National Emergency Response Telephone Number, initiated and funded in 1973 by the Robert Wood Johnson Foundation, which has saved countless lives by dispatching emergency help to accident and disaster victims, turns out to be incapable of communicating data via cellular telephones.[10] In November 2015, Tom Wheeler, chairman of the Federal Communications Commission, in a *New York Times* opinion column, urged the federal government to finance that updating, but, as we know all too well, Congress was and still is in a state of gridlock. If you care about bringing technology to the aid of Americans who need instant assistance in the face of threatening circumstances, perhaps you can help update 911.[11]

If you are determined to focus on a problem, you should see if anyone else has taken a first step to solve it with the kind of rigor, passion, and determination that you have. If you are fortunate, you will find someone who has started at the level of quality that you demand but who doesn't have the resources to take it to scale. That is exactly what Donald and Doris Fisher, cofounders of Gap Inc., did with their desire to put considerable resources behind charter schools for America's underprivileged youngsters. They identified two highly effective charter schools called KIPP Academies (Knowledge Is Power Program), one in Houston, Texas, established in 1994, and the other in New York's South Bronx, established in 1995. The schools were founded by Mike Feinberg and Dave Levin, former Teach for America volunteers. In 2000, the Fishers launched a nonprofit partnership with them called the KIPP Foundation, based in San Francisco, with an initial gift of $10 million with which to scale the growth of KIPP Academies nationwide. As of 2016, in part thanks to the continuing support of the Fisher Fund, there are 190 KIPP Academies across the United States.

If, after scouring the landscape, you cannot find an organization that suits your purposes, you may have to create and run your own initiative, just as Laurene Powell Jobs did. The widow of Apple founder Steve Jobs was intent on transforming the high school experience for American teenagers, but as far as she could tell, there was no existing organization that could and would be willing to undertake that task at the level of quality on which she would insist. She reached that judgment after consulting with some of America's leading education reformers, including Arne Duncan, who was then US Secretary of Education, and Ted Mitchell, the Under Secretary. So Ms. Jobs decided to create XQ: The Super School Project and committed $50 million to establishing it. As of the writing of this book, it is in its very early stages but appears quite promising. The XQ staff members are dynamic and creative and have organized an impressive nationwide tour of the XQ Super School Bus that travels the country to meet with groups of students and teachers who have volunteered to help "rethink high school." Some 10,000 people have submitted 1,400 concepts for how to do so; 700 of the proponents have been invited to submit applications to XQ for funding of their experiments. Like many others, I am excited to see which ones get funded and what happens next.[12]

Finally, for those who are determined to achieve the greatest impact for dollars spent but don't have a particular problem in mind, I suggest you consider the model that Facebook cofounder Dustin Moskovitz and his wife, former journalist Cari Tuna, are following.

Moskovitz and Tuna, two of the "new players in philanthropy" we encountered in Chapter 2, rejected the idea of a perpetual foundation at the outset. As Tuna says:

> For us, there was never a question of whether we would have a spend-down foundation or have a foundation that would exist in perpetuity. We always knew it was going to be spend-down and there are a few reasons for that. Our highest intention is to do as much good as we can with our giving. If you're creating a foundation to live in perpetuity, you have to preserve that endowment, and that leaves you with so much less to work with while you're alive.
>
> We think that we are best positioned to work on the problems that exist today and that future generations will be much better positioned to work on the problems of the future.
>
> To set up a structure that's going to remain relevant beyond our deaths seems really difficult. We hope and expect that people are going to be much better off in the future than they are today. That could mean it's going to cost a lot more in 30 years than it does today to improve lives significantly via philanthropy. Finally, as more wealth is created, we expect there to be much more philanthropy in the coming years and decades as

well. And so, those feel to us, in addition to our desire to alleviate suffering now, like really strong arguments for giving as soon as we can do so confidently.

In the first few years, we moved relatively slowly while we laid the foundation for our future philanthropic giving. But we're beginning to scale up our giving, and we hope within the next 30 or 40 years to have given most of our wealth away.[13]

Tuna and Moskovitz are casting a wide net to identify the areas in which they might be able to achieve significant impact and are actively seeking advice from experts on the range of subjects they find to be of interest to them. In my 2016 interview of her, Tuna reported:

Our overarching goal is to do as much good as possible for others with the resources we have. In service of that goal, we set out to learn about four broad categories of work that seemed especially promising: policy-oriented giving, global catastrophic risks, scientific research, and global health and development. As our team looked at the history of philanthropy, we came to realize that many of philanthropy's biggest successes have come from improving policy and funding scientific research. We are interested in mitigating global catastrophic risks—risks that could seriously threaten humanity's survival or progress—because such work seems to us a good conceptual fit for our philanthropy, given the long time horizon that we are able to have. We're interested in global health and development because dollars can go very far when focused on improving the lives of extremely low-income people.

Dollars donated today can go surprisingly far toward improving people's lives in a meaningful way. Our biggest grants [to date] have been to GiveWell's top charities—Give Directly, which makes direct cash transfers, the Against Malaria Foundation, the Schistosomiasis Control Initiative, and the Deworm the World Initiative. They are delivering evidence-backed, cost-effective, scalable global health and development interventions as well as cash transfers. In working to improve policy or fund scientific research, we might not see an impact for many, many years, and therefore we seek to balance those initiatives with giving cash now and giving bed nets now. We want to have a meaningful impact on people's lives today alongside the slow payoff of our longer-run, higher-risk-of-failure initiatives.[14]

One cannot help but be impressed by the genuine humility with which Tuna and Moskovitz have approached their philanthropic mission. They don't name programs after themselves. Tuna radiates an unpretentious zeal for doing the most good possible with the resources that she and her husband have available. She asks good questions but in a deferential way, and her manner of dealing with prospective donors contrasts strikingly with the high-handed ego and hyper self-confidence with which many of her fellow Silicon Valley philanthropic peers go about doing their good work.

For those wishing to spend all of their philanthropic resources during their lifetimes, the Tuna/Moskovitz model of impeccable due diligence, carefully analyzed choices, and admirable dealings with their recipients would be an excellent model for anyone to emulate, whether or not you are intent on "giving while living" and whether or not you have a predetermined notion of the problems you wish to solve or mitigate philanthropically.

The lesson to be learned from the above examples is this: First, crystallize a philanthropic mission consonant with your values and commensurate with your philanthropic means. Next, define your vision of what success will look like. Then craft a strategy or strategies to achieve that mission, complete with performance benchmarks to track your fidelity to those strategies and to reveal where fine-tuning of the strategies is necessary.

Then pray for good fortune and success!

Don't Neglect the Organizations You Have Supported in the Past

While many limited-life foundations have targeted late-year support for some of the organizations they have supported prior to and during the spend-down years, none have done so with the laser-like focus, generosity, and persistence that the S. D. Bechtel Jr. Foundation has. By formally establishing an Organizational Effectiveness team of program officers, and creating a "Resiliency Guide" to keep the foundation staff's attention on the foundation's critical obligation to fulfill its role of strengthening recipient organizations' capacity and resiliency, Bechtel raised that obligation to the highest possible level of attention.

Give yourself plenty of time to plan the spend-down. Don't fool yourself into thinking that you have all the time in the world to complete the responsible payout of your assets. You don't! What about the organizations to which you have contributed? Will they be able to survive when you exit from your role as donor? Spare no effort to prepare them for the day when your financial support will cease. That means ensuring that they have learned how to raise money from other donors. Create a trajectory of gradually declining support over multiple years. If your practice was to start new organizations or to provide a substantial proportion of an organization's funding, such a slowly diminishing schedule of support is all the more essential to help recipients learn how to compensate for the absence of your support.

PERPETUITY: ENSURING FIDELITY TO YOUR INTENTIONS

Despite all the alarm bells from those with an ideological ax to grind, the most important thing to understand about the prospect of creating a permanent foundation is that the future is not a hostile and dangerous terrain. It is possible—indeed, it is not at all unusual—to create a lasting institution that remains faithful to the vision, values, and purposes for which it was created. However, to achieve that goal, it is crucial to spell out, as precisely as you and your lawyer can, the areas on which you do and do not wish your philanthropic successors to focus. These nine guidelines should be helpful:

1. Embody your intentions in the founding legal document creating the foundation and in a letter you send to your trustees and executor of your estate. Make it as specific as possible. On the other hand, if, like Andrew Carnegie, you wish to grant your trustees some flexibility to adapt the foundation to future needs, you could follow the example of the letter he sent, quoted at length in Chapter 6, in which he explicitly gave his trustees "full authority to change policy or causes" as they saw fit, and assured them that "They shall best conform to my wishes by using their own judgment."[15]

2. Commission a video recording of you speaking directly to your successor trustees, in which you spell out your philanthropic intentions, why they are important to you, and what you'd like the boundaries of the trustees' grantmaking to be. James B. Duke, the donor/founder of Duke University and The Duke Endowment, required that his Trust Indenture be read aloud annually at a meeting of all of the trustees. You might require that your video be viewed annually in a meeting assembled for that purpose.

3. Think about the role you would like your family to play in your foundation—your spouse, your children, if any, and your grandchildren. In doing so, consider the alignment of their interests with yours.

4. Consider carefully the variety of structures that are available for creating your foundation.

5. Recruit and appoint a trusted attorney who is knowledgeable about laws regulating nonprofits and foundations as well as tax policies affecting exempt organizations.

6. Learn about the alternative structures that could define the governance of your foundation. Are you satisfied with one governing board of trustees with the power to select their successors in office? Perhaps you should consider a two-tier governance structure with a small group of carefully chosen members of the foundation corporation, who will have the power to select and terminate the trustees of your foundation. Perhaps you will wish to qualify your foundation as a supporting organization of the university you attended or of any other nonprofit institution with which you have trusting relationships, which will enable you to reduce the number of logistical chores you and your successors will have to perform if your foundation is a freestanding corporation or trust. You should seek the advice of an attorney who specializes in the practice of nonprofit and foundation law.

7. Recruit and appoint foundation trustees whom you trust, who share your values, and on whom you can depend absolutely.

8. Recruit and appoint at least two experienced practitioners and/or academic experts from the fields of nonprofit organizations in which you have primary interests.

9. Recruit and appoint at least two experienced businesspeople with knowledge about financial management, investment policies, and strategic and business planning.

These principles apply regardless of the kinds of goals a foundation may embrace and regardless of the ideology with which it is founded. My recommendations for structuring a foundation are almost the same, with one major exception, as those advanced by Adam Meyerson, president of the Philanthropy Roundtable, in an essay he wrote for the *Wall Street Journal*. I have made my disagreements with Meyerson clear in earlier chapters, but his guidance here is nearly unassailable:

> To avoid such problems, donors—whether large or small—need to take concrete action to safeguard their philanthropic principles:
>
> Clearly define your charitable mission. Write it down in your founding documents. Add a long written or oral record about your likes and dislikes in charitable giving.
>
> Choose trustees and staff who share your fundamental principles. Family members, friends, and close business associates such as lawyers, bankers, and accountants may not be good choices, unless you share the same worldview.
>
> Separate your philanthropic interests from your interests in maintaining control of your company. Donor intent frequently suffers when the two are mixed, as happened at the Ford Foundation. [Note: Here, as I explained in Part Two of this book, I disagree with the reference to the Ford Foundation, but the caution against mixing business and foundation concerns is sound.]
>
> . . .
>
> If you do establish a foundation in perpetuity, create strong procedures for electing future trustees who share your principles, and make respect for donor intent part of their fiduciary duty.[16]

In this quotation, I have omitted a passage with another bit of advice, which I cannot endorse: "If you establish a foundation, strongly consider a sunset provision, perhaps a generation or two after your death."[17] As I hope this book has shown, there may be a few good reasons to follow that advice under certain circumstances, but there are also many excellent reasons to ignore it. Any perpetual foundation whose donor heeds Meyerson's final recommendation, along with the other guidance I have offered in this chapter, has little to fear and much satisfaction to gain from bestowing a lasting gift on future generations.

Epilogue

Anticipate charity by preventing poverty; assist the reduced fellow man, either by a considerable gift of a sum of money or by
teaching him a trade or by putting him in the way of business so
that he may earn an honest livelihood and not be forced to the
dreadful alternative of holding out his hand for charity. This is
the highest step and summit of charity's golden ladder.
   —Maimonides[1]

PHILANTHROPY FOR TODAY OR INVESTING FOR TOMORROW?

Clearly the answer to that question is *both*. (And if this book's publisher had
not feared unduly complicating the title of this volume by giving that secret
away, the title would have read so.) By definition, one cannot deal with today's great social needs without simultaneously benefiting the future. Nor
can one invest wisely for the future without learning the ropes today. Every
major philanthropist who decided at some point to create a presumably perpetual foundation initially began by acting philanthropically to benefit present society. That is undoubtedly the reason the unlimited-life foundations
they later established usually got off on the right foot and have continued
performing so well. Similarly, it is inspiring to witness today's burgeoning
class of wealthy individuals who seem eager to tackle the great problems
of today. I would be willing to place a (small) bet, however, that many of
those who have publicly declared their intentions to give away their wealth
during their lifetimes will change their minds somewhere along the way, as
did Andrew Carnegie and George Soros, and instead create foundations to
carry on their philanthropy after their deaths.

Other wealthy individuals will come to the conclusion that the problems they care most about cannot be solved during their lifetimes, but even they will start tackling them today because they recognize that, for any continuing social problem, dealing with it effectively in the present will likely diminish its harm in the future.

As noted earlier, the Bridgespan Group focuses on helping nonprofit organizations and foundations develop and scale solutions to social problems affecting America's underserved. Yet, at a symposium on April 6, 2016, at Duke University's Sanford School of Public Policy's Center for Strategic Philanthropy and Civil Society, Thomas Tierney, Bridgespan's founding board chair, and Jeff Bradach, its cofounder and president, drew from Bridgespan's experience a significant conclusion: Despite its clients' successes, the number of people who benefit directly from these philanthropic initiatives is invariably a very small fraction of the overall population affected by the problems the initiatives are intended to solve or mitigate. That is both a great national shame and a tremendous opportunity.[2] Moreover, Results for America, a bipartisan organization, has been created with the mission of "improving outcomes for young people, their families, and communities by shifting public resources toward evidence-based, results-driven solutions."[3]

Tierney's and Bradach's point leads me to the following conclusion for this book: the most urgent, as well as the likely most effective, use of financial resources over the short run is for advocacy aimed at decisions to deploy public funds to take to the largest possible scale the proven solutions to major socioeconomic problems, such as the educational and health components of racial inequality in America. The Edna McConnell Clark Foundation has made the scaling of nonprofit solutions to some of such problems its primary mission and has succeeded in achieving impressive results. In persuading other foundations as well as individual philanthropists to partner with it in its most recent fund, Blue Meridian Partners, discussed above—which has a goal of raising $1 billion to be used in scaling already successful organizations—the Edna McConnell Clark Foundation's experience underscores the huge gap between what philanthropy and nonprofits can achieve and what American society's pressing needs are.

To succeed in filling that gap requires three indispensable ingredients:

1. Advocacy success in persuading the public and lawmakers to make available from government revenues the necessary funds to deploy in scaling to meet the full need;

2. Advocacy success in recruiting and training the nonprofit/public entrepreneurs to be charged with administering the scale-up process as well as the public/private ventures that will implement the scaled-up programs; and

3. *Great patience*, because a great deal of time will be required to persuade the public and the lawmakers as well as to train the implementers. Deeply rooted, resistant attitudes almost always require decades to change.

The success of such policy advocacy to achieve the scale-up-to-need will surely depend on much greater political participation by those in the center and on the left of the political spectrum to counter the massive, professionally implemented political and policy funding network created by right-leaning donors and foundations. The latter have been overwhelmingly successful at maintaining broad-scale opposition to government provision of funds to strengthen America's safety net for the poor, while funders on the left have not been nearly as effective in counteracting their influence.

This is not the same as arguing that American philanthropy needs to be more left-leaning. It is to say, rather, that institutions whose purposes *do* incline toward reducing poverty and inequality or expanding the social safety net need to be more effective in delivering that message to policy-makers and to the broad public. Conservative opponents of such ideas—including some foundations I have cited admiringly in this book and elsewhere for the focus and effectiveness of their work—have shown no reluctance to wage vigorous campaigns of both public advocacy and pressure on government. On the contrary, they have both excelled at these practices and shown extraordinary willingness to cooperate with one another to achieve their ends. (For an angry but compelling description of this success, see Jane Mayer's brilliant, meticulously researched *Dark Money: The Hidden History of the Billionaires Behind the Rise of the Radical Right.*[4]) Donors and foundations with a more progressive social agenda need to move from decrying their adversaries' success to emulating their methods.

Rebalancing America's politics is the single most important precondition for restoring sanity to American public policy. The recent triumphs of the radical right have short-circuited America's capacity to maintain its nearly 300-year history of achieving an ever-greater measure of social justice for our least well-off residents and citizens, while at the same time fostering equal opportunity and freedom for all Americans to realize their full potential as human beings. The only way to rebalance our politics is for progressive-leaning wealthy Americans, who are far more numerous than the wealthy of the radical right, to put their energies and wealth into the political process to counter the attack on that vision of equality.

Such extensive political engagement cannot legally be done by America's many law-abiding perpetual foundations because the Internal Revenue Code contains limits on what foundations can do. But it can be done by individuals who have created foundations and who are willing to devote non-tax-benefited dollars to lobbying and support for political candidates, which is what their counterparts on the right have been doing for decades. Some of the wealthy foundation founders of the left and center, such as George Soros, Mike Bloomberg, Tom Steyer, Pierre Omidyar, Jeff Skoll, and Tim Gill have already been engaging in more extensive political participation, often with significant success. Other liberal donors have recently come together in The Democracy Alliance and often coordinate their efforts to help elect their desired political candidates.

Most of the wealthy who express the intention of "giving while living" are contemplating solving or making a significant dent directly in major social problems. As I have written, I fear too frequently in this book, such head-on attacks on complex problems pose great risks of failure and, in any event, with respect to large, complex problems, such impact as is achieved will be, by definition, years or decades in the future. Large investments in political campaigns, on the other hand, can achieve major impact in the short run with the election of supported candidates. The experience of donors on the political right has proven that this is so. What other form of socially beneficial investment can be rewarded with significant impact in two, four, or six years, which are the durations of most political offices in the United States?

In a very real sense, carefully directed political giving is *the* gift that goes on giving long after an election is over. Giving for policy advocacy and in support of candidates who promise to effect desirable policy changes constitutes the greatest opportunity to achieve impact from intended socially beneficial giving, whether from tax-benefited dollars or from after-tax dollars. Moreover, unlike large substantive problem-solving initiatives, policy advocacy and political elections can not only benefit from huge infusions of cash over the short run and demonstrate clear impact but are likely to help rebalance American politics for decades to come. Unlike any other uses of "giving while living" funds, these purposes have to be the highest priority for anyone with the wealth and the passion for a fairer, freer, and more just America.

Appendix A: Firsthand Accounts of Philanthropy Under Time Limits and in Perpetuity

In the text of this book, I have often drawn on the track record of many of the time-limited foundations listed below and believe that it would be useful to you, the readers, to have available a fuller description of what these foundations are doing or have done. Half of them have completed their spend-down process and half continue to be in the midst of that process. Many of the points I make about the character of the initiatives that time-limited foundations support during the years after they resolved to spend down will be clearer to you, I think, if you have available a fuller picture of their aims, activities, and achievements.

In order to be sure that this book would accurately portray what the foundations themselves regard as their most important initiatives during their spend-down, I asked representatives of most of them to furnish an account in their own words. My editor and I have slightly edited the following entries but have not substantively altered the information provided by the authors in any significant ways. Consequently, the style and format of the following descriptions vary considerably. We chose not to impose any uniformity on them, preferring instead to let each institution represent itself in its own way. As the later chapters of this book reflect my views of how these foundations handled, or are going about, their spending down, I wanted to ensure that the foundations involved would be provided a place in the book where they could speak for themselves. That is the reason for this appendix.

FOUNDATIONS THAT HAVE COMPLETED THEIR SPEND-DOWN

Aaron Diamond Foundation[1]

Foundation established: 1955
Spend-down year: 1996
Year spend-down decision made: 1987

Rationale: Foundation was designed to spend down within 10 years of Aaron Diamond's death. Aaron Diamond died in 1984, and in 1994 Irene Diamond established the Irene Diamond Fund.[2]

Mission: To support medical research programs; specifically, AIDS research (Aaron Diamond AIDS Research Center)

Programmatic focus: Medical research (40% of activities), minority education (40% of activities), and cultural institutions (20% of activities), primarily in New York City

Grant allocation: Total of $200 million for spend-down over a decade; $50 million earmarked for AIDS research, including support for Aaron Diamond AIDS Research Center; $30 million for overall school improvement; and $2 million to start new schools[3]

Impact: In the area of medical research, according to *Philanthropy News Digest*, the "Aaron Diamond AIDS Research Center . . . pioneered the use of combination drug therapy to control the disease—a development that has helped reduce the death rate of HIV in America and Western Europe to one-fifth of what it was in the late '80s and 1990s."[4]

Former Executive Director Vincent McGee reports: "Though we initially set out to keep the foundation's AIDS work focused on medical research . . . we quickly became aware of the problem of AIDS in other settings—for example, children having parents with AIDS or being infected themselves, and how people living with HIV/AIDS were discriminated against at school and in the community. We discovered the importance of educating young people and teachers about AIDS, as well as the absence of AIDS in health education curricula. As a result, we quickly moved AIDS as a focus into our education and, later, human rights work. When people began to recognize our work as being ahead of the curve, particularly when we started a program for AIDS education and condom availability in the public schools, Mrs. Diamond would say, 'I'm a grandmother. We ought to be talking about this candidly. This is a disease that can be avoided, but people have to know how it's transmitted, and they have to change their behavior based on the facts.' The Aaron Diamond Foundation was seen as a model because there was a consistency and integrity across the spectrum of our program activities."[5]

Some of the foundation's "board members wanted to focus on increasing minority enrollment in prep schools and elite institutions of higher education. That was not Mrs. Diamond's interest. . . . [but, in time, the foundation] pioneered many of the things that are now known as the New Visions Schools, into which the Gates Foundation, Carnegie Corporation, and others are putting hundreds of millions of dollars around the country—breaking up big schools and creating smaller, themed schools where young people connect to a specific focus and get more attention. To make that work, [the foundation] also helped start minority recruitment programs for principals and teachers and collaborated with Agnes Gund's Studio in a School and others to bring the arts, which had been eliminated from most public schools during the city's fiscal crisis in the mid-70s, back into the curriculum. Toward the end of the foundation, [it] also funded a survey of arts education in the city that laid the groundwork for a special Annenberg Foundation grant which prompted city funding for a restructuring of the arts curriculum in the schools.

In the area of arts and culture, [the foundation] developed a focus on performing arts as a career vehicle for young people in music and dance, with film as a smaller area of interest. Because of Mrs. Diamond's long-standing interest in free speech, personal liberties and human rights, [the foundation] also developed programs in those areas. Mrs. Diamond also made large personal grants outside the foundation to expand the minority presence at Julliard and gave $30 million over fifteen years to Human Rights Watch."[6]

The Beldon Fund[7]

Beldon's overarching legacy is that of a bold funder that planted "seeds" that are still bearing fruit today. Another way of conceptualizing this overall legacy is that they were an "early adopter," advocate, and catalyst of many strategies and tools that today are seen as best practices in the fields of civic engagement, advocacy, and environmental health.

Beldon's living legacy and influence can be seen in the strong 501(c)(3) [collaborative nonprofit organization recipients] tables in many states across the country. It can also be seen in the continued work and progress of the environmental health community, a field that Beldon helped bring to life. These are just two highlights of the following list of 11 legacies of the Beldon Fund. Collectively, these are areas where, five years later, the Beldon Fund has had a continuing impact and Beldon's investments are either still flourishing or have evolved in a relevant manner.

1. Beldon's efforts to marry policy, organizing, advocacy, and nonpartisan civic engagement work in the environmental community are widely perceived to have been successful; the melding of policy advocacy with civic engagement remains particularly relevant today.

2. As a national funder, Beldon helped pioneer an approach of investing heavily in state-based work, a practice that has become more common today.

3. Beldon prioritized collaboration and the need for strong collaborative infrastructures; in many states, these collaborative efforts remain robust, although they have evolved in different ways both within and beyond the environmental community.

4. Beldon encouraged the use of tools, technology, metrics, and evaluation in ways that were new to many grantees at the time but now represent a best practice in the nonpartisan civic engagement field.

5. Beldon helped shape the field of environmental health, leading to significant shifts in public awareness, corporate behavior, and governmental policies.

6. The infrastructure connecting environmental health advocates remains strong, despite Beldon's exit and the absence of increased funding.

7. Health professionals and health-affected organizations continue to bring powerful voices to a range of environmental campaigns, building on work that was seeded by Beldon more than a decade ago.

8. Beldon's influence on philanthropy continues today and can be seen in the culture, strategies, and collaborations among funders, particularly environmental grantmakers.

9. Beldon's funding and leadership support significantly strengthened League of Conservation Voters Education Fund's affiliates in Michigan, Minnesota, North Carolina, and Wisconsin, helping increase the capacity of the environmental movement in those states in a manner that remains impactful today.

10. By creating a roadmap for spend-out foundations, Beldon's work has informed and advanced the field for a growing number of donors.

11. Core Beldon staff (and others in the "Beldon family") represent a living Beldon legacy, as they continue to champion many of Beldon's theories of change, and they remain active leaders in the field of environmental philanthropy.

The Julius Rosenwald Foundation[8]

Foundation established: 1917
Spend-down year: 1948
Year spend-down decision made: 1927
Rationale: In Rosenwald's view, as discussed at length in the text of this book, "Permanent endowment tends to lessen the amount available for immediate needs; and our immediate needs are too plain and too urgent to allow us to do the work of future generations."[9]
Mission: "For the well-being of mankind."[10]
Programmatic focus: Education, health, African Americans (education and health)
Grantmaking allocation: In total, the fund donated over $70 million to colleges and universities, Jewish charities, and African American schools.
Impact: The fund donated large grants for the construction of "Rosenwald Schools" in poor, majority African American school districts in 15 southern states. In addition, Rosenwald donated "over two million dollars to Black University Centers at Tuskegee, Howard, Fisk, Atlanta and Dillard Universities. The Rosenwald Foundation gave approximately 1,000 scholarships or fellowships to African American students."[11]

According to Karl Zinsmeister of the Philanthropy Roundtable, "America would be a very different, and lesser, nation absent this philanthropic inspiration (which outflanked a scandalous dereliction of duty by a variety of governments)."[12]

The John M. Olin Foundation[13]

Foundation established: 1953
Spend-down year: 2005
Year spend-down decision made: 1993

Rationale: As discussed in the text, Olin was influenced by Julius Rosenwald's opposition to establishing foundations in perpetuity. Olin's decision to limit the life of his foundation appears to have been catalyzed by Henry Ford II's resignation from the Ford Foundation Board of Trustees.

Mission: "The general purpose of the John M. Olin Foundation is to provide support for projects that reflect, or are intended to strengthen, the economic, political, and cultural institutions upon which the American heritage of constitutional government and private enterprise is based. The foundation also seeks to promote a general understanding of these institutions by encouraging the thoughtful study of the connections between economic and political freedoms, and the cultural heritage that sustains them."[14]

Programmatic focus: Free enterprise, individual liberty

Grantmaking overview: The foundation disbursed over $400 million in grants to conservative think tanks, universities, publications, and other organizations.[15]

Impact: As discussed in Chapter 5, the activities of the Olin Foundation led to the founding of the Federalist Society, which "would go on to transform legal education and shape the federal judiciary. . . . The foundation also supported pioneering researchers, journalists, and public intellectuals in producing influential new arguments and books. These included Allan Bloom's *The Closing of the American Mind*, Linda Chavez's *Out of the Barrio*, Dinesh D'Souza's *Illiberal Education*, Milton Friedman's *Free to Choose*, Francis Fukuyama's *The End of History?*, Samuel Huntington's *The Clash of Civilizations*, Richard John Neuhaus's *The Naked Public Square*, and Michael Novak's *The Spirit of Democratic Capitalism*. . . . Organizations that relied on Olin support as they grew into important roles in American intellectual life and public policy debates included the American Enterprise Institute, the Center for Individual Rights, the Heritage Foundation, the Hoover Institution, the Manhattan Institute, the National Association of Scholars, the New Criterion, Philanthropy Roundtable, and many others. Olin research funding was crucial in launching new analyses that ended up driving consequential national reform movements in areas like school choice, welfare reform, and colorblind public policy."[16]

The Whitaker Foundation and Helen F. Whitaker Fund[17]

Foundation established: 1975
Spend-down year: 2006
Year spend-down decision made: 1991/1992

Rationale: The foundation made the decision to spend down its funds in order to further the field of biomedical engineering. "Whitaker did not mandate a limited life for his foundation, but he did state in the trust document that 'settlor desires, but does not require, that the entire principal and income of [the] trust be completely distributed within 40 years following his death.'"[18]

Mission: To legitimate/strengthen/advance the field of biomedical engineering

Programmatic focus: Biomedical engineering research and education (Whitaker Foundation); training for classical musicians (Helen F. Whitaker Fund)

Grantmaking overview: "The foundation contributed more than $700 million to universities and medical schools to support faculty research, graduate students, program development, and construction of facilities. Most of its efforts were directed toward the establishment and enhancement of formal educational programs and the support of especially talented students and faculty."[19]

Impact: "Some 80 universities, among them some of the most prominent universities in the country, now have biomedical engineering programs, and it is generally recognized in the biomedical engineering community that the foundation was the catalyst in the rapid expansion of such programs over the past decade. This in turn was possible only because the foundation's committee was prepared to utilize both income and principal to advance its mission."[20]

Andrea and Charles Bronfman Philanthropies (ACBP)[21]

Foundation established: 1986
Spend-down year: 2016
Year spend-down decision made: 2001

Rationale: A June 2011 letter explains the foundation's reasoning: "The decision gradually to divest all of ACBP's resources was made by Charles and Andy after robust family conversations. It became clear that their philanthropic interests were an expression of their own particular values, experiences, and interests, and therefore that ACBP should phase out its grant-making as they began to anticipate entering a less engaged chapter in their own lives. Tragically, Andy [died] in 2006. . . . At the heart of the family decision is the desire that each generation should be at liberty to engage philanthropically in support of their individual commitments and passions in their own ways. . . . Charles did not want to be the cold fist trying to rule from the grave. . . .

"In 2001, Andy and Charles, along with Jeff [Solomon, president and CEO of the foundation], chose 2016 as the date by which ACBP would accomplish the goal of ensuring that the missions of the organizations that ACBP has incubated would continue. . . . After 2016, our involvement will change. . . . We will still be active donors but without the infrastructure and support built over the years.

"To align with our values, we have taken the following steps in preparation for 2016:

1. We have been transparent with our grantees about the grant support that would be available to them between now and then;

2. We have continued to nurture these organizations, providing advice and back office assistance on a regular basis;

3. We play fluid and varied roles as these organizations grow and mature. From governance to advocacy, development to technical assistance, we attempt to help with a light touch . . . to champion and cheerlead, only occasionally offering "tough love." . . .

4. We have retained an outside firm, Cambridge Leadership Associates (CLA), and other outside advisors to work with us, with the grantees, and with their constituencies, to

    a. maximize the potential that the missions of these incubated organizations will be preserved going forward;

b. ensure as much as possible that the organizations themselves, if they are to continue, will be sustainable and best in class, and;

c. make certain that the people involved will be treated with sensitivity and concern throughout this transition.

5. Future letters and brief papers will discuss the roles played and the lessons learned as we chronicle the sunset process."[22]

Mission: "[ACBP is] a family of charitable foundations operating in Canada, Israel, and the United States. [They] seek to nourish the deep and fundamental human desire to belong to a community and to help individuals forge connections between their identity and community."[23]

Programmatic focus: To strengthen the unity of the Jewish people, to improve the quality of life in Israel, and to promote Canadian heritage[24]

Grantmaking overview: The foundation funded operating programs and made as major grants.

Grant allocation: As of June 2011, ACBP reported that it had "granted more than $325,000,000 to some 1,700 organizations. While believing dearly in good citizenship and relationship grants, we are proud that our strategic giving has generally been at 65 percent or above of all grantmaking. Much of the operating support of nearly $59,000,000 went to the day-to-day work of incubating and developing the organizations/programs at the heart of the Philanthropies' mission."[25]

Here is a partial list of grants:

- Association of Israel's Decorative Arts (AIDA): $921,852 from 7/22/2003 to 1/1/2015

- Museum of Arts and Design: $955,900 from 4/24/1992 to 1/1/2017

- Musicians on Call: $160,750 from 3/21/2001 to 1/1/2016

- The Israel Museum, Jerusalem: $15,013,423 from 5/22/1991 to 5/13/2023

- The Israel Philharmonic Orchestra: $10,000,000 from 3/23/1992 to 1/1/2019

- The Raymond F. Kravis Center for the Performing Arts: $850,750 from 1/4/1987 to 1/1/2016

- Brandeis University: $6,993,358 from 10/12/1990 to 1/1/2016

Impact: The foundation "has guided the creation of a dozen start-ups in three countries, most famously Birthright Israel, a program that has already exposed more than three hundred thousand young Jewish adults to life in Israel for ten days, all expenses paid; 21/64, a program that fosters an inter-generational approach to strategic philanthropy; and the Historica-Dominion Institute, the leading NGO focused on Canadian history and heritage. One of the more interesting experiments of the Foundation was designed by Charles's late wife, Andrea, a few days after the tragedy of 9/11, and then enacted by Jeff. Rather than simply provide charitable money contributions to the families who lost loved ones, Andy and Jeff sought to find a way to help them heal. They arranged for every one of the arts, cultural, entertainment, and sports venues in the tri-state area to provide free tickets to those in grief. The hope was that a museum, a baseball game, or a circus would help a grieving child find a reason to smile. Andy and Jeff built the Gift of New York to execute this idea and opened it by Christmas 2001—and they closed it, as planned, on Easter Sunday 2003. Ten thousand people took advantage of the program."[26]

FOUNDATIONS THAT HAVE NOT YET REACHED THEIR SPECIFIED WINDOW FOR SPENDING DOWN

The Bill and Melinda Gates Foundation[27]

Foundation established: 2000
Estimated spend-down year: 20 years after the death of the survivor of Bill Gates and Melinda Gates
Year spend-down decision made: 2000
Mission: To ensure more children and young people survive and thrive; to empower the poorest, especially women and girls, to transform their lives; to combat infectious diseases that particularly affect the poorest; and to inspire people to take action to change the world[28]

Programmatic focus: Education, world health, and population, as well as community giving in the Pacific Northwest

Grant allocation and impact (selected initiatives):

Global Health

Global Polio Eradication Initiative (GPEI). In 1988, wild poliovirus was endemic in 125 countries and about 350,000 people, primarily young children, were paralyzed by polio annually. That year, the world resolved to eradicate the disease. GPEI was formed as a public-private partnership led by national governments and spearheaded by the WHO, Rotary International, the CDC, and UNICEF. The foundation has committed more than US$1 billion to support GPEI's efforts to eradicate polio. To date, polio has been 99 percent eliminated. India was certified polio free in 2014. There are now only three countries where transmission has never been stopped: Nigeria, Pakistan, and Afghanistan.

Gavi, the Vaccine Alliance. The need to find innovative, market-based ways to cut vaccine costs led the foundation to provide the seed money to create Gavi, the Vaccine Alliance. That initial seed grant was for $750 million; the foundation has granted about $2.5 billion to Gavi to date. The alliance has helped increase the capacity and competitiveness of manufacturers willing to produce vaccines for the developing world and to reduce prices. In just a two-year period (2010–2012), the cost of immunizing a child with pentavalent, pneumococcal, and rotavirus vaccines went down by 35 percent. Since its inception, Gavi has helped low-income countries reach an additional 440 million children with lifesaving vaccines, averting an estimated 6 million deaths.

MenAfriVac (Sub-Saharan Africa Meningitis Group A Vaccine). After the biggest meningitis epidemic ever recorded in Africa killed 25,000 people in 1996–1997, the continent's health ministers were desperate for an alternative that was more effective and easier to administer than the existing vaccine. In 2001, the foundation committed a 10-year, $70 million grant to support PATH's Meningitis Vaccine Project (MVP), a partnership between PATH (an international NGO working in public health), the World Health Organization, African health ministries, and the Serum Institute of India. Since

December 2010, at a cost of just 50 cents per dose, MenAfriVac has been rolled out across Sub-Saharan Africa's meningitis belt: Burkina Faso, Mali, Niger, Cameroon, Chad, and Nigeria. More than 150 million people have received the vaccine. A hallmark in the history of vaccines, it is the first time a vaccine has been designed specifically for Africa.

Global Development

AfSIS (African Soil Information Service). By far the most ambitious and innovative soil-mapping effort ever undertaken in Africa, AfSIS was established with a $15.6 million Gates Foundation grant in 2008.

bKash (Financial Services in Bangladesh). In order to address Bangladesh's low-income population without access to banks, the foundation funded ShoreBank International, Ltd. to support bKash, a financial services provider that allows Bangladeshis to store, transfer, and receive money safely via their mobile phones and to deposit/withdraw cash through a network of community-based agents. Just four years after being founded, bKash processes roughly 1.5 million transactions per day, which amounts to nearly $1 billion each month. It is a collaboration with the BRAC Bank Ltd. (a private commercial bank focused on reaching Bangladesh's unbanked by facilitating small and medium enterprises) and a US company called Money in Motion.

Mobile money platforms similar to bKash are springing up in other developing countries, enabling more low-income customers to utilize the services and build financial futures for themselves and their families.

M-PESA. The Gates Foundation supported the accelerated expansion of Vodafone's highly used M-PESA mobile money service (originally in Kenya) to reach more than two million of Tanzania's poorest people.

London Summit on Family Planning and FP2020. In 2012, the foundation partnered with the UK Government's Department for International Development (DFID) to galvanize global political commitments to enable access to voluntary family-planning services for 120 million more women and girls by 2020. The summit raised $2.6 billion to support family-planning efforts. The priorities discussed at the summit are enacted through Family Planning 2020, an organization that helps women and girls gain access to contraceptives.

United States

Gates Millennium Scholars (GMS). The foundation's signature scholarship program will enable roughly 18,000 high-achieving, low-income minority students to attend college through an advanced degree at full cost. GMS recipients have a college graduation rate of 90 percent. The program demonstrates that if the financial barriers to college for high-achieving, low-income minority students are removed, they can succeed and graduate from elite colleges and universities at the same rate as anyone else. (Note: This program is sunsetting; final GMS cohort will be selected in 2016.)

US Libraries. The foundation accomplished its earliest goal of getting computers with Internet access in nearly every public library in the United States. By 2003, after investing $240 million, 99 percent of US public libraries were Internet ready with trained staff on hand.

Pacific Northwest. The foundation has invested more than $1 billion in its home state of Washington to ensure a quality education for all children, reduce family homelessness, and support the most vulnerable families.

The Atlantic Philanthropies[29]

Foundation established: 1982
Spend-down year: 2019
Year spend-down decision made: 2001
Rationale: "In keeping with the Giving While Living philosophy of [its] founder, Charles 'Chuck' Feeney, [the foundation] believe[s] in making large investments to capitalize on significant opportunities to solve urgent problems now, so they are less likely to become larger, more entrenched and more expensive challenges later."[30]
Mission: "To bring about lasting changes that will improve the lives of disadvantaged and vulnerable people"

Programmatic focus: Children & Youth, Aging, Population Health, Reconciliation & Human Rights, Higher Education, Biomedical Research, Philanthropy/Giving While Living

Selected grant/cluster (total spent since 2001) and impact (post-limited life decision):

US Health Reform ($190,944,304): Big, bold, substantial bet with long-term impact, affording millions of uninsured and underinsured people access to quality care

US Death Penalty Abolition ($59,117,516): Momentum building toward fixing a broken, discriminatory criminal justice system that disproportionally affects the poor and people of color. Well-timed strategic collaboration of funders and advocates resulting in Supreme Court decision outlawing juvenile death penalty. Seven states have abolished the adult death penalty, four others have declared moratoria, and death sentences, executions, and public support of death penalty are at lowest levels in over 20 years.

Elder Care & Dementia, US, Ireland, No. Ireland ($305,417,700): Helped catalyze changes in public narrative about role and contributions of older people, and engaged government to fund and implement national dementia policy and practice across Ireland

Public Health Transformation, Viet Nam ($286,591,316): Created academic and research infrastructure to establish the public health field, transform training of physicians and public health professionals, and provide essential services for millions of Vietnamese. Built or renovated over 900 health centers, dramatically reduced morbidity and mortality, and improved health outcomes.

UCSF Mission Bay Campus ($299,900,000): Transforming a derelict neighborhood into a thriving residential/commercial center organized around research and clinical care

Cornell NYC Tech ($350,000,000): Catalytic investment building to scale, leveraging massive investments by government and private sector. Creating new applied research and technology industry in New York City to rival Silicon Valley.

S. D. Bechtel, Jr. Foundation[31]

Foundation established: 1957
Spend-down year: 2020

Year spend-down decision made: 2009

Rationale: The foundation's board of directors made the momentous decision to invest all of the assets by 2020 so that more could be invested in solutions over a shorter period of time. An internal process refocused the grantmaking on a small number of discrete lines of work, where increased funding for timely opportunities might lead to significant progress within the foundation's time horizon.

Mission: The S. D. Bechtel, Jr. Foundation invests in a vibrant, sustainable future through development of young people and management of natural resources. The majority of the foundation's grants have been directed toward organizations in California, the Bechtel family's home state.

Programmatic focus: Strategic work in education and the environment emphasizes systems change, field building, policy advocacy, and strengthening key grantees so that they can continue the work beyond the foundation's sunset.

Grant allocation and impact (selected):

Education

Math in Common Initiative®. (Initiated 2013, projected to conclude in 2018.) The Common Core State Standards outline what a student should know and be able to do following the completion of each grade, and charge states that adopt these standards (42 and the District of Columbia have so far) with aligning curriculum to meet the standards. California's adoption of the Common Core State Standards for Mathematics (CCSS-M) has the potential to transform student learning. A key component of the foundation's five-year, $53 million initiative is ensuring that educators are working with the knowledge and resources to address these standards. As of this writing, the foundation is midway through the Math in Common Initiative®, which engages 10 school districts that collectively serve over 300,000 California students.

Next Generation Science Standards Early Implementation Initiative. (Initiated 2014, projected to conclude in 2018.) Similar to the Common Core State Standards, the Next Generation Science Standards (NGSS) provide educators with an internationally benchmarked science education framework, developed by national organizations including the National Science Teachers

Association. The California K–8 NGSS Early Implementation Initiative is a four-year demonstration project that supports NGSS implementation in 11 local education agencies, including eight school districts supported by the foundation. The initiative consists of leadership training for teachers and administrators, professional development in content and pedagogy, and support to develop and implement a K–8 districtwide NGSS plan. Participating districts also form a cross-district learning community.

Instructional Leadership Corps (ILC). (Initiated in 2014, projected to conclude in 2019.) The ILC Initiative facilitates successful implementation of both CCSS-M and NGSS by building the instructional leadership capacity of a select corps of strong California educators, who can then grow the capacity of local educators and administrators through professional learning experiences. These trainings reach up to 8,000 teachers and 900 school site-leaders. There will be a conference for the members of the leadership corps to share their results and to plan regional summer institutes. The proceedings will be videotaped and made available for those not able to attend the events. A longer-term goal of developing the ILC is to create regional professional development expertise that can add value long after the foundation's sunset.

Environment

Conserving California's Landscapes. (Initiated prior to 2008, projected to conclude in 2020.) The foundation's Land Portfolio works to advance land management and conservation systems to ensure the long-term vitality of California's land resources. The foundation's conservation efforts were inspired by an interest in supporting sustainable populations of migratory waterfowl and providing outdoor recreation opportunities to California's communities. The Partnership's efforts have enhanced the management of over 100,000 acres for the benefit of migratory birds.

Advancing Water Management. (Initiated 2008, projected to conclude in 2020.) The foundation's Water Portfolio works to ensure that the management of water in California is informed by research and good data, grounded in best practice, and enabled by sound policy so that California transitions to a sustainable water management system that meets the needs of people and nature over the intermediate and longer term.

Foundation water investments to date—totaling approximately $50 million—helped set the stage for important advances in water policy and management, including the 2014 historic groundwater management reform and a $7.5 billion water bond, a series of governance reforms for the Sacramento-San Joaquin Delta, urban water efficiency improvements, and improvements to California's flood management system. By continuing its water investments and capitalizing on the heightened awareness and commitment to act due to California's drought, the foundation seeks to spur continued focus on high-impact water issues—such as fundamentally improving California's water data systems—and to generate additional philanthropic support for water beyond 2020.

Support for Grantee Capacity and Resiliency

Along with program-specific outcomes, the foundation is committed to building the capacity, adaptability, and resiliency of its grantees so that they can carry on their important work long after the foundation's sunset. The foundation supports grantees to enhance effectiveness and resiliency, including efforts to engage other funders, diversify and grow revenue, and reduce dependence on the foundation. The foundation's Organizational Effectiveness team developed a Resiliency Guide—a checklist of factors and resources related to organizational resiliency—to help frame dialogue between foundation staff and grantees in developing goals and approaches to enhancing effectiveness and resiliency.

Recently Concluded Initiatives

Alzheimer's Disease Research. (Initiated in 1998, concluding in 2016.) Starting in 1998, the foundation provided grants to promising early-career researchers studying Alzheimer's disease. The foundation received advice from experts regarding the current gap in funding for research that occurs between the end of a doctoral program and the first government grant. Aiming to address that gap, the foundation's portfolio of Alzheimer's research grants grew to include 15 promising scientists across 7 research institutions and 5 states. These grants also supported Alzheimer's disease-focused conferences, which promoted collaboration and innovative research. As of this writing, 10 supported researchers are running their own labs at prominent universities or interdisciplinary research centers.

Civic Learning. (Initiated in 2012, concluding in 2016.) Stemming from interest by the Founder, the foundation supported programs that encourage young people to engage in their communities and with local and state government. The grants funded research on best practices in civic education as well as a professional development program for teachers in elementary schools regarding civics lessons. The foundation also supported meetings of policy-makers and stakeholders regarding civic education as well as communication campaigns on relevant research findings.

Founder Grants

While the main focus of staff efforts is appropriately on achieving defined outcomes through strategic grantmaking, our Founder remains active and, from time to time, directs grants to take advantage of compelling opportunities to advance STEM in higher education settings and to excite young people about the possibilities of careers in engineering. Budgeting for the spend-down years included a substantial set-aside pool to allow for these special projects without the need to redirect funds from strategic program priorities.

The AVI CHAI Foundation[32]

Foundation established: 1984
Spend-down year: 2019
Year spend-down decision made: 2005
Rationale: Arthur Fried, the first chairman of AVI CHAI after founder Zalman Bernstein's passing, quoted him as follows: "Those who knew me should spend the money in their lifetime. I do not know who is coming next. The history of philanthropy in America is that the vision of the founder often becomes corrupted in the years following his passing."[33]
Mission: "Whereas AVI CHAI is committed to the perpetuation of the Jewish people, Judaism, and the centrality of the State of Israel to the Jewish people, the objectives of AVI CHAI are simply stated:

- To encourage those of the Jewish faith towards greater commitment to Jewish observance and lifestyle by increasing their understanding, appreciation, and practice of Jewish traditions, customs, and laws.

- To encourage mutual understanding and sensitivity among Jews of different religious backgrounds and commitments to observance."[34]

Programmatic focus: While the mission of the foundation is common across the three geographic areas in which AVI CHAI funds, the focus and programmatic agendas are different. In North America, the focus has been to nurture the core group of Jewish youth who have the values, motivation, and skills to lead the Jewish people intellectually, spiritually, communally, and politically in the 21st century. One-half of AVI CHAI's grants budget is focused on its North American activities. AVI CHAI Israel seeks to engage Israeli Jews in the study and celebration of diverse expressions of Jewish tradition and culture and to develop Israeli Jews' commitment to Israel as a Jewish and democratic state. Forty percent of AVI CHAI's grants budget is focused on its Israeli activities. The central focus of AVI CHAI's work in the Former Soviet Union (FSU) has been the reseeding of Jewish life after the fall of the Soviet Union. Ten percent of AVI CHAI's annual grants budget is directed to the Former Soviet Union.

Grant allocation and impact (selected projects):

North America

Curricular Programs: TaL AM[35] and NETA/Bishvil Ha'Ivrit.[36] AVI CHAI has funded two curricular and teacher training programs, one for the elementary grades and one for middle school/high school. The TaL AM curricular program is taught to over 30,000 elementary school students annually at 350 day schools in North America (and other countries outside Israel). The initial investments enabled TaL AM to expand its integrated Hebrew language and Jewish studies program through Grade 5. New AVI CHAI funding is helping the organization join forces with Compedia, a for-profit educational technology company, to develop an interactive digital version of the curriculum. The foundation hopes that the nonprofit organization formed through this joint venture will be a long-term, sustainable home for the project.

NETA/Bishvil Ha'Ivrit is a Hebrew-language curriculum and teacher training program used by 15,000 students in 110 middle and high schools. NETA has now become part of a thriving Israeli nonprofit organization, the Center for Educational Technology (CET), which has helped develop a digital version of NETA, called Bishvil Ha'Ivrit, and has agreed to take long-term responsibility for the project.

Building Loan Programs.[37] AVI CHAI made available $150 million in interest-free loans for construction and renovation at day schools and summer camps, assisting in capital projects of nearly $1 billion. The capital projects enabled enrollment growth, increased the attractiveness of the facilities, and/or supported educational improvement. The program addressed a critical timing mismatch in capital campaigns: donors typically fulfill their capital pledges over a few years, but the contractor needs to be paid at the time of construction. To alleviate this timing challenge, AVI CHAI made loans of up to $1 million, repayable over five years (after an initial six-month grace period) and secured by a standby Letter of Credit issued by an acceptable commercial bank. AVI CHAI agreed to pay the annual Letter of Credit fee. After AVI CHAI ceased making loans because of its spend-down, the Maimonides Fund agreed to provide the funding needed to continue the program for summer camp construction and renovation.

Israel

The AVI CHAI Film and Television Project.[38] In 1999, AVI CHAI established an in-house effort to promote quality treatment of Jewish life, history, and culture on Israeli television and cinema. Prior to this, Jewish content on the Israeli television screen was superficial, laden with stereotypes, or nonexistent. The Foundation helped develop over 300 hours of programming that have obtained impressive ratings and numerous awards, have become an effective educational tool in schools and cultural centers, and have inspired filmmakers to create what has now become legitimate content for film and television—the Jewish-Israeli story.

Pre-army *Mechinot* (Zionist Leadership Academies).[39] Since 1997, AVI CHAI has supported the development of pre-army social leadership academies. As of 2015, 23 *mechinot* supported by AVI CHAI attract annually over 1,500 high school graduates to an intensive year-long residential program. These academies, each with its distinctive character, seek to engage participants in the significant study of Jewish and Zionist texts, to foster dialogue across diverse religious identities, and to nurture a commitment to Judaism, democracy, and civic responsibility. A disproportionate number of *mechinot* graduates continue on as officers in the Israel Defense Forces and can be found later in positions of social and civic leadership in Israeli society.

Tzohar.[40] Tzohar began as a small group of rabbis interested in providing secular couples with an alternative to the impersonal weddings officiated by Israel's Chief Rabbinate. Over a period of 15 years, beginning in 1997, AVI CHAI's support enabled this modest organization to grow into a powerful movement of 1,000 Zionist rabbis and female volunteers, which offers, among other things, training for rabbis to counter trends of religious extremism, religious services for the secular public, and a voice of rabbinic moderation in public discourse over issues and policies of religion and state.

Former Soviet Union (FSU)

Judaic and Academic Enhancement in Jewish Day Schools across the FSU. Over a period of 12 years, AVI CHAI's efforts to enhance Jewish Day School education in the FSU included a two-pronged effort: strengthening the Jewish experiences of students attending Jewish Day Schools and, with an eye to bolstering registration, creating stronger academic departments in 30 Jewish day schools in 18 cities across the FSU. Supported programs included Jewishly themed after-school clubs and activities, expansion of Jewish and academic libraries, tutorials, preparations for interschool academic and Jewish Olympics, stipends to attract outstanding teachers, a curriculum-based study of the Hebrew language via an adapted version of the TaL AM and NETA programs for the FSU (currently used as the core Jewish studies curriculum by 28 schools with a combined total of over 2,000 students), and a Youth Leadership initiative for high school students in these schools. Support for these programs came in partnership with Israel's Ministry of Education/Jewish Agency for Israel, the Leviev Fund, the Mirilashvili Family, and local donors. With AVI CHAI's sunset in the FSU, these programs continue with support from these partners.

Booknik.ru. Booknik.ru is the first Russian-language Internet portal focusing on Jewish and Israeli history, religion, society, and thought; Jewish arts and culture; and the Jewish spirit, with a section for children and families as well as a subsection that focused on bringing Booknik.ru's articles and postings to Russia's rapidly developing world of social networking.

By July 2015, Booknik's traffic exceeded 825,000 viewers per month. In addition, the overall total number of participants in the social networking efforts surpassed 90,000, and Booknik's biannual "Booknik-party" drew several thousand people to the center of Moscow to celebrate "Booknik and Jewish/Israeli Life and Culture." Booknik is currently working on identifying new partners that can ensure the unique project's continued growth in the years following AVI CHAI's sunset.

Publication of Books on Jewish Themes in the Russian Language.[41] Research showed that most treasures of Jewish/Israeli literature and thought were locked away for most Russian speakers even a decade after the fall of the Iron Curtain. To combat this, AVI CHAI launched a major publishing effort that to date has resulted in over 500,000 books in circulation in the fiction series, 130,500 in the nonfiction series, 180,000 illustrated books for children on Jewish themes, 25,000 in the Pearls of Yiddish Literature series, and 15,700 in the Hebrew and classical series. The foundation's efforts were buttressed by the support of Jewish/Israeli Book Festivals across the FSU, aggressive marketing in bookstores and literary venues, and visits of Israeli and Jewish authors and an app called JKniga for mobile and handheld devices that digitized published books. In addition to AVI CHAI, these efforts are supported by local and international donors, with several local philanthropists providing significant gifts to name individual series in their families' honor.

The Gill Foundation[42]

Foundation established: 1994
Spend-down year: 20 years after death of founder, Tim Gill
Rationale: To make largest impact possible during lifetime of founder
Mission: "To advance equality for LGBT Americans further, faster"[43]
Programmatic focus: LGBT advocacy
Grantmaking overview: The foundation's grantmaking priorities are equal treatment and family recognition of LGBT individuals, safe schools for

them, and a prosperous Colorado. As of 2013, grants represented 61 percent of the foundation's money spent. The foundation's total grants in 2013 were $11 million, with $3.4 million specifically for the state of Colorado. See Table A.1 below.

A.1 Gill Foundation 2013 Grant Allocation[44]

Initiative	Grant Amount	% of total
National LGBT	$2,822,828	26%
State LGBT	$1,825,000	17%
National Allies	$779,625	7%
Federal Agency Project	$750,000	7%
Colorado LGBT & HIV	$711,500	6%
Colorado Civic Engagement/Roundtable	$649,600	6%
GF Communications Projects	$636,500	6%
Colorado Communications Network	$618,325	6%
Latino Initiative	$565,000	5%
Colorado STEM Initiative	$421,100	4%
School Culture Initiative	$416,000	4%
African American Initiative	$380,000	3%
Board Discretionary	$190,000	2%
ED Programs & Oppty Fund	$45,000	<1%
National Donor Development	$30,500	<1%
Employee Matched	$27,460	<1%
ED Discretionary Grants	$7,500	<1%
TOTAL	$11,000,938	

Impact:

Equal Treatment

"In 32 states, LGBT people are not fully protected from discrimination. In 2013, Gill Foundation and [its] funding partners invested in a two-year research project to understand how the public thinks about policies that protect LGBT people from discrimination. This messaging initiative is impacting how advocates talk about these policies in public education campaigns across the country." In addition, "18 states (plus DC) now have employment nondiscrimination laws that protect hardworking LGBT employees."

Family Recognition

"For years, the Gill Foundation has supported strategic, high-impact litigation. And in 2013 that work led to a monumental win before the Supreme Court in *Windsor v. United States*. This decision laid the groundwork upon which future cases were built, creating nationwide momentum for the freedom to marry."

Safe Schools

"In 2013, Gill Foundation grantee One Colorado Education Fund hosted a statewide training for educators with a special focus on transgender students, providing guidance on topics such as gender-segregated facilities, identity documentation, and working with families."[45]

Prosperous Colorado

"Colorado kids spend less time on science than those in 45 other states. In 2013, [the foundation] funded organizations to strengthen science, technology, engineering, and math (STEM) education for all students. STEM competencies prepare students to be critical thinkers, to persevere through failure, to communicate and collaborate across real and perceived barriers, and to solve complex and ever-changing problems."[46]

The Brainerd Foundation[47]

Foundation established: 1995
Spend-down year: 2020

Year spend-down decision made: 2008

Rationale: According to Paul Brainerd, president of the foundation: "Despite all that we have accomplished, the ecological challenges before us are as significant as humanity has ever faced. I believe we must each do whatever we can to protect the natural resources that sustain this planet because the need is nothing short of urgent. There are many ways to accomplish this, of course, and mine is to see that the foundation's entire endowment is spent in my lifetime. After much thought, I have decided to spend-out the foundation's assets over the next ten to twelve years and then pass the baton to a new generation of conservationists and philanthropists."[48]

Mission: "To protect the environment of the Northwest and to build broad citizen support for conservation."[49]

Programmatic focus: Conservation policy, place-based conservation, conservation capacity

Grantmaking overview: The foundation invests in nonprofit organizations in Alaska, Idaho, Montana, Oregon, Washington, and British Columbia. Since 1995, the foundation has invested in more than 300 organizations; since 2007, the foundation has funded 38 organizations within its funding areas: conservation policy, place-based conservation, conservation capacity, a grassroots fund, and an opportunity fund.[50]

Grant allocation: 2014:

Conservation policy grants: $705,000

Place-based grants: $920,000

Conservation capacity grants: $893,000

Grassroots grants: $30,000

Opportunity fund grants: $76,500

Other funding: $76,000

TOTAL: $2,700,500[51]

Impact: "President Obama's 2016 Budget recommends $17,930,000 from the Land and Water Conservation Fund for conservation in the High Divide of Montana and Idaho. This funding will support proposals developed by the High Divide Collaborative for conservation easements, property acquisition, habitat restoration, and protection of wildlife connectivity and cultural values. Brainerd Foundation grantees involved in this effort include the Heart of the Rockies Initiative, Salmon Valley Stewardship, Lemhi Regional Land Trust, Centennial Valley Association, Big Hole Watershed Committee, TNC/MT, Madison Valley Ranchlands Group, and Wildlife Conservation Society.

In December 2014, the North Fork Watershed Protection Act was approved by the Senate and sent to President Obama for his signature. The legislation designates 245,000 new acres of wilderness and shields 430,000 acres along the North Fork of the Flathead River near Glacier National Park in Montana from future mining and drilling. This legislation complements actions taken by the B[ritish] C[olumbia] government to protect lands in the Canadian portion of the Flathead River from energy development. Brainerd grantees supporting this legislation included Headwaters Montana, National Parks Conservation Association, and Trout Unlimited.

In December 2014, the Rocky Mountain Front Heritage Act passed Congress, adding 67,000 acres of new wilderness to the Bob Marshall Wilderness Complex, creating a 208,000-acre Conservation Management Area where current uses can continue and directing federal agencies to prioritize noxious weed management on the Front. The Brainerd Foundation supported the work of Montana Wilderness Association, National Parks Conservation Association, and The Wilderness Society in this effort.

In October 2014, a Montana district judge closed a Montana regulatory loophole that allowed developers to drill as many wells as they wanted to provide water to subdivisions, encouraging ill-planned developments and growth in rural areas. [This] decision will help keep development in check on landscapes that are valuable for wildlife habitat and connectivity. The Brainerd Foundation supported Western Environmental Law Center on this challenge to state water well permit rules.

In December 2014, the Yukon Supreme Court ruled in favor of First Nations and the conservation community, overturning a Yukon government decision that would have opened up the 17-million-acre Peel River Watershed to mining and resource development. The court decision reiterates the government's responsibility to consult with First Nations on land management plans affecting aboriginal lands and rights. The Brainerd Foundation supported the work of CPAWS [Canadian Parks and Wilderness Society] and the Yukon Conservation Society in their strong endorsement of First Nations rights and conservation in the Peel Watershed."[52]

The Bloomberg Philanthropies[53]

Foundation established: 2006

After about two decades of significant individual giving, both personally and by pass-through gifts to other foundations, including the Carnegie Corporation of New York, and also after establishing a private foundation, the Bloomberg Family Foundation, as a freestanding 501(c)(3) foundation, Mayor Michael Bloomberg decided that, for the sake of future flexibility and convenience, he would establish one umbrella organization that would, to the extent permitted by US law, coordinate his philanthropic and public policy interests. That organization is now The Bloomberg Philanthropies.

Spend-down year: Unspecified as of 2016

Year spend-down decision made: Uncertain date, according to Mayor Bloomberg in my interview of him for this book

Mission: To ensure better, longer lives for the greatest number of people

Programmatic focus: Focuses on five key areas for creating lasting change: public health, environment, education, government innovation, and the arts. These five areas encompass the issues about which Michael Bloomberg, three-term mayor of New York City and founder of Bloomberg LP, and his team are most passionate and where they believe they can achieve the greatest good.

Public-private partnerships were a hallmark of Bloomberg's approach as mayor. Bloomberg Philanthropies takes a similar approach, bringing together people, ideas, and resources from across sectors toward a common purpose and amplifying their impact.

Grantmaking overview: In 2015, Bloomberg Philanthropies distributed $510 million. Michael Bloomberg's lifetime giving is more than $4 billion.

Grant allocation and impact (selected):

Public Health

A primary focus of Bloomberg Philanthropies' public health program is on noncommunicable diseases, like those caused by obesity, which receive minimal funding from governments and philanthropies around the world. Activities include:

- The Bloomberg Initiative to Reduce Tobacco Use, an unprecedented global campaign to save lives by protecting people from the devastating effects of tobacco. When Bloomberg Philanthropies began spreading these effective solutions in 2007, only 11 countries had passed comprehensive smoke-free tobacco control laws; today 50 countries have these types of laws in place.

- The Global Road Safety Program advocates for stronger road safety legislation in five countries. Bloomberg Philanthropies also works with ten cities to implement proven solutions to improve road safety like seat-belt and helmet wearing and road infrastructure, including promoting sustainable urban transport. The program supports crash testing for cars sold regionally in Latin America and Asia, which can provide evidence for advocates to demand better safety standards. Since 2010, nearly 1.95 billion people are covered by new or improved road safety laws in eight countries or localities.

- The Obesity Prevention Program has supported research and advocacy in Mexico to raise awareness of the country's obesity epidemic and to implement policies and interventions like banning junk food advertising for children and raising taxes on sugar-sweetened beverages (the first such national tax ever). Efforts include rigorous evaluations of the impact of these policies to better determine what works and spread the results to other jurisdictions. The program is preparing to replicate the Mexico model in Brazil, Colombia, South Africa, and Turkey and is tracking and supporting efforts to tax sugar-sweetened beverages in the United States as well.

- The Maternal and Reproductive Health Program started as an initiative to reduce maternal deaths and injuries in Tanzania and later expanded to include reproductive health services, like expanding access to contraceptives and providing postabortion care. Between 2009 and 2015, 67,000 babies were delivered in upgraded maternal health centers in Tanzania. The program formed a partnership with the Gates Foundation to expand contraception to 120 million women around the world by 2020. In addition, the program invests in advocacy programs in four countries—Burkina Faso, Uganda, Nicaragua, and Senegal—to improve access to reproductive health services, including contraception and medical abortion.

- The Partnership to Eradicate Polio supports the Global Polio Eradication Initiative in partnership with the Bill and Melinda Gates Foundation and other donors through on-the-ground activities such as vaccination campaigns in high-risk countries.

Environment

Bloomberg Philanthropies' Environment program seeks to address some of the most serious threats to our environment, including:

- The Clean Energy Initiative aims to halve the amount of electricity generated by coal in America by supporting the Sierra Club's Beyond Coal campaign and by working with states to develop and implement common-sense clean energy policies.

- As UN Secretary-General's Special Envoy for Cities and Climate Change, Michael Bloomberg launched the Compact of Mayors, a common reporting platform to capture the collective impact of global cities in reducing greenhouse gas emissions and addressing climate risk through consistent, public reporting of their efforts—which, in turn, will continue to push nations to increase their carbon-cutting commitments. With the merger of the Compact and European Union's Covenant of Mayors, the new Covenant of Mayors includes almost 7,000 cities. Bloomberg Philanthropies also supports the C40 Cities Climate Leadership Group, a global network of mayors from the largest cities committed to tackling climate change.

- Vibrant Oceans aims to end overfishing worldwide by piloting efforts to reform both industrial and small-scale fishing practices in Brazil, Chile, and the Philippines, which together constitute approximately 7 percent of the global catch. The program also works to increase private capital for sustainable fishing by exploring and publicizing effective vehicles for investment.

Government Innovation

Solutions to many of the greatest challenges we face can be found in cities. Bloomberg Philanthropies works to support public sector innovation capacity and spread proven and promising solutions among cities worldwide. Major government innovation initiatives include:

- The Mayors Challenge competitions use prizes to encourage cities to develop bold and innovative solutions that have the potential to spread and be replicated by cities worldwide. As of 2016, there have been challenges in the United States, Europe, and Latin America, and the Caribbean.

- Bloomberg Philanthropies' Innovation Teams (i-teams) are in-house consultants that work across city agencies and report directly to mayors on a priority issue. Using Bloomberg Philanthropies' Innovation Delivery approach, the i-teams help agency leaders and staff go through a data-driven process to assess problems, generate responsive new interventions, develop partnerships, and deliver measurable results.

- What Works Cities helps city governments in midsized US cities. The program empowers leaders to use data to drive decision-making, supports implementation and enhancement of open data and performance management programs, and helps cities conduct real-time, low-cost evaluations of programs so they can continually improve services.

- The Bloomberg Harvard City Leadership Initiative is a joint program between Harvard Business School and Harvard Kennedy School of Government to provide 40 mayors and 60–80 key aides per year access to a robust leadership program, including a convening in New York and virtual learning over a 12-month period. The program will also generate the world's largest open-source hub of new case studies and curriculum focused on innovative city leadership. It will also include a significant internship component for Harvard students to be placed in participating city halls.

Bloomberg Associates, a team of globally recognized experts who formerly served as commissioners and deputy mayors in the Bloomberg administration, has developed into a highly sought-after pro bono municipal consulting firm. The team focuses on developing deep relationships in a select number of cities across multiple disciplines, helping mayors around the world tackle some of the most complex and difficult challenges.

The Arts

Bloomberg Philanthropies promotes the critical economic and cultural role the arts play in helping cities flourish. Major arts initiatives include:

- The Arts Innovation and Management program provides management training developed specifically for small and midsized nonprofit arts organizations. Participating organizations are required to secure matching funds, reach 100 percent board participation in fundraising, and maintain up-to-date information in DataArts, an online financial management tool that assists arts organizations across the country to collect and use data effectively.

- Bloomberg Connects aims to expand public access to cultural institutions by funding the development of digital tools and other technology that enhance the visitor experience. There have been 15.7 million users of technologies developed through Bloomberg Connect since 2013.

- The Public Art Challenge helps US city leaders partner with artists to use public art as an effective tool to celebrate creativity, enhance urban identity, and catalyze economic development. The inaugural competition was held in 2015, and four winners were chosen out of 237 applicants.

Education

Bloomberg Philanthropies works to improve education in America with an innovative program to strengthen educational leadership, advance good public policies in communities across the United States, and help ensure that the best and brightest, whatever their economic backgrounds, make it to America's top universities and colleges. Major education initiatives include:

- CollegePoint works to increase the number of high-achieving, low- to moderate-income students who enroll in the 265 most selective US colleges and universities. The program's goal is to help as many as 65,000 students apply to, enroll in, and graduate from these schools. CollegePoint helps students by providing them with free virtual college advising (via the phone and online). The program also engages college and university presidents and leading experts to change higher education policies so that more high-achieving, low- to moderate-income students enroll and graduate from top schools.

- Bloomberg Philanthropies also makes strategic investments in targeted areas to elect, protect, and support education reform leaders so that those leaders can strengthen the US education system, improve student performance substantially, and reduce the achievement gap. All advocacy work is done with Mike Bloomberg's personal money.

- The Career and Technical Education program works to fill the gap in vocational training in the United States by supporting promising programs that provide training for "middle-skill" jobs that require postsecondary training but not a college career. Support is currently in areas where the Education program is already active and include Denver; Colorado; New Orleans; Louisiana; Philadelphia; Pennsylvania; Washington, D.C.; Rhode Island; and New Jersey.

Founder's Projects

Bloomberg Philanthropies funds projects that are of special interest to its founder, including:

- Support of Johns Hopkins University, his alma mater, which has surpassed $1 billion, and includes a gift to hire 50 interdisciplinary professors ("Bloomberg Distinguished Scholars") to work across at least two departments at the institution; undergraduate merit-based scholarships; an endowment of the Charlotte R. Bloomberg Children's Center, a globally renowned pediatric hospital; and funding for the Bloomberg-Kimmel Institute for Cancer Immunotherapy. In recognition of Bloomberg's deep support of the university, the School of Public Health was named the "Johns Hopkins Bloomberg School of Public Health" in his honor.

- Everytown for Gun Safety is a national organization cofounded by Michael Bloomberg with the goal of protecting Americans from gun violence. Everytown advocates for life-saving laws state by state, blocks dangerous bills pushed by the gun lobby at both the state and federal level, and conducts research on gun violence and safety.

- Bloomberg Philanthropies' Economic Development in Africa program is helping women in Rwanda and Congo gain skills, like farming and hospitality, which enable them to support their families and be economically self-sufficient. Nearly 150,000 women have completed the program since it launched in 2007.

STORIES OF PERPETUITY

For the sake of balance and to represent a sampling of the many perpetual foundations and their achievements, I asked the heads of the following institutions to write short descriptions of one or more of the significant achievements of the foundations over which they preside. My editor and I have compressed some of them, but they are presented here in the authors' own words. In some other cases, I have drawn on already existing short summaries of the foundations' work, with appropriate crediting.

Samuel N. and Mary Castle Foundation, Hawaii[54]

Founded in 1894 in Hawaii, the Castle Foundation is now the oldest family foundation in the United States. It continues to be animated by Mary Castle's "dramatic vision for Hawaii, one of greater equity, social justice, and opportunity. 'Her social change theory was the theory of early education,' said Al Castle, the foundation's executive director, noting the founder's close association with Chicago progressives like John Dewey and George Herbert Mead, her son-in-law. 'She asked: "How long will it take to get to the type of community that we want in Hawaii?" To get to that kind of community, every child had to have access to high quality kindergarten, to care, nutrition, to good family support, to safe and healthy community. It was at least a century-long project.' . . . Today, the family is still focusing on education."[55]

The Grable Foundation, Pittsburgh, Pennsylvania[56]

The Grable Foundation, located in Pittsburgh, Pennsylvania, was founded in 1976 by Minnie K. Grable, the widow of Errett M. Grable, the founder and lifetime director of Rubbermaid, Inc., which grew to become an international housewares company. As longtime residents of Pittsburgh, the Grables were deeply concerned about the welfare of the Pittsburgh region and all its citizens; in particular, they were firmly committed to education and the important role it can play in helping children build productive, self-sustaining, and meaningful lives. Following the death of Mrs. Grable in 1990, the assets from her estate began to be distributed to the foundation, and the first professional staff members were hired in 1991. Today, the foundation's eight-member board of trustees, most of whom are members of the Grable family, are guided by Minnie Grable's desire to help young people lead fulfilling lives with hope for the future. The foundation retains an endowment of approximately $300 million and currently distributes nearly $13 million in grant awards each year, with a focus on its key areas of early education, improving K–12 school systems and out-of-school time, and building community vitality in the Pittsburgh region.

What began with just a handful of people and organizations has grown into a diverse network of more than 200 organizations, including more than 2,000 educators and professionals in schools, museums, libraries, afterschool programs, community centers, university research centers, educational technology companies, local philanthropies, and youth civic groups.

Recognizing the need to sustain momentum, leaders across the Pittsburgh region reaffirmed their commitment in 2014 and formed the Remake Learning Council. The Council brings together leading executives and learning scientists in business, higher education, public education, civic and cultural organizations, foundations, and government to support the greater Pittsburgh region's efforts strategically so as to remake learning in all the places where children and youth learn.

The Remake Learning Network has established a solid ecosystem for learning innovation in the greater Pittsburgh region, attracting visitors from around the world to examine firsthand how a handful of people—with foundation guidance and funding—worked together to transform school districts and build effective partnerships between educators, cultural institutions, and research universities, all while providing children and youth with the best available opportunities to learn and be creative.

The Charles H. Revson Foundation, New York, New York[57]

Created in 1956 by Charles H. Revson, founder of Revlon, the Revson Foundation focuses on four program areas: urban affairs, education, biomedical research, and Jewish life. With a current endowment of $160 million and annual spending of $8–10 million, the foundation remains dedicated to Mr. Revson's self-professed "zeal to learn" and love of New York City.

In recent years, the trustees turned their attention to a philanthropic opportunity overlooked but in plain sight: New York City's branch libraries. Over a century ago, Andrew Carnegie began construction of many local public libraries. There are now 207 branches, touching every city neighborhood, serving over 40 million visitors annually, more than all the city's cultural institutions and sports arenas combined. Millions of New Yorkers rely on libraries for Internet access, job-search assistance, English-as-a-second-language classes, homework help, community and cultural programs, and a safe and horizon-expanding place to go after school. According to a 2010 analysis conducted by the Center for an Urban Future, a prominent local urban-affairs think tank, in the past decade the city's branch libraries have seen a 27 percent increase in program offerings, a 40 percent increase in program attendance, and a 59 percent increase in circulation. They rank among the nation's top 10 in each of these categories, despite diminishing budgets that left most branches open only four to five days a week. Unlike most major urban public libraries, which are under the auspices of city government, the New York, Brooklyn, and Queens public libraries operate as separate nonprofit organizations. And unlike other city services such as parks and education, the three systems had no organized constituency and no designated public official advocating for increased resources.

In 2008, the Revson Foundation set out to secure desperately needed capital funds for the branch libraries while addressing a high priority of the Bloomberg administration: the development of affordable housing in a land-starved city. A feasibility study commissioned by the foundation found 20–30 library branches in need of significant capital investment that were also suitable for redevelopment with a state-of-the-art library on the lower floor(s) and affordable housing above. At least 50 apartments could be developed on each site. Development under this mixed-use model would lower the costs of library construction by 40–50 percent.

Through a proposed partnership among the City of New York, the three library systems, and a collaborative group of foundations, "Living Libraries" was born. Ten library sites were selected for the pilot program, and lead philanthropic commitments were in hand from the Revson and Wallace Foundations. Unfortunately, the financial crisis of 2008 and the recession that followed decimated the foundation's plans. With no sources of financing, extremely limited philanthropic support, and no government champion (the city housing commissioner left to work in the new Obama administration), all that remained of Living Libraries was a feasibility study showing that— someday, perhaps—the model could still work.

Despite the setback, the Revson trustees agreed that New York's branch libraries were too important a community asset to abandon. Over the next

seven years, the foundation pursued several strategies to build public awareness and support for libraries, including encouraging collaboration among the
three library systems and providing ways for the patrons and staff of branch
libraries to tell their stories. Thanks to the foundation's 2015 "Tri-Library"
"Invest in Libraries" campaign, the outpouring of activity by tens of thousands of New Yorkers reenergized the city council to fight vigorously for the
libraries. By the end of the fiscal year 2016 budget process, six-day-a-week
service was restored citywide, with some branches open seven days a week.
And, for the first time, libraries were included in the city's 10-year capital
plan, with an allocation close to $400 million.

By 2015, New York's economy had fully recovered, and Bill de Blasio,
the recently elected mayor, had made affordable housing among his highest
priorities—thus seeming to present a renewed opportunity for "Living Libraries." After a period of exploration and due diligence, the Robin Hood
Foundation offered to join Revson in a five-site pilot program, in which
Robin Hood would raise $25 million to finance 30 percent of the library
capital costs, if the city would finance the housing component and 30 percent of the library capital costs. The remaining financing would be derived
from the value of the land and cost savings accrued from employing the
"mixed-use" model.

Robin Hood worked closely with enthusiastic partners from all three library systems to identify at least 30 viable sites for the project, now renamed
"New Stories." It then approached city hall to negotiate the public share of
the funding. After six months of negotiations, the city offered considerably
less than requested, and Robin Hood was unwilling to double its funding
commitment to make up the difference. The Revson Foundation was again
compelled to rescind its grant, and the project returned to a holding pen.

Despite significant improvements in cooperation among the libraries and
major funding increases from city government, the Revson Foundation's
business with the city's branch libraries continues. Among other things, it is
currently underwriting "Innovation Funds" at New York Public Library and
Brooklyn Public Library, with the goal of cross-fertilization and scaling of innovation both within and across systems. And it is exploring the potential to
establish a first-ever fellowship program for up-and-coming branch librarians
and the feasibility of allowing branch libraries to lend local museum passes
to their patrons—an idea that has been successfully implemented in many
other systems across the country.

The Meadows Foundation, Dallas, Texas[58]

The mission of this foundation, which was founded by Algur Meadows and his wife, Virginia, in 1948, is to serve Texans in every county of the state. During its past history, its grants totaled around $800 million, and its endowment has now grown to about $1 billion. It is widely known for its preservation, starting in 1981, of 22 acres of land in downtown Dallas, called the Wilson Historic District, to provide rent-free offices exclusively for Dallas nonprofit organizations. It built the Dallas Center for Contemporary Art and provided land for the Volunteer Center of North Texas as well as Dallas's Latino Cultural Center. In the wake of Hurricanes Katrina and Rita, the Meadows Foundation was a major contributor to efforts to serve the needs of the evacuees of those hurricanes to Dallas, Houston, and other parts of Texas.

The Z. Smith Reynolds Foundation, Winston-Salem, North Carolina[59]

The Z. Smith Reynolds Foundation was established in 1936 by Mary Reynolds Babcock and her siblings as a memorial to their brother Zachary Smith Reynolds, who died under mysterious circumstances from a shooting at the family estate when he was 20 years old. Eighty years later, that family foundation has a governing board composed of both family and nonfamily members and aims to support worthwhile civic-sector initiatives across North Carolina. Much to the chagrin of right-wing zealots,[60] the foundation has maintained the centrist commitment of its founding family to the goal of advancing social justice in North Carolina by supporting new and previously existing social service–delivering organizations, educational institutions, and advocacy organizations committed to a just and fairer state and communities.

The foundation's most visible grants were made to attract Wake Forest College from the tiny hamlet of Wake Forest, North Carolina, to a new campus in Winston-Salem, North Carolina, for which members of the Reynolds family provided the land as well as some of the building costs, and the foundation constructed some of the buildings to house it and guaranteed in perpetuity annual support starting at $420,000 a year, which has now grown to about $2 million a year. Thanks to the foundation's efforts, Wake Forest

University has attained international stature. In 2016, it tied for 10th place in the *US News and World Report* rankings for "Best Undergraduate Teaching" in the United States and as 27th best overall university in the United States. In addition to its promised support, the foundation has made gifts to endow distinguished faculty professorships, one of which was filled by Maya Angelou for many years until her death in 2014. Over the 60 years since Wake Forest College moved to Winston-Salem, the foundation has given it more than $100 million.

Among the other statewide initiatives that were founded with major support from the foundation are the North Carolina Fund, which was the first statewide "War on Poverty" program in the United States after President Lyndon B. Johnson established the national Office of Economic Opportunity;[61] the North Carolina School of the Arts, which, at its founding in 1963, was the first statewide, publicly supported conservatory of the arts and is now a branch of the University of North Carolina System; the North Carolina Center for Public Policy Research, founded in 1977, which is the principal "watchdog" think tank covering state government; the Public School Forum of North Carolina, the leading nonprofit advocacy organization for the North Carolina public schools; and the Commission on Higher Education for North Carolina, which charted the development of North Carolina's statewide system of community colleges and technical institutes.

All but the closed-minded right-wing critics applaud the foundation's hand-in-glove relationship with North Carolina's state and municipal governments that has helped generate North Carolina's reputation for progressive change, at least until recently.

The Robert W. Woodruff, Lettie Pate Whitehead, Lettie Pate Evans, and Joseph B. Whitehead Foundations, Atlanta, Georgia[62]

The Robert W. Woodruff Foundation and its six related foundations, all of which grew out of the Coca-Cola fortune, constitute the wealthiest philanthropic group in Georgia. Joseph B. Whitehead was the founder of the Coca-Cola Company, and Mr. Woodruff presided over it from 1923 until his death in 1985. Despite his celebrity as the head of Atlanta's leading company, he sought to avoid the limelight by giving anonymously as he engaged in his generous philanthropic endeavors, which included major endowment gifts that helped elevate Emory University to its present stature as one of the nation's leading private universities. It is said that there was hardly a civic initiative of any significance in which Mr. Woodruff was not a prime mover and generous donor. He left a large part of his fortune to these foundations, which were also supported by his relatives for whom they are named. The annual giving of these related foundations is over $321 million, and their $10 billion in assets places them among the largest 100 foundation groupings in the United States. These foundations have steadily made unique contributions over many years to the building of Atlanta into one of the major metropolitan areas in the United States and have been a constant mainstay of the large, diverse, and dynamic nonprofit sector in the city. The Woodruff Foundation describes itself as a "social venture philanthropy fund for Atlanta."[63] The Robert Woodruff Foundation is a continuing major partner with the Greater Atlanta Community Foundation and many other private foundations.

The Virginia G. Piper Charitable Trust, Phoenix, Arizona[64]

Four years before Virginia G. Piper died in 1999, she established the Virginia G. Piper Charitable Trust, under the terms of which the trustees were given the authority to determine whether her trust would have unlimited life or would be spent down in a time period of their choosing. When her estate was settled in 2001, the trust received $600 million, making it one of the 100 largest foundations in the United States. The trust makes annual grants of about $15 million in program areas, including arts and culture, children, education, health care and medical research, older adults, and religion; and it partners frequently with the Arizona Community Foundation, which gives away about double the amount of the Piper Trust's annual grantmaking. Over the following decade, the trustees pondered the pros and cons of perpetuity or limited life and concluded that, as the largest general purpose foundation in the state of Arizona, it was too important to Maricopa County's nonprofit sector to be spent down and chose instead to continue for an indefinite period.

Appendix B: Signers of the Giving Pledge[1]

NAME, COUNTRY

Bill & Karen Ackman, USA

Margaret & Sylvan Adams, Canada

Paul G. Allen, USA

HRH Prince Alwaleed Bin Talal Bin Abdulaziz AlSaud, Saudi Arabia

Sue Ann Arnall, USA

Laura & John Arnold, USA

Lord Ashcroft KCMG PC, England

Lynne & Marc Benioff, USA

Nicolas Berggruen, Germany

Manoj Bhargava, USA

Steve Bing, USA

---

[1]As of 3/6/17; http://givingpledge.org/.

Sara Blakely, USA

Arthur M. Blank, USA

Nathan & Elizabeth Blecharczyk, USA

Michael R. Bloomberg, USA

Richard & Joan Branson, British Virgin Islands

Eli & Edythe Broad, USA

Charles R. Bronfman, Canada

Edgar M. Bronfman, USA

Warren Buffett, USA

Jean & Steve Case, USA

John Caudwell, England

Brian Chesky, USA

Scott Cook & Signe Ostby, USA

Lee & Toby Cooperman, USA

Joe & Kelly Craft, USA

Joyce & Bill Cummings, USA

Ray & Barbara Dalio, USA

Jack & Laura Dangermond, USA

John Paul DeJoria, USA

Mohammed Dewji, Tanzania

Barry Diller & Diane von Furstenberg, USA

Ann & John Doerr, USA

Glenn & Eva Dubin, USA

Larry Ellison, USA

Henry Engelhardt CBE & Diane Briere de l'Isle-Engelhardt OBE, WALES, UK

Judy Faulkner, USA

Charles F. Feeney, USA

Andrew & Nicola Forrest, Australia

Ted Forstmann (d. 2011), USA

Phillip & Patricia Frost, USA

Bill & Melinda Gates, USA

Joe Gebbia, USA

Dan & Jennifer Gilbert, USA

Ann Gloag OBE, Scotland

Dave Goldberg (d. 2015) & Sheryl Sandberg, USA

David & Barbara Green, USA

Jeff & Mei Sze Greene, USA

Harold Grinspoon & Diane Troderman, USA

Gordon & Llura Gund, USA

Harold Hamm, USA

Reed Hastings & Patty Quillin, USA

Lyda Hill, USA

Barron Hilton, USA

Christopher Hohn, England

Elie & Susy Horn, Brazil

Sir Tom & Lady Marion Hunter, Scotland

Jon & Karen Huntsman, USA

Dr. Mo Ibrahim, England

Carl Icahn, USA

Joan & Irwin Jacobs, USA

John W. "Jay" Jordan II, USA

George B. Kaiser, USA

Brad & Kim Keywell, USA

Vinod & Neeru Khosla, USA

Sidney Kimmel, USA

Rich & Nancy Kinder, USA

Beth & Seth Klarman, USA

Robert & Arlene Kogod, USA

Elaine & Ken Langone, USA

Liz & Eric Lefkofsky, USA

Gerry & Marguerite Lenfest, USA

Peter B. Lewis (d. 2013), USA

Lorry I. Lokey, USA

George Lucas & Mellody Hobson, USA

Duncan & Nancy MacMillan, USA

Alfred E. Mann (d. 2016), USA

Joe & Rika Mansueto, USA

Bernie & Billi Marcus, USA

Richard Edwin & Nancy Peery Marriott, USA

Strive & Tsitsi Masiyiwa, England

Kiran Mazumdar-Shaw, India

Craig & Susan McCaw, USA

Red & Charline McCombs, USA

PNC & Sobha Menon, India

Dean & Marianne Metropoulos, USA

Gary K. Michelson, M.D., USA

Michael & Lori Milken, USA

Yuri Milner, Russia

George P. Mitchell (d. 2013), USA

Thomas S. Monaghan, USA

Gordon & Betty Moore, USA

Tashia & John Morgridge, USA

Michael Moritz & Harriet Heyman, USA

Dustin Moskovitz & Cari Tuna, USA

Patrice & Precious Motsepe, South Africa

Elon Musk, USA

Arif Naqvi, UAE

Jonathan M. Nelson, USA

Gensheng Niu, China

Pierre & Pam Omidyar, USA

Natalie & Paul Orfalea, USA

Bernard & Barbro Osher, USA

Bob & Renee Parsons, USA

Ronald O. Perelman, USA

Jorge M. & Darlene Perez, USA

Peter G. Peterson, USA

T. Boone Pickens, USA

Victor Pinchuk, Ukraine

Hasso Plattner, Germany

Vladimir Potanin, Russia

Azim Premji, India

Terry & Susan Ragon, USA

Julian H. Robertson Jr., USA

David Rockefeller (d. 2017), USA

Edward W. (d. 2016) & Deedie Potter Rose, USA

Stephen M. Ross, USA

David M. Rubenstein, USA

David Sainsbury, England

John & Ginger Sall, USA

Henry & Susan Samueli, USA

Herb & Marion (d. 2012) Sandler, USA

Denny Sanford, USA

Vicki & Roger Sant, USA

Lynn Schusterman, USA

Ruth & Bill Scott, USA

Walter Scott Jr., USA

Tom & Cindy Secunda, USA

Craig Silverstein & Mary Obelnicki, USA

Annette & Harold Simmons, USA

Jim & Marilyn Simons, USA

Liz Simons & Mark Heising, USA

Paul E. Singer, USA

Jeff Skoll, USA

John A. & Susan Sobrato, John Michael Sobrato, USA

Michele B. Chan & Patrick Soon-Shiong, USA

Ted (d. 2016) & Vada (d. 2013) Stanley, USA

Mark & Mary Stevens, USA

Tom Steyer & Kat Taylor, USA

Jim (d. 2014) & Virginia Stowers, USA

Dato' Sri Dr. Tahir, Indonesia

Vincent Tan Chee Yioun, Malaysia

Tad Taube, USA

Claire (d. 2014) & Leonard Tow, USA

Ted Turner, USA

Albert Lee Ueltschi (d. 2012), USA

Hamdi Ulukaya, USA

Sunny & Sherly Varkey, UAE

Dr. Romesh & Kathleen Wadhwani, USA

Sanford & Joan Weill, USA

Dr. Herbert & Nicole Wertheim, USA

Shelby White, USA

Sir Ian Wood, Scotland

Hansjörg Wyss, USA

Samuel Yin, Taiwan

Charles Zegar & Merryl Snow Zegar, USA

Mark Zuckerberg & Priscilla Chan, USA

Appendix C: People Interviewed for This Book

Bannick, Matthew. Managing Partner, Omidyar Network, 3/11/14.

Bell, Susan. Former Vice President, The William and Flora Hewlett Foundation, 3/12/15.

Bennack, Frank, Jr. Vice Chairman and CEO, Hearst Corporation, 5/11/15.

Berresford, Susan. Former President, Ford Foundation, 5/5/14.

Bloomberg, Michael. Former Mayor of New York City; Founder, Bloomberg Philanthropies, 2/19/15.

Bowen, William. Former President, The Andrew W. Mellon Foundation, 12/11/13.

Brest, Paul. Former President, The William and Flora Hewlett Foundation, 10/8/13.

Canales, James, Jr. President and CEO, Barr Foundation, 3/7/14.

Crown, Lester. Chairman, Crown Family Philanthropies, 2/20/14.

Dachs, Laurie and Kibbe, Barbara. President, S. D. Bechtel, Jr. Foundation; Director of Organizational Effectiveness, S. D. Bechtel, Jr. Foundation, 3/7/14.

Dale, Harvey. Founding President and CEO, The Atlantic Philanthropies, 2/3/14.

Esposito, Virginia. Director, National Center for Family Philanthropy, 5/14/15.

Fanton, Jonathan. Former President, The John D. and Catherine T. MacArthur Foundation, 5/5/14.

Fineberg, Dr. Harvey. President and CEO, Gordon and Betty Moore Foundation, 3/11/15.

Fried, Arthur. Former President and CEO, Now a Trustee, The AVI CHAI Foundation, 2/3/14

Gallucci, Robert. Former President, John D. and Catherine T. MacArthur Foundation, 2/21/14.

Gund, Agnes. Founding Trustee, The Agnes Gund Foundation, 3/28/14.

Heintz, Stephen. President, Rockefeller Brothers Fund, 12/13/13.

Joskow, Paul. President, Alfred P. Sloan Foundation, 1/31/14.

Kramer, Larry. President and CEO, The William and Flora Hewlett Foundation, 3/14/14.

LaMarche, Gara. Former President and CEO, The Atlantic Philanthropies, 5/5/14.

Larson, Carol. President and CEO, The David and Lucile Packard Foundation, 10/9/13.

McCormick, Steven. Former President and CEO, Gordon and Betty Moore Foundation, 3/12/14.

McGee, Vincent. Former Executive Director, Aaron Diamond Foundation and the DJB Foundation; Senior Advisor, The Atlantic Philanthropies, 12/11/13.

Meehan, William. Lecturer in Strategic Management and Raccoon Partners Lecturer, Stanford Graduate School of Business, 3/12/15.

Miller, Will. President, The Wallace Foundation, 3/28/14.

Morrisett, Lloyd. Former President of the Markle Foundation; Vice President, Carnegie Corporation of New York, 2/25/15.

Oechsli, Christopher. President and CEO, The Atlantic Philanthropies, 5/6/14.

Osberg, Sally. President, Skoll Foundation, 10/11/13.

Piereson, James. William E. Simon Foundation, 3/28/14.

Pritzker, J. B. President, Pritzker Family Foundation, 2/20/14.

Randel, Don. Former President, The Andrew W. Mellon Foundation, 12/9/13.

Rapson, Rip. President and CEO, The Kresge Foundation, 10/21/14.

Rimel, Rebecca. President and CEO, The Pew Charitable Trusts.

Robertson, Julian. President, Robertson Foundation, 12/17/13.

Rockefeller, David, Jr. Chairman of the Board of Trustees, The Rockefeller Foundation, 1/31/14.

Rodin, Judith. President and CEO, The Rockefeller Foundation, 5/6/14.

Rothschild, Lord Jacob. President, The Rothschild Foundation, 9/3/14.

Rubenstein, David. Managing Partner, The Carlyle Group, 2/4/15.

Sall, John and Ginger. President and Cofounder, Sall Family Foundation, 5/20/15.

Sandler, Herbert. President, Sandler Foundation, 3/7/14.

Schroeder, Steven. Former President and CEO, Robert Wood Johnson Foundation, 3/10/14.

Schusterman, Lynn. Chairman, Charles and Lynn Schusterman Family Foundation, 12/10/14.

Solomon, Jeffrey. President, The Charles and Andrea Bronfman Foundation, 5/8/15.

Steinhardt, Michael. President, The Steinhardt Foundation for Jewish Life, 3/27/14.

Stone, Christopher. President, Open Society Foundations, 1/29/14.

Tuna, Cari. President, Good Ventures, 3/9/15.

Vachon, Michael. Advisor to the Chairman, Soros Fund Management LLC, 12/15/14.

Walker, Darren. President, Ford Foundation, 6/20/14.

Weiss, Ariel. CEO, Yad Hanadiv (The Rothschild Foundation Israel), 5/23/14.

Notes

PREFACE

1. Moses Maimonides, *Guide for the Perplexed* (Friedlander translation, 1903), chapter 31, accessible at sacred-texts.com/jud/gfp/.
2. Joel L. Fleishman, *The Foundation: A Great American Secret* (New York: PublicAffairs, 2007); paperback edition 2009.
3. Peter M. Ascoli, "Julius Rosenwald's Crusade: One Donor's Plea to Give While You Live," *Philanthropy*, May/June 2006, http://www.philanthropyroundtable. org/topic/excellence_in_philanthropy/julius_rosenwalds_crusade.
4. Christopher G. Oechsli, "30 Years of Giving While Living: Our Final Chapter" (July 10, 2012), http://www.atlanticphilanthropies.org/news/30-years-giving -while-living-our-final-chapter; and The Atlantic Philanthropies, "Giving While Living," http://www.atlanticphilanthropies.org/giving-while-living.

INTRODUCTION

1. Edwin Rekosh, "Impact Investing Might Help Nonprofits Overseas Asphyxiat-ed by Their Governments," *The Chronicle of Philanthropy*, February 22, 2016, https://philanthropy.com/article/Opinion-Impact-Investing/235392.
2. Jennifer Ablan, "Russia Bans George Soros Foundation as State Security 'Threat,'" November 30, 2015, http://www.reuters.com/article/2015/11/30 /russia-soros-idUSL1N13P22Y20151130?elq=315797deafc04b5babe6f03 f9bce61ef&elqCampaignId=1958&elqaid=7061&elqat=1&elqTrackId= 23043a84d1ed4a0d9b47f4602bf12cca#Z2i3fs7iBQFrSyqL.97.
3. See Kendra DuPuy, James Ron, and Aseem Prakash, "Foreign Disentangle-ment," *Stanford Social Innovation Review*, Fall 2015, http://ssir.org/articles/entry /foreign_disentanglement#sthash.0ULqpEeM.dpuf.

4. Edward Wong, "U.S. Denounces Chinese Law Restricting Foreign Organizations," *New York Times*, April 29, 2016, http://www.nytimes.com/2016/04/30/world/asia/china-foreign-ngo-law.html.

5. Kendra DuPuy, James Ron, and Aseem Prakash, "Foreign Disentanglement," *Stanford Social Innovation Review*, Fall 2015, http://ssir.org/articles/entry/foreign_disentanglement#sthash.0ULqpEeM.dpuf; see also Julie Makinen, "China's Move Toward Restricting Foreign NGOs Spurs Anxiety in Many Organizations," *Los Angeles Times*, July 5, 2015, http://www.latimes.com/world/asia/la-fg-china-ngos-20150705-story.html; Christopher Marquis, Yanhua Zhou, and Zoe Yang, "The Emergence of Subversive Charities in China," *Stanford Social Innovation Review*, Winter 2016, http://ssir.org/articles/entry/the_emergence_of_subversive_charities_in_china?utm_source=Enews&utm_medium=Email&utm_campaign=SSIR_Now&utm_content=Title; Andrew Jacobs, "Foreign Groups Fear China Oversight Plan," *New York Times*, June 17, 2015, http://www.nytimes.com/2015/06/18/world/foreign-groups-fear-china-oversight-plan.html?_r=0; Charles Digges, "New Crackdown on 'Undesirable' Foreign Organizations Becomes Law with Putin's Signature," May 26, 2015, http://bellona.org/news/russian-human-rights-issues/russian-ngo-law/2015-05-new-crackdown-undesirable-foreign-organizations-becomes-law-putins-signature; and Ruth McCambridge, "Proposed Draconian Law on Associations in Egypt Further Threatens Civil Society," *Nonprofit Quarterly*, July 15, 2014, http://nonprofitquarterly.org/2014/07/15/proposed-draconian-law-on-associations-in-egypt-further-threatens-civil-society/.

6. John Gardner, "Giving Back the Future: Philanthropy in the Twenty-First Century," *Community Foundations of the San Francisco Bay Area*, Oakland, CA, September 28, 1998.

7. Ibid.

8. National Center on Charitable Statistics, "Quick Facts About Nonprofits," *Business Master File*, May 20, 2015, http://nccs.urban.org/statistics/quickfacts.cfm. The figures for religious congregations are as of August 2015.

9. National Center on Charitable Statistics, *NCCS Core File 2013*, http://nccs.urban.org/statistics/quickfacts.cfm.

10. Eugene Steuerle, Alan Abramson, et al., "Meeting Social Needs through Charitable and Government Resources," in *Nonprofits and Government*, ed. Elizabeth Boris and C. Eugene Steuerle, 3rd ed. (Washington, DC: Urban Institute Press, 2015), 94.

11. Ibid.

12. Giving USA, *Giving USA 2016: The Annual Report on Philanthropy for the Year 2015* (Chicago: Giving USA Foundation, 2016), 46.

13. Slightly different figures, published by the Johns Hopkins Center for Civil Society Studies, are available for all countries at http://ccss.jhu.edu/wp-content

/uploads/downloads/2013/02/Comparative-data-Tables_2004_FORMATTED
_2.2013.pdf, Table I.1, but they confirm that the United States continues to
have the significantly highest percentage among all countries.

14. Giving USA, *Giving USA 2016*, 244.

15. Ibid., 45.

16. Ibid., 48; see also http://www.bea.gov/newsreleases/national/pi/2016/txt/pi0516
    .txt, Table 2.

17. Ibid. 27.

18. Giving USA, *Giving USA 2016*, 39.

19. Ibid., 48.

20. Ibid., 40.

21. "Angel" is the term for start-up investors; mezzanine investors provide funding
    close in time afterwards.

22. See Congressional Research Service, "CRC Reports on Tax Issues Relating to
    Charitable Contributions and Organizations," January 24, 2013, http://www.
    pgdc.com/pgdc/crs-reports-tax-issues-relating-charitable-contributions-and
    -organizations, 1.

23. The Joint Committee on Taxation estimates that the total cost to the Treasury
    in 2015 of all individual charitable contributions is about $46 billion. See "Es-
    timates of Federal Tax Expenditures for Fiscal Years 2015–2019," December 7,
    2015, JCX-141R-15, 36, 38.

24. As my Duke colleague Kristin Goss pointed out in an e-mail message to me on
    October 30, 2015, "The best new research suggests that elected officials do not
    represent majority will, except when it is aligned with the preferences of elites."
    See, for example, the frequently cited work of Martin Gilens and Benjamin I.
    Page in "Testing Theories of American Politics: Elites, Interest Groups, and Av-
    erage Citizens," https://scholar.princeton.edu/sites/default/files/mgilens/files
    /gilens_and_page_2014_-testing_theories_of_american_politics.doc.pdf.

25. See Brian Galle, "Pay It Forward? Law and the Problem of Restricted-Spending
    Philanthropy," *Washington University Law Review* 92, no. 5 (2016), http://
    openscholarship.wustl.edu/law_lawreview/vol93/iss5/5.

26. See Wikipedia entry on "intergenerational equity," https://en.wikipedia.org
    /wiki/Intergenerational_equity.

27. James Tobin, "What Is Permanent Endowment Income?" *The American Eco-
    nomic Review* 64, no. 2 (May 1974), http://www.jstor.org/stable/1816077.

CHAPTER 1

1. The Kresge Foundation, *Annual Report 2014: A Bold Urban Future Is Unfolding
   in America's Cities* (Troy, MI: The Kresge Foundation, 2015), 4–5.

2. Ibid.

3. Ibid., 11–13.

4. Julia Stasch, "Time for Change," August 2015, https://www.macfound.org/annual -report/2014/essay/.

5. Michael Bailin, "Re-Engineering Philanthropy: Field Notes from the Trenches," http://www.emcf.org/fileadmin/media/PDFs/history/Bailin_Reengineerin Philanthropy.pdf.

6. See Neil F. Carlson, "Making Evaluation Work," http://www.emcf.org/fileadmin /media/PDFs/history/EMCF_MakingEvaluationWork.pdf.

7. For an excellent summary of the way the Edna McConnell Clark Foundation makes its decisions, see the video of President Nancy Roob's presentation at Duke University on September 30, 2015, "A Decade of Capital Aggregation," http://cspcs.sanford.duke.edu/learning-resources/video-archive/decade-capital -aggregation.

8. See William P. Ryan and Barbara E. Taylor, *An Experiment in Scaling Impact: Assessing the Growth Capital Aggregation Pilot* (New York: The Edna McConnell Clark Foundation, December 2012), http://www.emcf.org/fileadmin/media /PDFs/GCAPReport_Final.pdf.

9. In the interest of full disclosure, The Bridgespan Group's initial major funding was provided by Atlantic Philanthropies, where I was then president of its US Program Staff. I have served as a consultant and advisor to The Bridgespan Group since I resigned from Atlantic Philanthropies in 2003.

10. Sangwon Yoon, "From Ackman to Musk, Charity Giving Takes on Stock-Picking Feel," December 2015, http://www.bloomberg.com/news/articles/2015-12-23 /from-ackman-to-musk-charity-giving-takes-on-stock-picking-feel.

11. Ibid.

12. "Doing Good by Doing Well: Lessons from Business for Charities," *The Economist*, May 23, 2015, http://www.economist.com/node/21651815/print.

13. (New York: HarperCollins, 1990).

14. For a superb account of the "pay-for-success" experiments, as well as an analysis of their future and this particular benefit, see V. Kasturi Rangan and Lisa A. Chase, "The Payoff of Pay-for Success," *Stanford Social Innovation Review* 13, no. 4 (Fall 2015), 28–39.

15. Alex Daniels, "The $1.6 Billion Barr Foundation Expands Its Reach," *The Chronicle of Philanthropy*, February 5, 2016, https://philanthropy.com/article /Barr-Fund-Expands-Its-Grant/235199.

16. See https://centers.fuqua.duke.edu/case/knowledge_items/the-meaning-of-social -entrepreneurship/.

17. *Harvard Business Review* (March-April 1997), https://hbr.org/1997/03/virtuous -capital-what-foundations-can-learn-from-venture-capitalists.

18. Devin Thorpe, "Heron Foundation Leads Foundations Toward 100 Percent Impact Investment," *Forbes*, July 2015, http://www.forbes.com/sites/devinthorpe/2015/07/01/fb-heron-foundation-leads-foundations-toward-100-percent-impact-investment/.

19. Valerie Bauerlein, "Activist Foundations Impact Investing Pays Off, Sometimes After Court Fights," *Wall Street Journal*, October 2015, http://www.wsj.com/articles/activist-foundations-impact-investing-pays-off-sometimes-after-court-fights-1444901401?cb=logged0.9912678744332917; see also Ben Gose, "Impact Investing Requires Foundations to Think and Act in New Ways," *The Chronicle of Philanthropy*, November 17, 2013, https://philanthropy.com/article/Impact-Investing-Requires/154051; and Steven Godeke and William Burckart, "Impact Investing Can Help Foundations Avoid Obsolescence," *The Chronicle of Philanthropy*, March 18, 2015, https://philanthropy.com/article/Opinion-Impact-Investing-Can/228569.

20. See www.fordfoundation.org/the-latest/news/ford-foundation-commits-1-billion-from-endowment-to-mission-related-investments/.

21. Ben Gose, "Foundations Are Cautious on Impact Investing," *The Chronicle of Philanthropy*, December 1, 2015, https://philanthropy.com/article/Foundations-Are-Cautious-on/234356.

22. Drew Lindsay, "Foundation Puts Emphasis on No-Strings-Attached Grants," *The Chronicle of Philanthropy*, July 6, 2015, https://philanthropy.com/article/Foundation-Puts-Emphasis-on/231317.

23. Darren Walker, "Moving the Ford Foundation Forward," Ford Foundation, November 8, 2015, https://www.fordfoundation.org/ideas/equals-change-blog/posts/moving-the-ford-foundation-forward/.

24. Ibid.

25. Suzanne Perry, "2 Nonprofits Get Surprise $1-Million Grants," *The Chronicle of Philanthropy*, October 14, 2015, https://philanthropy.com/article/2-Nonprofits-Get-Surprise/233699?cid=pt&utm_source=pt&utm_medium=en&elq=b725602df0594a63a5ee964e2bf461c7&elqCampaignId=1616&elqaid=6579&elqat=1&elqTrackId=433591a916e942c5a87fd0ad470e2e53.

CHAPTER 2

1. Rebecca Koenig, "Chan Zuckerberg Initiative Pledges $3 Billion for Science Research," *The Chronicle of Philanthropy*, September 21, 2016, https://www.philanthropy.com/article/Chan-Zuckerberg-Initiative/237865.

2. See Megan O'Neil, "Wringing the Most Good Out of a Facebook Fortune," *The Chronicle of Philanthropy*, December 1, 2015, https://philanthropy.com/article/Wringing-the-Most-Good-Out-of/234366.

3. See Benjamin Soskis, "Time for the Public to Weigh Good and Bad of the Zuckerberg-Chan Gift," *The Chronicle of Philanthropy*, December 11, 2015, https://philanthropy.com/article/Opinion-Time-for-the-Public/234584?cid=pt&utm_source=pt&utm_medium=en&elq=691bf6c34ac743ef9ed3f94ad6df0bd4&elqCampaignId=2051&elqaid=7208&elqat=1&elqTrackId=eb8b342490334d0c887db5b11a1a6167.

4. Bradford K. Smith, "Version 2.0. The Giving Pledge Globalizes," Philantopic Blog, March 1, 2013, http://pndblog.typepad.com/pndblog/2013/03/version-20-the-giving-pledge-globalizes.html#more.

5. See https://www.omidyar.com/.

6. Quoted from Participant Media website, http://www.participantmedia.com/.

7. Joel L. Fleishman, *The Foundation: A Great American Secret* (New York: Public-Affairs, 2007), 82–83.

8. For a more exhaustive report on this "grand bargain," see Nathan Bomey, John Gallagher, and Mark Stryker, "How Detroit Was Reborn," November 2014, http://www.freep.com/longform/news/local/detroit-bankruptcy/2014/11/09/detroit-bankruptcy-rosen-orr-snyder/18724267/.

9. See http://www.ef.org/.

10. See http://www.ef.org/programs/energy-foundation-china/.

11. See https://www.livingcities.org/about/members.

12. See http://www.climateworks.org/.

13. Michael Anft, "Seeking $1 Billion for Research That Takes Time," *The Chronicle of Philanthropy* (July 2015): 23a; http://www.sciencephilanthropyalliance.org/who-we-are/members/.

14. See http://hewlett.org/programs/special-projects/madison-initiative.

15. See https://philanthropy.com/article/2-Nonprofits-Get-Surprise/233699?cid=pt&utm_source=pt&utm_medium=en&elq=b725602df0594a63a5ee964e2bf461c7&elqCampaignId=1616&elqaid=6579&elqat=1&elqTrackId=433591a916e942c5a87fd0ad470e2e53.

16. Staff, "Freedom Fund Website," as accessed December 2016 http://freedomfund.org/about/our-vision-and-mission/.

17. See http://www.mbkalliance.org/about.

18. See http://www.pewtrusts.org/en/projects/global-ocean-legacy.

19. Ibid.

20. See http://www.emcf.org/capital-aggregation/.

21. See http://www.emcf.org/our-strategies/blue-meridian-partners.

22. See http://www.emcf.org/our-next-chapter/.

23. See www.hewlett.org/fund-for-shared-insight.

24. Paul Sullivan, "Kevin Spacey and Cal Ripken Jr. to Team Up for Fund-Raising Gala," *New York Times*, September 4, 2015, http://www.nytimes.com/2015/09/05/your-money/kevin-spacey-and-cal-ripken-jr-to-team-up-for-fund-raising-gala.html.

25. See Michael Lipsky, "Statehouse Scrutiny," *Stanford Social Innovation Review*, Spring 2016, http://ssir.org/articles/entry/statehouse_scrutiny#sthash.vQ4zDjQ7.dpuf.

26. See http://www.nationalservice.gov/programs/social-innovation-fund/about-sif.

27. Tony Proscio, "Common Effort, Uncommon Wealth: Lessons from Living Cities on the Challenges and Opportunities of Collaboration in Philanthropy," *Living Cities*, April 2010, https://livingcities.s3.amazonaws.com/resource/79/download.pdf.

28. See Megan E. Tompkins-Stange, *Policy Patrons* (Cambridge, MA: Harvard Education Press, 2016).

29. See Naomi Rothwell, "Bold Advocacy: How Atlantic Philanthropies Funded a Movement," June 18, 2013, http://www.grantcraft.org/blog/bold-advocacy-how-atlantic-philanthropies-funded-a-movement.

30. See Sylvia Yee, "Equal Effort: How Intentionality and Collaboration Have Helped Gay Rights Progress," *Perspectives*, August 21, 2014, http://www.haasjr.org/perspectives/equal-effort; Joanne Weiss, "Competing Principles," *Stanford Social Innovation Review* 13, no. 6 (Fall 2015): 57–60; and The Proteus Fund, "Hearts and Minds: The Untold Story of How Philanthropy and the Civil Marriage Collaborative Helped America Embrace Civil Marriage Equality," http://www.proteusfund.org/sites/default/files/upload/inline/29/files/heartsandmindsnov5.pdf.

31. See Staff, "Bloomberg to Launch $50 Million Gun Control Initiative," *Philanthropy News Digest*, April 17, 2014, http://philanthropynewsdigest.org/news/bloomberg-to-launch-50-million-gun-control-initiative; Catherine Ho, "Inside the Bloomberg Backed Gun Control Group's Effort to Defeat the NRA," *Washington Post*, June 20, 2016, https://www.washingtonpost.com/news/powerpost/wp/2016/06/20/everytowns-survivors-network-stands-on-the-front-lines-of-the-gun-control-battle/?tid=ss_mail.

32. See http://www.atlanticphilanthropies.org/news/ending-well-maximizing-lasting-impact.

33. See Tompkins-Stange, *Policy Patrons*.

34. See http://www.nytimes.com/2016/03/05/education/oakland-district-at-heart-of-drive-to-transform-urban-schools.html?_r=0.

35. Tony Proscio, e-mail message to the author, June 22, 2016.

36. Megan O'Neil, "For Calif. Nonprofits, Advocacy Work on $15 Minimum Wage Pays Off," *The Chronicle of Philanthropy*, March 31, 2016, https://philanthropy.com/article/For-Calif-Nonprofits/235934.

37. Stephen Greenhouse, "How the $15 Minimum Wage Went from Laughable to Viable," *New York Times*, April 1, 2016, http://www.nytimes.com/2016/04/03/opinion/sunday/how-the-15-minimum-wage-went-from-laughable-to-viable.html.

38. For a full list, see http://flackpedia.org/National_Employment_Law_Project#Foundation_Funding.

39. See Motoko Rich, "Teacher Tenure Is Challenged Again in a Minnesota Lawsuit," *New York Times*, April 13, 2016, http://www.nytimes.com/2016/04/14/us/teacher-tenure-is-challenged-again-in-a-minnesota-lawsuit.html.

40. Valerie Reitman, "Benefactor's Final Gift Shakes a Foundation," *Los Angeles Times*, October 30, 2006, http://articles.latimes.com/2006/oct/30/local/mebequest30.

41. Staff, "Texas Cinema Magnate's Foundation Bequest Tops $600 Million," *The Chronicle of Philanthropy*, December 15, 2015, https://philanthropy.com/article/Tex-Cinema-Magnates/234614.

42. Paul Grogan, "The Boston Foundation in the City of Ideas," presentation to the Foundation Impact Research Group, Center for Strategic Philanthropy and Civil Society, Sanford School of Public Policy, Duke University, September 9, 2015, http://cspcs.sanford.duke.edu/learning-resources/video-archive/boston-foundation-city-ideas.

43. Ibid.

44. Ibid.

45. See *Thriving People, Vibrant Places: A Five-Year Progress Report from the Boston Foundation*, which is available by writing the foundation at The Boston Foundation, 75 Arlington Street, 10th floor, Boston, MA 02116.

46. Kelvin Taketa, e-mail message to the author, January 6, 2016.

47. Lucy Bernholz, Katherine Fulton, and Gabriel Kasper, "On the Brink of New Promise: The Future of U.S. Community Foundations," Blueprint Research & Design, Inc. and the Monitor Institute, 2005, http://www.monitorinstitute.com/downloads/what-we-think/new-promise/On_the_Brink_of_New_Promise.pdf, 35.

48. See http://www.cfleads.org/about/about.php.

49. James Covert, "Star-Studded Robin Hood Foundation Galas Raise $101M," *New York Post*, May 13, 2015, http://nypost.com/2015/05/13/star-studded-robin-hood-foundation-galas-raise-101m/.

50. Daniel Lurie, e-mail message to the author, December 17, 2015.

51. See "Super Bowl 50 Redefined," https://www.youtube.com/watch?v=JWO2D-cboq6U; and Alex Davidson, "Super Bowl Fund to Launch on Giving Tuesday," *The Chronicle of Philanthropy*, December 1, 2014, https://philanthropy.com/article/Super-Bowl-Fund-to-Launch-on/152163; see also "Superbowl 50 Sets Records Across the Board," February 10, 2016, http://www.sfbaysuperbowl.com/super-bowl-50-sets-records-across-the-board#xCzvekivsyGItbqj.97.

52. See http://www.vppartners.org/.

53. See http://www.ptech.org/ and http://www.aspeninstitute.org/policy-work /economic-opportunities/skills-americas-future/models-success/ibm.

54. IBM, "2015 Corporate Social Responsibility Report," http://ibm.com/responsibility/2015.

55. See http://www.goldmansachs.com/our-thinking/investing-in-women/bios-pdfs /womenomics-pdf.pdf.

56. See http://www.goldmansachs.com/our-thinking/investing-in-women/bios-pdfs /women-half-sky-pdf.pdf.

57. See http://www.goldmansachs.com/citizenship/10000women/news-and-events /10kwprogressreport.html.

58. Ibid.

59. See http://www.goldmansachs.com/citizenship/10000women/news-and-events /10000women-ifc.html.

60. See http://www.goldmansachs.com/our-thinking/public-policy/gmi-folder/gmi -report-pdf.pdf.

61. See https://www.opic.gov/press-releases/2015/opic-announces-plans-join-goldman -sachs-10000-women-and-ifc-women-entrepreneurs-opportunity-facility -committ.

62. See http://www.goldmansachs.com/citizenship/10000-small-businesses/US/about -the-program/index.html.

63. See http://www.goldmansachs.com/citizenship/10000-small-businesses/US /program-impact/report.pdf.

CHAPTER 3

1. See http://www.fidelitycharitable.org/about-us.shtml.

2. See Ray Madoff, "5 Myths About Pay Out Rules for Donor-Advised Funds," *The Chronicle of Philanthropy*, January 13, 2014, https://philanthropy.com /article/5-Myths-About-Payout-Rules-for/153809; and Alex Daniels, "Role of Donor-Advised Funds Prompts Heated Debate," *The Chronicle of Philanthropy*, October 23, 2015, https://philanthropy.com/article/Role-of-Donor-Advised -Funds/233916.

3. See Alex Daniels, "Donor-Advised Funds Navigate a Deluge of Year-End Gifts and Grants," *The Chronicle of Philanthropy*, December 10, 2015, https:// philanthropy.com/article/Donor-Advised-Funds-Navigate-a/234567.

4. Sacha Pfeiffer, "Fidelity Charitable Fund Donations Reach Record $3.1b," *The Boston Globe*, January 28, 2016, https://www.bostonglobe.com/business /2016/01/28/fidelity-charitable-savings-arm-makes-record-donations/ccXkEi CB4yteR56I8CeHIP/story.html.

5. See http://www.fidelitycharitable.org/2014-annual-report/growth-in-grantmaking .shtml; and http://www.nptrust.org/daf-report/market-overview.html.

6. See http://www.nptrust.org/daf-report/giving-vehicle-comparison.html.

7. See http://www.nptrust.org/daf-report/projections-and-observations.html.

8. See Roger Colinvaux, "Congress Needs to Send a Message That Commercial Advised Funds Are About Giving, Not Saving," *The Chronicle of Philanthropy*, December 29, 2015, https://philanthropy.com/article/Opinion-Congress-Needs-to/234712.

9. See Alex Daniels, "Role of Donor-Advised Funds Prompts Heated Debate," *The Chronicle of Philanthropy*, October 23, 2015, https://philanthropy.com/article/Role-of-Donor-Advised-Funds/233916/.

10. See National Philanthropic Trust 2015 Donor-Advised Fund Report, http://www.nptrust.org/daf-report/sponsor-type-comparison.html#community-foundations.

11. See http://www.newprofit.org/about-us/our-story/.

12. See http://foundationcenter.org/media/news/20150924.html.

13. See http://foundationcenter.org/about/.

14. See http://www.fidelitycharitable.org/private-donor-group/advisors/philanthropic-initiative.shtml.

15. Ibid.

16. See http://www.mckinsey.com/about-us/social-impact/generation.

17. See http://www.generationinitiative.org/.

18. See http://www.rockpa.org/donzelina-barroso-named-director-global-philanthropy-rockefeller-philanthropy-advisors/.

19. Ibid.

20. Ibid.

21. See "Facebook Hints at Powerful New Tools for Fundraising and Crisis Response," *The Chronicle of Philanthropy*, October 21, 2015, https://philanthropy.com/article/Facebook-Hints-at-Powerful-New/233848.

22. Megan O'Neill, "Facebook New Donate Button Helps Charities Build Donor Lists," *The Chronicle of Philanthropy*, August 25, 2015, https://philanthropy.com/article/Facebooks-New-Donate-Button/232595.

23. Giving USA, *Giving USA 2016: The Annual Report on Philanthropy for the Year 2015* (Chicago, IL: Giving USA Foundation), 77.

24. See http://www.networkforgood.org/digitalgivingindex, accessed August 29, 2015.

25. See http://nonprofitquarterly.org/2015/04/23/in-2015-m-r-benchmarks-study-online-and-monthly-giving-are-up.

26. See https://www.blackbaudhq.com/corpmar/cgr/how-nonprofit-fundraising-performed-in-2014.pdf.

27. Giving USA, *Giving USA 2016*, 26.

28. Corporation for National and Community Service. See http://www.volunteeringinamerica.gov/national and http://www.volunteeringinamerica.gov/research.cfm.

29. Ibid.

30. Eden Stiffman, "Indiegogo Launches Free Crowdfunding Site for Nonprofits," *The Chronicle of Philanthropy*, October 21, 2015, https://philanthropy.com /article/Indiegogo-Launches-Free/233839.

31. Ibid.

32. See www.fastcompany.com/3064808/future-of-philanthropy/gofundme-just-hit-3-billion-in-total-donations.

33. See http://www.universalgiving.org/.

34. Roger Martin and Sally Osberg, *Getting Beyond Better: How Social Entrepreneurship Works* (Cambridge, MA: Harvard Business Review Press, 2015), 130.

35. See http://www.givedirectly.org/.

36. See http://www.givingtuesday.org/.

37. Eden Stiffman, "Donors Give $116.7 Million on Giving Tuesday," *The Chronicle of Philanthropy*, December 2, 2016, https://philanthropy.com/article /Donors-Give-1167-Million-on/234443.

38. Meredith Myers, Eden Stillman, and Ariana Giorgi, "Online Giving Trends," *The Chronicle of Philanthropy*, accessed March 1, 2017, https://philanthropy .com/interactives/online-giving-dashboard.

39. Sara Reardon, "Pete Frates: Ice-Bucket Challenger," in "365 Days: Nature's 10: Ten People Who Mattered This Year," *Nature*, December 18, 2014, http:// www.nature.com/news/365-days-nature-s-10-1.16562; see also "Nancy Frates: How Did a Simple Challenge Become a Worldwide Phenomenon?," *TED Radio Hour*, August 14, 2015, http://www.npr.org/2015/08/14/431543256/how -did-a-simple-challenge-become-a-worldwide-phenomenon.

40. See http://www.elle.com/culture/celebrities/news/a15448/celebrities-ice-bucket -challenge/; see also http://www.alsa.org/about-us/ice-bucket-challenge-faq.html for the fuller history, under the heading "Who Started the ALS Ice Bucket Challenge?" The site explains that the challenge already "existed in the sporting world and had been used with other causes in the past. It started with a professional golfer named Chris Kennedy, who challenged his sister, Jeanette Senerchia in Pelham, New York. Jeanette's husband Anthony has ALS. Through Facebook, one of her friends was connected to Pat Quinn in Yonkers, New York, who was connected to Pete Frates in Boston, Massachusetts. Pat and Pete are both young men battling the disease and their social networks blasted the ALS Ice Bucket Challenge out of the Northeast to places across the country and even the globe."

41. James Surowiecki, "Philanthropic Fads," *The New Yorker*, July 25, 2016, 19, http://archives.newyorker.com/?i=2016-07-25#folio=18.

42. See http://bikefls.nationalmssociety.org/site/PageServer?pagename=BIKE_FLS _history.

43. See http://www.bikingbis.com/charity-bicycle-rides/ for some of the countless such charity bike rides, which could not possibly be organized and orchestrated without social media.

44. See, for example, Suzanne Perry, "Red Cross Report Gets Strong Critique from Dan Pallotta's New Venture," *The Chronicle of Philanthropy*, August 11, 2015, https://www.philanthropy.com/article/Red-Cross-Report-Gets-Strong/232305.

45. See http://www.thelifeyoucansave.org/Blog/ID/222/Peter-Singers-Best-Charities -for-2016.

46. See http://www.curealz.org/.

47. See http://www.fastercures.org/about/.

CHAPTER 4

1. Patricia L. Rosenfield, *A World of Giving: Carnegie Corporation of New York—A Century of International Philanthropy* (New York: PublicAffairs, 2014), 21.

2. See a brief summary of the principal writers on that subject in Jesse Brundage Sears, "Philanthropy in the History of American Higher Education," in *Department of the Interior, Bureau of Education, Bulletin, 1922, No. 26* (Washington, DC: Government Printing Office, 1922), 1–8.

3. Ibid., 2.

4. Ibid., 4.

5. Sir Arthur Hobhouse, *The Dead Hand: Addresses on the Subject of Endowments and Settlements of Property* (London: Chatto & Windus, 1880).

6. John Stuart Mill, *Dissertations and Discussions* (London: Savill and Edwards, 1859), 2:28–67.

7. Ibid., 2:60–62.

8. Ibid., 2:7–11.

9. Reprinted in Andrew Carnegie, *The Gospel of Wealth and Other Timely Essays* (New York: The Century Co., 1900).

10. Ron Chernow, *Titan, The Life of John D. Rockefeller, Sr.* (New York: Random House, 1998), 313.

11. Many philanthropically knowledgeable individuals have recollections that Carnegie actually wrote this, as this author does, but no one, including professional archivists familiar with Carnegie's writings, has been able as of this writing to verify its authenticity.

12. See *North American Review* 148, no. 391 (December 1889): 682–699, later republished as Carnegie, *Gospel of Wealth*.

13. Carnegie, *Gospel of Wealth*.

14. Joel L. Fleishman, J. Scott Kohler, and Steven Schindler, *Casebook for The Foundation: A Great American Secret* (New York: PublicAffairs, 2007), 17.

15. Ibid.
16. Ibid.
17. Rosenfield, *A World of Giving*, 8–9.
18. Ibid., 28–29.
19. See https://en.wikipedia.org/wiki/Julius_Rosenwald.
20. Sears Archives, "What Is the Julius Rosenwald Foundation?" http://www.searsarchives.com/people/juliusrosenwald.html.
21. Peter M. Ascoli, *Julius Rosenwald: The Man Who Built Sears, Roebuck and Advanced the Cause of Black Education in the American South* (Bloomington: University of Indiana Press, 2006).
22. See Steven Schindler, "Carnegie Public Libraries for America's Communities," in *Casebook for The Foundation: A Great American Secret* (New York: PublicAffairs, 2007), 14–18; and Steven Schindler, "Building Schools for Rural African Americans," ibid., 27–30.
23. Ibid., 29.
24. See trailer for the film at http://www.rosenwaldfilm.org/.
25. Julius Rosenwald, "The Principles of Public Giving," *Atlantic Monthly* (May 1929): 605.
26. See *The Saturday Evening Post*, January 5, 1929.
27. Ascoli, *Julius Rosenwald*, 320.
28. Julius Rosenwald, "The Burden of Wealth," *The Saturday Evening Post*, January 5, 1929, 12.
29. Ascoli, *Julius Rosenwald*, 406.

CHAPTER 5

1. Verne S. Atwater and Evelyn C. Walsh, *The Ford Foundation: The Early Years—1936–1968—An Insider View of the Impact of Wealth and Good Intentions* (New York: The Ford Foundation, 2011), 18.
2. *Report of the Study for the Ford Foundation on Policy and Program* (Detroit, MI: Ford Foundation, November 1949), 9–10.
3. Ibid., 10–12.
4. Atwater and Walsh, *Ford Foundation*, 26.
5. Warren Weaver and George Wells Beadle, *U.S. Philanthropic Foundations: Their History, Structure, Management, and Record* (New York: Harper and Row, 1967), 86.
6. Atwater and Walsh, *Ford Foundation*, 26–27.
7. Ibid., 52–53.
8. Ibid., 173–174.
9. Ibid., 173–174.

10. Ibid., 183.
11. Ibid., 5.
12. Ibid., 20.
13. See Letter of Resignation by Henry Ford II at http://www.philanthropyroundtable .org/topic/donor_intent/henry_ford_2_letter_of_resignation.
14. Ibid.
15. William E. Simon, *A Time for Truth* (New York: McGraw-Hill, 1978), 230–231.
16. Letter of December 11, 1976, to Mr. Alexander Heard, chairman of the board, Ford Foundation, from the Ford Foundation Archives.
17. Interview by Charles T. Morrissey with Henry Ford II for the Ford Foundation Oral History Project, Dearborn, MI, August 1, 1973.
18. Julie Cantwell Armstrong and Michelle Krebs, "The Worst Mistake: Henry Ford II's Ceding of Ford Foundation Control Has Cost Detroit Area," *Crain's Detroit Business* 19, no. 22 (Summer 2003 supplement): 76, http://connection .ebscohost.com/c/articles/10073141/worst-mistake-henry-ford-iis-ceding-ford -foundation-control-has-cost-detroit-area.
19. See Adam Meyerson, "When Philanthropy Goes Wrong," *Wall Street Journal*, March 9, 2012, https://www.wsj.com/articles/SB10001424052970203370604577263820686621862; see also Adam Meyerson, foreword to *Protecting Donor Intent: How to Define and Safeguard Your Philanthropic Principles*, by Jeffrey J. Cain (Washington, DC: Philanthropy Roundtable, 2012), vii–ix.
20. See http://www.philanthropyroundtable.org/topic/donor_intent/the_ford_foundation_and_donor_intent.
21. For a dramatic, blow-by-blow description of the events of that weekend, see George Lowery, "A Campus Takeover That Symbolized an Era of Change," *Cornell Chronicle*, April 16, 2009, http://www.news.cornell.edu/stories/2009/04/campus-takeover-symbolized-era-change.
22. Ibid.
23. Ibid.
24. See James Piereson, "Switching Off the Lights at the Olin Foundation," *Philanthropy*, March/April 2002, http://www.philanthropyroundtable.org/site/print /the_insiders_guide_to_spend_down.
25. Ibid.
26. Steven Schindler, "Conservative Legal Advocacy," in *Casebook for The Foundation: A Great American Secret—How Private Wealth Is Changing the World*, ed. Joel L. Fleishman, J. Scott Kohler, and Steven Schindler (New York: PublicAffairs, 2007), 135.
27. Piereson, "Switching Off the Lights," 2.
28. Ibid.
29. Fleishman et al., *Casebook*, 148–151.
30. Schindler, "Conservative," 136–137.

31. Deanne Stone, *Alternatives to Perpetuity: A Conversation Every Foundation Should Have* (Washington, DC: National Center for Family Philanthropy, 2005).

32. See https://www.nccivitas.org/2015/z-smith-reynolds-foundation-roots-radicalism/.

33. Adam Meyerson, "When Philanthropy Goes Wrong," *Philanthropy Roundtable*, http://www.philanthropyroundtable.org/topic/donor_intent/when_philanthropy _goes_wrong.

34. See http://www.philanthropyroundtable.org/site/print/the_contested_legacy_of _j._howard_pew.

35. The debate continued, with a response to Rimel's letter written by Evan Sparks, the editor of *Philanthropy*, the Roundtable's magazine, ibid.

36. See Adam Meyerson, "Why Donors Must Protect Their Philanthropic Principles," http://www.philanthropyroundtable.org/topic/donor_intent/why_donors _must_protect_their_philanthropic_principles.

37. Evan Sparks, "Back to Bill: How the Daniels Fund Lost Sight of Bill Daniels, Clawed Its Way Back—and Is Preserving Donor Intent into the Far Future," *Philanthropy*, Fall 2011, http://www.philanthropyroundtable.org/topic/donor _intent/back_to_bill; Mark O'Keefe, "The Daniels Fund: A Rocky Mountain Commitment to Donor Intent," *Philanthropy*, May/June 2006, http://www .philanthropyroundtable.org/topic/excellence_in_philanthropy/the_daniels _fund.

38. See Evan Sparks, "Duke of Carolina: Was James B. Duke More Successful than Andrew Carnegie and John D. Rockefeller?," *Philanthropy*, Winter 2011, http:// www.philanthropyroundtable.org/topic/donor_intent/duke_of_carolina.

CHAPTER 6

1. For more extensive descriptions of these foundations, as well as of foundations that ended their existence prior to 2016, see http://cspcs.sanford.duke.edu /time-limited-philanthropy/time-limited-foundations.

2. See https://hbr.org/1997/03/virtuous-capital-what-foundations-can-learn-from -venture-capitalists.

3. Ibid., 10–11.

4. Patricia Rosenfield, *A World of Giving: Carnegie Corporation of New York* (New York: PublicAffairs, 2014), 19.

5. For those interested in the litigation over The Buck Trust, see Robert R. Augsburger, Victoria Chang, and William F. Meehan III, "The San Francisco Foundation: The Dilemma of the Buck Trust," *Harvard Business Review*, January 1, 1998, https://hbr.org/product/the-san-francisco-foundation-the-dilemma-of-the -buck-trust-a/an/SI106A-PDF-ENG; and John G. Simon, "American Philanthropy and the Buck Trust," *Yale Law School Legal Scholarship Repository*, January 1,

1987, http://digitalcommons.law.yale.edu/cgi/viewcontent.cgi?article=2998& context=fss_papers.

6. In my interview of David Rockefeller Jr. for this book, he confirmed that his father made that statement and the younger Rockefeller continues to regard his father's sentiment as accurate. It is nonetheless a fact that other descendants of John D. Rockefeller Sr., including his son John D. Jr. and his great-grandchildren Peggy Delany and Senator Jay Rockefeller, did serve on The Rockefeller Foundation's board. Moreover, his great-grandson David Jr. agreed to join the foundation's board, was subsequently elected to serve as its chairman, and presided in that role during The Rockefeller Foundation's Centennial celebration in 2013. He completed his 5-year term as chairman and 10-year term as trustee in mid-2016.

7. (New York: PublicAffairs, 2013, the revised paperback edition).

8. Interview with John and Ginger Sall, Cary, NC, March 20, 2015.

9. *Wall Street Journal*, June 26, 2015, http://www.wsj.com/articles/sean-parker -philanthropy-for-hackers-1435345787.

10. (New York: PublicAffairs, 2007).

11. *Wall Street Journal*, June 26, 2015, http://www.wsj.com/articles/sean-parker -philanthropy-for-hackers-1435345787.

12. Julius Rosenwald, "The Burden of Wealth," *The Saturday Evening Post*, January 5, 1929, 12.

13. Ibid., 13.

14. Ibid., 12.

15. Alice Buhl, "Irwin Sweeney Miller Foundation: A Study in Spend-Down," *PASSAGES Issue Brief*, November 2013, https://cspcs.sanford.duke.edu/sites /default/files/2013-Passages-ISMF-Spend-Down-Web%20(2).pdf.

16. Ibid., 18.

17. See http://www.bridgespan.org/Philanthropy-Advice/Philanthropist-Spotlights /Stories/Donors/Bernie-Marcus/RecentVideos/Bernie-Marcus-explains-why -he-gives-while-he-lives.aspx#.VtJnCE0UVD8.

18. James Schulman, e-mail to the author, December 9, 2016.

19. Geraldine Fabrikant, "Yale Endowment Earned 3.4% in a Year When Many Peers Lost," *New York Times*, September 23, 2016, B2, http://www.nytimes .com/2016/09/24/business/yale-university-endowment.html.

20. Ibid.

21. Speech delivered by Martin Luther King Jr. on April 4, 1967, at a meeting of Clergy and Laity Concerned about Vietnam at Riverside Church in New York City.

22. Rosenwald, "Burden of Wealth," 14.

23. See http://www.atlanticphilanthropies.org/our-story.

24. Attributed to Maimonides, probably by derivation from his "greatest level of giving" in Mishneh Torah Laws of Charity 10:7–14, which states that "the greatest level of charity is finding employment for a poor person."

25. Attributed to Andrew Carnegie.

26. Kenneth Prewitt, *Social Sciences and Private Philanthropy: The Quest for Social Relevance* (Indianapolis: Indiana University Center on Philanthropy, 1995), 13.

27. For more on the Aaron Diamond Foundation, see Mitch Nauffts's interview with foundation CEO Vincent McGee, "Vincent McGee, Aaron Diamond Foundation: Spending Out as a Philanthropic Strategy," *Philanthropy News Digest*, January 10, 2007, http://philanthropynewsdigest.org/newsmakers/vincent-mcgee-aaron-diamond-foundation-spending-out-as-a-philanthropic-strategy. For more on the "AIDS cocktail," see "Combination Antiretroviral Therapy: The Turning Point in the AIDS Pandemic," at the website of The Rockefeller University Hospital, where the Aaron Diamond AIDS Research Center is now housed: http://centennial.rucares.org/index.php?page=Combination_Antiretroviral_Thera.

28. Charles F. Feeney, letter to Bill Gates, February 22, 2011, http://www.atlantic philanthropies.org/news/atlantics-founding-chairman-chuck-feeney-joins-giving-pledge.

29. Michael Klausner, "When Time Isn't Money: Foundation Payouts and the Time Value of Money," *Stanford Social Innovation Review* 1, no. 1 (Spring 2003): 56.

30. See http://www.atlanticphilanthropies.org/our-story.

31. Interview with David Rubenstein, cofounder of The Carlyle Group, February 4, 2015.

32. Interview with Michael Steinhardt on March 27, 2014, in New York City.

33. Stephen Greenhouse, "How the $15 Minimum Wage Went from Laughable to Viable," *New York Times*, April 1, 2016, http://www.nytimes.com/2016/04/03/opinion/sunday/how-the-15-minimum-wage-went-from-laughable-to-viable.html.

34. Tony Proscio, e-mail to the author, November 1, 2016.

35. Willa Seldon and Meera Chary, "Why Success Sometimes Eludes Community Efforts to Fight Social Problems," *The Chronicle of Philanthropy*, September 4, 2015, https://philanthropy.com/article/Opinion-Why-Success-Sometimes/232223.

36. Ibid.

37. See David Kroll, "What '60 Minutes' Got Right and Wrong on Duke's Polio Virus Trial Against Glioblastoma," *Forbes*, March 30, 2015, http://www.forbes.com/sites/davidkroll/2015/03/30/60-minutes-covers-dukes-polio-virus-clinical-trial-against-glioblastoma/.

38. See http://fortune.com/2016/04/13/parker-institute-launch-cancer-immuno therapy/.

39. See http://www.sfgate.com/health/article/UCSF-gets-177-million-grant-to-address
    -dementia-6636858.php.

CHAPTER 7

1. (New York: Crown, 1991).
2. See http://clearwaymn.org/about/annual-reports/2013-annual-report/.
3. See http://www.newsday.com/long-island/hagedorn-foundation-to-wind-down
   -operations-by-2018-1.7626632.
4. See http://gillfoundation.org/priorities/family-recognition/.
5. Karl Zinsmeister, "Julius Rosenwald," http://www.philanthropyroundtable.org
   /almanac/hall_of_fame/julius_rosenwald; Steven Schindler, "Building Schools
   for Rural African Americans: Julius Rosenwald Fund, 1920," in *Casebook for
   The Foundation: A Great American Secret*, ed. Joel L. Fleishman, J. Scott Kohler,
   and Steven Schindler (New York: PublicAffairs, 2007), 27–30.
6. Scott Kohler, "The Aaron Diamond AIDS Research Center," in ibid., 183–
   187; "Vincent McGee, Aaron Diamond Foundation: Spending Out as a
   Philanthropic Strategy," *Philanthropy News Digest*, January 10, 2007, http://
   philanthropynewsdigest.org/newsmakers/vincent-mcgee-aaron-diamond
   -foundation-spending-out-as-a-philanthropic-strategy.
7. See http://clearwaymn.org/quitting/quitplan-services/.
8. See John J. Miller, "John Olin," http://www.philanthropyroundtable.org/almanac
   /hall_of_fame/john_m._olin; see also Steven Schindler, "Conservative Legal Advocacy: John M. Olin Foundation, 1975," in *Casebook for The Foundation: A
   Great American Secret*, ed. Joel L. Fleishman, J. Scott Kohler, and Steven Schindler
   (New York: PublicAffairs, 2007), 135–137; and Steven Schindler, "Revolution-
   izing Legal Discourse: Law and Economics, John M. Olin Foundation 1978,"
   ibid., 148–151.
9. Nancy Roob, Edna McConnell Clark Foundation CEO, e-mail message to the
   author on the subject of "Our Next Chapter," December 13, 2016.
10. See June 11, 2014, letter from Charles Bronfman and Jeffrey Solomon on the
    ACBP website, "Spend Down / Strategy: June 2011 Letter from Charles Bron-
    fman and Jeffrey Solomon Announcing ACBP Spend-down," http://www.acbp
    .net/strategy.php.
11. See Francie Ostrower, "Foundation Sunset: A Decision-Making Guide," http://
    www.aspeninstitute.org/sites/default/files/content/docs/pubs/DecisionGuide2.pdf.
12. See president and CEO Christopher Oechsli's public letter about both of these
    post-sundown initiatives at http://www.atlanticphilanthropies.org/news/ending
    -well-maximizing-lasting-impact.

13. See http://www.atlanticphilanthropies.org/racial-equity-us.

14. See http://www.beldon.org/about-beldon.html.

15. See Ben Gose, "Small Grant Maker, Closing Down in 4 Years, Is a Force in Immigration," *The Chronicle of Philanthropy*, May 9, 2013, http://hagedorn foundation.org/downloads/Chronicle.pdf.

16. See https://www.jmfund.org/program-areas/clean-energy/.

17. See Staff, "The John Merck Fund to Spend Out, Refocus Programs," *The John Merck Fund*, October 2011, http://www.jmfund.org/news/the-john-merck -fund-to-spend-out-refocus-programs; and an interview with Olivia H. Farr and George W. Hatch, "Changing a Mindset," *Faith & Leadership*, July 28, 2014, https://www.faithandleadership.com/qa/olivia-h-farr-and-george-w-hatch -changing-mindset.

18. See http://www.brainerd.org/about/successes.php.

19. See http://clearwaymn.org/2014-annual-report/.

20. See http://www.theeleosfoundation.com/who_we_are.html; see also http:// www.alliancemagazine.org/interview/eleos-foundation-to-spend-down-and -use-assets-for-impact-investing-interview-with-john-duffy/.

21. See http://www.gatesfoundation.org/Who-We-Are/General-Information/ Foundation-Factsheet.

22. See http://dealbook.nytimes.com/2014/05/26/as-his-foundation-has-grown-gates -has-slowed-his-donations/?_r=0.

23. Deanne Stone, *Alternatives to Perpetuity: A Conversation Every Foundation Should Have* (Washington, DC: National Center for Family Philanthropy, 2005), 5.

CHAPTER 8

1. For an excellent, readable summary of the history of Birthright Israel, see Leonard Saxe, "Taglit-Birthright Israel: A New Paradigm for Engaging American Jews with Israel," available from the author; other research reports are accessible at http://www.brandeis.edu/cmjs/researchprojects/taglit/index.html.

2. See Leonard Saxe, "Reflections on the Science of the Social Scientific Study of Jewry: Marshall Sklare Award Lecture," *Contemporary Jewry* 34, no. 1 (2014): 3–14; and Leonard Saxe et al., (2011). Intermarriage: The Impact and Lessons of Taglit-Birthright Israel," *Contemporary Jewry* 31, no. 2 (2011): 151–172.

3. Joel L. Fleishman, J. Scott Kohler, and Steven Schindler, *Casebook for The Foundation: A Great American Secret* (New York: PublicAffairs, 2007).

4. George Soros, "My Philanthropy," in Chuck Sudetic, *The Philanthropy of George Soros: Building Open Societies* (New York: PublicAffairs, 2011), 41.

5. Interview with Chris Stone, January 29, 2015, Durham, NC.

6. Caroline Preston, "With an Expected $9-Billion Windfall, the Cargill Philanthropies Could Become America's Third Largest Grant Maker," *The Chronicle of Philanthropy*, January 21, 2011, https://philanthropy.com/article/A-9-Billion-Philanthropic/159185.

7. Staff, "The Legacy of Margaret A. Cargill," The Borgen Project Blog, October 18, 2013, https://borgenproject.org/legacy-margaret-cargill/.

CHAPTER 9

1. Quotation courtesy of Virginia Esposito, Director, National Center for Family Philanthropy.

2. See http://www.surdna.org/about-the-foundation/mission-and-history.html?id=683.

3. See http://www.florafamily.org/about.html.

4. See http://www.hewlett.org/about-us/board-members-and-officers.

5. Interview with John and Ginger Sall, Cary, NC, March 20, 2015.

6. Interview with Lester Crown, February 20, 2014, in Chicago, IL.

7. See https://www.schusterman.org/mission-and-values.

8. Interview with Lord Rothschild, September 3, 2014, in London.

9. Ibid.

10. Ibid.

11. Ibid.

12. Interview with John and Ginger Sall, Cary, NC, March 20, 2015.

CHAPTER 10

1. See http://www.pewtrusts.org/en/topics/religion.

2. See http://www.lillyendowment.org/religion.html.

3. See http://hewlett.org/programs/special-projects/madison-initiative.

4. See Jane Mayer, *Dark Money: The Hidden History of the Billionaires Behind the Rise of the Radical Right* (New York: Doubleday, 2016).

5. Jack Anderson, "W. McNeil Lowry Is Dead," *New York Times*, June 7, 1993, http://www.nytimes.com/1993/06/07/obituaries/w-mcneil-lowry-is-dead-patron-of-the-arts-was-80.html.

6. Miles A. Smith, Associated Press, "Ford Foundation Grants Provide Boosts for American Symphony Orchestras," *The Register Guard*, February 6, 1966, https://news.google.com/newspapers?nid=1310&dat=19660206&id=VKx VAAAAIBAJ&sjid=DOEDAAAAIBAJ&pg=6117,1199313&hl=en.

7. See http://hewlett.org/programs/performing-arts.

8. See https://www.packard.org/what-we-fund/local-grantmaking/.
9. See http://www.surdna.org.
10. See http://www.ddcf.org.

CHAPTER 11

1. See http://www.hhmi.org/about.
2. See http://med.stanford.edu/allergyandasthma/about-us/sean-parker-gift.html.
3. See https://www.ucsf.edu/news/2015/11/249846/new-sean-n-parker-autoimmune -research-laboratory-launched-ucsf.
4. See http://fortune.com/2016/04/13/parker-institute-launch-cancer-immuno therapy/.
5. Ibid.
6. See Scott Kohler, "The Prostate Cancer Foundation," in *Casebook for The Foundation: A Great American Secret*, ed. Joel L. Fleishman, J. Scott Kohler, and Steven Schindler (New York: PublicAffairs, 2007), 234–236.
7. Ibid.
8. Arthur Koestler, *The Act of Creation* (New York: Penguin Arkana, 1996), 230.
9. For more details on the Sandler initiatives, see William E. Seaman, Richard M. Locksley, and Michael J. Welsh, "New Blood: Creative Funding of Disease -Specific Research," *Science Translational Medicine*, May 20, 2015, http://stm .sciencemag.org/content/7/288/288ed5.
10. For a description of the origin of 911, see Scott Kohler, "The Emergency Medical Services Program," in Fleishman et al., *Casebook for The Foundation*, 119–125.
11. Tom Wheeler, "The 911 System Isn't Ready for the iPhone Era," *New York Times*, November 23, 2015, http://www.nytimes.com/2015/11/23/opinion /the-911-system-isnt-ready-for-the-iphone-era.html.
12. See William Foster et al., "Making Big Bets for Social Change," *Stanford Social Innovation Review*, Winter 2016, http://ssir.org/articles/entry/making_big _bets_for_social_change#bio-footer.
13. Interview with Cari Tuna, March 9, 2015, San Francisco, CA.
14. Interview with Cari Tuna, March 15, 2016, San Francisco, CA.
15. Andrew Carnegie, "Deed of Gift to the Carnegie Corporation of New York," quoted in Patricia Rosenfield, *A World of Giving: Carnegie Corporation of New York* (New York: PublicAffairs, 2014), 19.
16. Adam Meyerson, "When Philanthropy Goes Wrong," *Philanthropy Roundtable*, http://www.philanthropyroundtable.org/topic/donor_intent/when_philanthropy _goes_wrong.
17. Ibid.

EPILOGUE

1. Maimonides is the most quoted and least well-documented source of ethical behavior. According to Quote Investigator, this quote is an 1826 translation by "The Religious Intelligences" of Maimonides highest degree of charity. Accessible at www.quoteinvestigator.com/tag/Maimonides.
2. Bradach and his coauthor, Abe Grindle, elaborated on that point in "Transformative Scale: The Future of Growing What Works," *Stanford Social Innovation Review*, Spring 2014 supplement, http://ssir.org/articles/entry/transformative_scale_the_future_of_growing_what_works.
3. See http://www.results4america.org/.
4. (New York: Doubleday, 2016).

APPENDIX A

1. Prepared by Vincent McGee, executive director from 1985 to 1996.
2. Sasha Abramsky, "Give It Away," *The Nation*, September 6, 2011, http://www.thenation.com/article/give-it-away/.
3. See "Aaron Diamond Foundation," http://www.sourcewatch.org/index.php/Aaron_Diamond_Foundation.
4. See "Vincent McGee, Aaron Diamond Foundation: Spending Out as a Philanthropic Strategy," *Philanthropy News Digest*, January 10, 2007, http://philanthropynewsdigest.org/newsmakers/vincent-mcgee-aaron-diamond-foundation-spending-out-as-a-philanthropic-strategy.
5. Ibid.
6. Ibid.
7. The following is the executive summary of this foundation's five-year-after "Final Impact Assessment," written by Dan Cramer and Keiki Kehoe of Grassroots Solutions, which was commissioned by the foundation and published in 2014. Accessible at http://www.beldon.org/final-impact.html.
8. Prepared by Jane Nicholson, research assistant, from various sources cited below.
9. Miles J. Gibbons Jr., "Going for Broke: Why It Often Makes Sense to Consider a Sunset Clause," *Philanthropy*, May/June 2001, http://www.philanthropyroundtable.org/topic/excellence_in_philanthropy/going_for_broke.
10. See https://en.wikipedia.org/wiki/Rosenwald_Fund.
11. Sears Archives, "What Is the Julius Rosenwald Foundation?," http://www.searsarchives.com/people/questions/rosenwaldfoundation.htm.
12. See Karl Zinsmeister, "Julius Rosenwald," http://www.philanthropyroundtable.org/almanac/hall_of_fame/julius_rosenwald.

13. Prepared by Jane Nicholson.

14. See "The Olin Foundation and Support for Law and Economics Research," *The Record*, Fall 2011, http://www.law.uchicago.edu/alumni/magazine/fall11/olin.

15. "From 1980 to its close in 2005, Mr. Piereson estimates that the Olin Foundation spent about $400 million." See the proceedings of the Open Society Institute, September 21, 2006, https://opensocietyfoundations.org/sites/default/files/how-strategic-funding-conservative-ideas-20060921_0.pdf.

16. See John J. Miller, "John Olin," http://www.philanthropyroundtable.org/almanac/hall_of_fame/john_m._olin.

17. Prepared by Jane Nicholson, from sources cited below.

18. Miles J. Gibbons Jr., "Going for Broke."

19. See "IIE/Program History," http://www.whitaker.org/about-us/iie-program-history.

20. Miles J. Gibbons Jr., "Going for Broke."

21. Prepared by Jane Nicholson and edited by Jeff Solomon, president and CEO of the foundation.

22. Charles Bronfman and Jeffrey Solomon, "Spend Down / Strategy: June 2011 Letter from Charles Bronfman and Jeffrey Solomon Announcing ACBP Spend-down," http://www.acbp.net/strategy.php.

23. See http://www.acbp.net/strategic-philanthropy.php.

24. Ibid.

25. Bronfman and Solomon, "Spend Down / Strategy."

26. Charles Bronfman and Jeffrey Solomon, *The Art of Doing Good: Where Passion Meets Action* (San Francisco, CA: Jossey-Bass, 2012).

27. Prepared by the foundation.

28. See http://www.gatesfoundation.org.

29. Prepared by David J. Morse, Chief Communications Officer.

30. See http://www.atlanticphilanthropies.org.

31. Prepared by Barbara Kibbe, Director of Organizational Effectiveness.

32. Prepared by Yossi Prager, Eli Silver, and David Rozenson of the AVI CHAI Foundation, http://avichai.org/.

33. Interview with Arthur Fried.

34. See http://avichai.org/about-us/mission/.

35. See http://www.talam.org/.

36. See http://neta.cet.ac.il/.

37. See http://avichai.org/program-listings/building-loan-program-day-schools-2/.

38. See http://www.bac.org.il/trailers.

39. See http://www.mechinot.org.il/english/about.

40. See http://www.tzohar.org.il/English/.

41. See http://www.knizhniki.ru.

42. Prepared by Jane Nicholson, from the foundation website.

43. See http://gillfoundation.org/.

44. Financial data available from "2013 Annual Report," http://annualreports.gill foundation.org/annual-reports/year-2013/2013-grants/2013-gill-foundation -grants/.

45. See http://annualreports.gillfoundation.org/annual-reports/year-2013/.

46. See http://gillfoundation.org/priorities/a-prosperous-colorado/.

47. Prepared by Jane Nicholson, from the foundation website.

48. Paul Brainerd, "Foundation Sunset: A Message from Paul Brainerd," March 1, 2008, http://www.brainerd.org/about/sunset.php.

49. See http://www.brainerd.org/funding/default.php.

50. Ibid.

51. Financial data obtained from "2014 Financial Statement," http://www.brainerd .org/about/default.php.

52. See http://www.brainerd.org/about/successes.php.

53. Prepared by Frank Barry, Bloomberg Newsroom.

54. Adapted from Kevin Laskowski, "Perpetuity Is a Long Time," *National Center for Family Philanthropy*, May 15, 2008, https://www.ncfp.org/blog/2008/may -perpetuity-is-a-long-time.html.

55. Ibid.

56. Prepared by Gregg S. Behr, executive director, The Grable Foundation.

57. Prepared by Julie Sandorf, president, The Charles H. Revson Foundation.

58. See http://www.philanthropyroundtable.org/topic/excellence_in_philanthropy /meadows_foundation.

59. Prepared by Thomas W. Lambeth, former executive director, The Z. Smith Reynolds Foundation.

60. See Staff, "From Tobacco to Politics: The Z. Smith Reynolds Foundation Works to Turn North Carolina into a Bastion of Liberalism," *Capital Research Center*, June 1, 2013, https://capitalresearch.org/2013/06/from-tobacco-to-politics/.

61. Robert Korstad and James Leloudis, *To Right These Wrongs: The North Carolina Fund and the Battle to End Poverty and Inequality in 1960s America* (Chapel Hill: University of North Carolina Press, 2010).

62. Russell Hardin, "Unabashedly Responsive Philanthropy: The Woodruff and Whitehead Foundations," *Center for Strategic Philanthropy and Civil Society*, www.cspcs.sanford.duke.edu/learning-resources/video-archive.

63. Ibid.

64. Website of *Virginia G. Piper Charitable Trust*, www.pipertrust.org. In addition, information in this paragraph came from discussions between the author and the Board of Trustees in Phoenix, Arizona, on August 13, 2013.

Index

Page numbers followed by *n* indicate note numbers.

Joel L. Fleishman is a professor of law and public policy; director of the Samuel and Ronnie Heyman Center for Ethics, Public Policy and the Professions; and director of the Center for Strategic Philanthropy and Civil Society at Duke University. From 1993 to 2001, Fleishman took a part-time leave from Duke University to serve as president of the Atlantic Philanthropic Service Company, the US Program Staff of Atlantic Philanthropies. Fleishman also serves as a director of Ralph Lauren Corporation.

PublicAffairs is a publishing house founded in 1997. It is a tribute to the standards, values, and flair of three persons who have served as mentors to countless reporters, writers, editors, and book people of all kinds, including me.

I. F. STONE, proprietor of *I. F. Stone's Weekly*, combined a commitment to the First Amendment with entrepreneurial zeal and reporting skill and became one of the great independent journalists in American history. At the age of eighty, Izzy published *The Trial of Socrates*, which was a national bestseller. He wrote the book after he taught himself ancient Greek.

BENJAMIN C. BRADLEE was for nearly thirty years the charismatic editorial leader of *The Washington Post*. It was Ben who gave the *Post* the range and courage to pursue such historic issues as Watergate. He supported his reporters with a tenacity that made them fearless and it is no accident that so many became authors of influential, best-selling books.

ROBERT L. BERNSTEIN, the chief executive of Random House for more than a quarter century, guided one of the nation's premier publishing houses. Bob was personally responsible for many books of political dissent and argument that challenged tyranny around the globe. He is also the founder and longtime chair of Human Rights Watch, one of the most respected human rights organizations in the world.

·　　·　　·

For fifty years, the banner of Public Affairs Press was carried by its owner Morris B. Schnapper, who published Gandhi, Nasser, Toynbee, Truman, and about 1,500 other authors. In 1983, Schnapper was described by *The Washington Post* as "a redoubtable gadfly." His legacy will endure in the books to come.

Peter Osnos, *Founder and Editor-at-Large*